A Circus of One

ADAM FRANCIS RABY

Deep Eddy
Publishing

Published by Deep Eddy Publishing, June 2013

ISBN: 978-1-482393-64-4

10 9 8 7 6 5 4 3 2 1

Cover and Interior Book Design by Coreen Montagna
(Cover image is a digital painting based on street art photographed from the side of a
building at Windansea Beach in San Diego, California, in 2008. It was gone the next day,
painted over by the city; the artist remains unknown.)

Back cover photography by Kent Horner (KentHorner.com)

Produced in the United States of America

To every human being that has entered my life
and to those I have yet to encounter.
My yoke of gratitude is heavy.

TABLE OF CONTENTS

AN ATOM CANNOT
BE CHANGED,
ONLY REARRANGED...

1
THE MAGIC COUCH

The energy at Windansea was noticeably different without the ritual chirping of the sparrows darting in and out of the sprawling hydrangea bush outside my front room window. It was a loud silence. Unfriendly.

Luckily, the ebb and flow of the light breeze broke this dreary silence when the vertical blinds fluttered in its wake, signaling it was time to get up. Quickly, my mind fired a message to my limbs to untangle the bed sheets from my torso — a sure remnant from a night of twisting and turning. I took my first conscious breath to inhale the sweet, yet slightly pungent smell of the ocean. I gasped for the next salty bouquet. My nostrils burned. My eyes opened. I was awake, but not really.

It was a morning not unlike thousands of others I'd experienced before in this short but long, exhausting life of mine. My oldest brother, Juno, framed my journey quite well when introducing me to strangers:

"This is my youngest brother, Adam. He's smarter than all of us, better looking, has a better golf game…but it's not the years of his life that make him unique, but the miles he has traveled."

Every time those words spilled from his lips, a piercing knife entered my side, cutting me deeply as I had no defense for his sarcasm. Without fail, his words intensified the unbroken desperation weighing down my life, taking my thoughts hostage. How did I get here? Who was I? Were my actions or inactions in life defining me? I was obese with worry. Bloated.

he doesn't feel exposed to life

Forty-two years, nine months, and twenty-three days of actual time outside the womb had passed by in this vessel. Indeed, it was those uncountable and undocumented miles cultivating a dreary feeling in me. A place of despair, emptiness, and complete isolation from who I really was, or for that matter, wanted to be. A dark place where the will to live life had faded away with my own willfulness. A place I knew so well, and understood was killing me physically, emotionally and spiritually since my first breath.

The unyielding struggle to entertain a different way of living never escaped me, although I found myself unwilling to muster the courage to halt what my ego had erected for survival. What was sustaining me was killing me. A circus of one, containing a thousand moving parts and performers, all choreographed by the actions of my own self-will.

I was lucky, some might say. But I never felt that way. Deep within the complexity of my circus, I was granted a reprieve of not being isolated physically from those surrounding me while I navigated through life. I was connected to others in a sense, but not in a genuine way. The guiding force behind my particular strain of humanness — my own self-inflicted disease, though not unique to the human condition but unique to my own experience — was extreme isolation in the power of my reason.

I was trapped. I was shackled. I was a slave to the first thought entering my mind. With no dexterity for a second thought, I quickly set my sights on acting on this first thought without restraint. I never realized people entertained multiple thoughts, sorted through them to make a decision, and then acted. In the human experience, the fantasy and delusion often accompanying the first thought is tempered with a second thought and then quashed by the third thought as being selfish, insane, or unattainable. I was powerless over the first thought entering my mind and as life played out, powerless over the trivial and not so trivial matters in life.

Early on, I recognized the ability to connect my first thought with an action. The desire to fulfill the needs of a young boy, like getting attention or something he wanted, was not the end game, but rather it served the more sinister, or should I say, dark areas of my life.

My actions on the outside resembled those of a child, but what was going on inside was not childlike. This bondage weighed heavy on my soul, prematurely accelerating its age. By the time I reached eight years old, the dark in my life was so overwhelming I had to find an outside cure for my internal condition. I had no idea what would bring clarity and refuge to the torturous dark-dream life I experienced. The uneasiness of whether I was going to make it to the next day was my constant battle.

The deep loneliness I experienced by not feeling connected to my five siblings was unwavering. Never feeling like I belonged perpetually looped in my thoughts during my waking hours, producing a feeling equally haunting and intriguing, which in time paralyzed my ability to reach out for help. I needed help.

Soon enough, a veil of isolation and desperation shrouded my growth. I needed a miracle, a cure to free me from this shackled, dark existence with the hope it might release me into the light of life without fear of the dark. It was equally conceivable this miracle cure would have the opposite effect beginning a life that would be riddled with extreme selfishness and self-centeredness, taking me to a depth of darkness that even in the light of life it would be unlivable. What course would this miracle cure take me?

These were my daily thoughts, thoughts no eight-year-old should have, but if you're human, it's possible. My footing was unstable and my grasp on life uncertain. I screamed in silence, "Please help!"

With no relief in sight, my life relentlessly percolated with fear and anxiety, but something had to change if living peacefully was possible. My thoughts of the future rambled on and on as the pain of the here and now was too much to bear. In which direction should I navigate?

Would I serrate a course creating destruction and despair within my own vessel, and would this course leave a swath of wreckage and debris behind me of people, places, and things? Would I ever be able to reconcile the battle between the light and dark, so I could have at least a reflection of peace in my life? How many miles would I travel before the pain of holding onto the life I willfully created would be greater than the fear of letting it go? Would my destiny have me standing alone at the center of the cavernous circus tent, my life, directing the cast of performers called "Me" to a destination planned only by the next thought entering my mind?

With fingers tightly crossed, I was hoping for a miracle, but tomorrow was never for certain in my eyes. If you're human, it never is.

The morning sun burned brightly Sunday, September twenty-third, 2007, when a perfect storm collapsed upon me, arousing the possibility of a different life, or for that matter, life for the very first time.

Awakening to a shortness of breath, the cruel haze of alcohol yearnings, and the sheer weight of my cranium as it lay uncomfortably wedged between the pillows on my two—piece, rust and green sectional couch. The monotonous feeling of being semi-conscious in the early morning, preceded always by a night overloaded with large quantities of alcohol and other mind-altering substances. This was the wrestling match I was all too familiar with — the match of myself against myself with the referee being myself.

The routine of waking up on the couch not sure of where I really was but instinctively looking for the items that would allow for the anxiety to subside when awaking in this stupor time after time. But this time was different because I felt like I had been in jail. I kind of remembered being in jail, but I was on my couch. I arose, stumbled, and then gathered my balance to see if my keys, car, and phone were accounted for. I found the keys and the phone; the car was in the backyard. It was a relief to find the car so close because sometimes it would be missing and I would have to scour the neighborhood like I had done so many times before. I was glad to not have to search this morning. My limbs were numb. Was it the night before? I honestly didn't remember.

Initially an overwhelming sense of relief was felt. "How long would it last?" was always the question. Was it possible I escaped the feelings that precede the impending consequences that are a part of a blackout when you're not sure exactly what happened the previous night? As my blurred vision swept across the room, I noticed a large pile of pink paperwork scattered across my desk, and I instantly knew I *had* been in jail and was a recipient of another DUI. All the feelings of anxiety quickly rushed back. No reprieve. Luckily, I had been in this situation numerous times before and knew exactly what to do to defer or absolve the consequences, but this time I felt things would be different. I didn't know how or why, but something was going to be different. It was purely a gut feeling, which I never trusted.

I waited for a few moments for my vision to clear and for my hands to stop shaking. I was in trouble, but it had nothing to do with the law. I pushed forward. Shuffling through the paperwork, I determined I needed to go pick up my wallet and pay my bond, which I had processed in a blackout. Apparently I'd been wheeling and dealing in my blackout. Without fail, the circus of one and all its performers were at work mitigating the pain and consequences once again.

After dragging my brain-swollen cranium and alcohol-infused frame off the magic couch to pay my bond and pick up my belongings, I quickly returned home, watchful of every twist and turn in the road. I had no idea how risky the previous seventy-two hours had been. I needed rest. If only I could rest, as my mind was racing and the planning and plotting was underway. I always pushed forward. To survive, I had no choice. I was stuck on the invisible tracks of life.

The stakes were a little higher this time around, and the situation was a little more precarious, as I had been driving a company-provided vehicle. The car was never impounded, leaving open the possibility I could fix the car out of my own pocket and never reveal the DUI to my employer. I had been in some type of accident, but my vehicle was in my backyard. Strange. The left, front quarter panel was damaged, but the car was very drivable, so I must not have been in too serious an accident. The pink paperwork provided very few details, and I knew through experience it would be several weeks and maybe up to a month to secure the police report to see what, in fact, I had hit. Was it a car, an alley trash can, a side of a building, or something more tragic? Had I injured someone in the accident? This all occurred in a blackout, a temporary loss of consciousness, sight, or memory.

By now my instincts alone were processing the available information to chart a plan of action, so my circus of one would go on. The show must go on! Drawing on my six other DUIs—of which I had only been convicted of two—was the well-spring of relief and confidence I had in my ability to keep afloat this life that I'd woven together since birth. Weaving together a life driven by the first thought entering my mind had proven to be extremely fruitful on so many different levels. In fact, from the perspective of our modern world, I had been successful. The people, places, and things in my life were extreme, honorable, and noteworthy. But the feeling rumbling in my belly when realizing I had been in jail once again with another DUI and that things would be different this time around kept rushing through my consciousness. Did I really want to keep the circus of one going? I was tired and weary and wanted the inside of my life, my soul, to match the outside of my life that seemed so fruitful.

In a flash it was Monday morning and I had not slept a wink. Uneasiness was settling in on what to do next. I knew with a little time and planning and some good counseling from an attorney I would be able to move through this seventh DUI and resume my life. But I experienced something strange—a yearning to reach out to another human being to share what was going on. That I would consider sharing my internal thoughts was very unusual for me, regardless of my current circumstances. Isolation in your own self-will doesn't allow for the time to share with others the victories in life, much less the troubling spots. Sharing feelings and thoughts only detracted from the next thought that came to mind, and that way of life, for the most part, had been a success, so why change now.

This unfamiliar energy stirred up my courage to share. Without the ability to have a second thought, I started calling some friends and family. At this point, a second thought would have served me well since sharing made me feel vulnerable. My secrets would no longer be secret. The dark side of my life that I protected with silence for so long suddenly poured out from my mouth. Most were aware of my previous brushes with the law, but no one was privy to the details. A miracle was happening before my eyes! I was telling the truth about my current situation with the facts I had uncovered so far. The facts and my will were not always on friendly terms. Who needs the truth? I surely navigated without it and prospered. Didn't I?

The facts and truth of everyday life for me was always a moving target. Lying as a form of communication never intrigued me, although I developed over time and then perfected a practice of stretching or detracting from the truth to get the desired outcome. This manipulation of the facts with intent distorted the truth, resulting in getting what I wanted or keeping what I had. It was simple. I would take the truth and add a little bit to make it sound better than the truth, or I would take the truth and leave out a couple of details so it wouldn't sound so bad. Either way, it wasn't the truth. This miracle of telling the simple truth delivered me into uncharted waters. I was lost and uncomfortable without the illusion of control. I was losing control, as I knew it. The truth is never simple.

I reached out with a purpose, morphing into a confession day for me to the small group of people surrounding me. I didn't quite know how to figure out my situation because I had been in a blackout. When piecing together my last week, I was starting to realize I couldn't remember anything past Thursday evening upon my return from San Francisco on a three day business meeting. My blackout was for several days, not the one night, and I didn't remember being in jail. Now, I've had blackouts and woke up in another city or for that matter another country, but for me, this was a new experience. I didn't have the necessary information to mitigate the damages with number seven looming in my future. Uncontrollably, my hand kept dialing.

A phone call to Richard propelled me to reach out to the light side of my life. Richard was one of the few people afforded a bird's eye view of the light and dark in my life, and when I called he led with compassion. He suggested getting some type of help, knowing my spiritual life was important to me and I should lean on its foundation in this time of healing.

I reached out to Paul. In April of 2007, Paul was going through proton therapy for prostate cancer at Loma Linda University, and he would spend the weekends in between treatments with me in La Jolla, California. It would be the best of times and the worst of times. Bottom line, I trusted Paul, and he knew about the dark portions of my life, but with limited details. We were connected spiritually. My intent was to set in motion with Paul the possibility of attacking number seven with some form of formal treatment, and I asked if he or his father knew of somebody on the West Coast I could ask for help.

At the same time, I was talking with Wayne my co-worker and friend who was aware of my dark side, but like Paul, did not know the details. So much information was missing to devise the necessary plan to help save my job, so I lobbied Wayne for his assistance. We went through several scenarios, all of which required me to not come clean with my employer, as I knew getting a seventh while driving a company car was a sure case for termination. I didn't want to lose my job, and the comfort on the outside of life it afforded, since without its presence as a cloaking device for my dark side, I would be exposed and naked to the duality my life had become. My secret was safe when clouded with the comforts my work provided. Material devices.

Once again I was battling the dark and light in my life: the light with Paul, a cleansing of the past to mitigate the consequences in my future; and the dark with Wayne, a covering of the past to mitigate the consequences in my future. I was working both sides of the aisle like a seasoned politician. But the aisle this time was not for some silly legislation to help a constituent and further my own electability. See, I knew how to make my situation better, and in fact, I knew how to make others feel better, but I never knew how to make myself better.

As it turned out, it would be the battle consuming my life since birth; the battle of who I really was and, more importantly, who I wanted to become. It's funny how when we turn to the simple (but not always easy) to enact foundations of a genuine life, honesty, that things start to move in a direction which is equally unplanned and unimaginable. The pressure to reconcile was mounting. Close to unbearable.

I was preparing for the ensuing battle over the next twenty-four hours, between the dark and light in my life and my inability or desire to reconcile the differences between these two polar constituents. I was in a tremendous amount of pain, and the time and effort it took to keep the warring factions of my life content had me in a state of complete exhaustion. I had not slept in almost two days and was detoxing from sure alcohol poisoning. In fact, I should have been in a physician's care after the amount alcohol I'd poured into my body over a seventy-two-hour period. I didn't know how much I consumed, due to my blackout, but the breath alcohol content reading that I had performed at the police station was a strong 0.39 on the first test. The officers giving me the test had been laughing at the high score and summoned me for another test to see if the first was somehow flawed. The second time I blew a 0.40. People die with this much alcohol in their bodies. I should have been dead.

Slowly I was piecing together my arrest, and now I remembered making a phone call around seven p.m. on Saturday night to Leigh Ann, my friend in New Mexico. We talked briefly about my upcoming trip back to New Mexico for business in mid-October and how much I wanted to spend some time with her to catch up on life. I vaguely remember getting off my couch and going down the street to The Rancherita to get some food and some more alcohol to curb the feeling of coming off my drunk state. I wanted to get something in my stomach but more importantly, to get enough liquor in my system so when I returned home, passing out until the morning would be possible. I had to get in my car to make this happen, since I was never a stay at home drinker.

It was a rare occasion for me to have liquor in my house. It wasn't a factor in my drinking routine. Drinking was not a solitary sport for me; it was always a team game. The ability to create an acquaintance at any bar/restaurant in any city, state, or country was always fun for me. I was equally comfortable at the Ritz in Paris as well as a strip club called The Stinky Bar in Mazatlan, Mexico—and trust me, stinky was not just a name. I was able to use all the performers in my circus of one to connect with people at whatever station in life they resided. I was truly at the top of my game when fueled by the alcohol. All of my shadow material, the ability to shape-shift to whom you wanted me to be or I needed to be for that encounter, was heightened in this forum.

With reflection, I was now able to remember a brief portion of the arrest. I was asleep on my couch after presumably making it home from The Rancherita, and I was being awakened by a police officer standing in my living room and asking me if my car was parked in the backyard. I apparently left my back door open when returning home, and the police walked in to drag me off my couch, placing me under arrest. I was asleep on my couch and being arrested for leaving the scene of an accident while under the influence. But a key piece of information was missing, and with the inability to see the police report for some time, I still didn't know what I hit and what type of damage was done. At that moment, this information had been the least of my concerns, as I recognized something powerful was stirring inside of me. This was evident by my desire to reach out to another person. Why was I feeling this way? I was also curious to know what would be my next thought to keep the show going. "How could I pull this off?" was my mantra.

The battle of which option to take to resolve this seventh—lucky number seven—was more than finding a way to lessen the consequences, but rather it was a question of what road to redemption I was going to take: the dark path of shape-shifting and truth manipulation to keep the show going while mitigating the pain, or was it going to be a path I had never traveled before, one of being genuine with the material in front of me without the cast of performers to help me keep the circus of one intact? I was leaning on old navigational routes hoping for something new. Tick-tock.

It was now Tuesday morning with no measurable sleep, and I was still unable to eat or drink any liquids. Every time I tried to take a sip of water to quench my parched lips, I would immediately throw up and endure three to five minutes of dry heaving. I desperately needed hydration, but I was afraid to drink anything, so I wouldn't have to repeat the gut wrenching pain one feels when trying to extricate the poison in their stomach. But this poison was no longer in my stomach; it was as if every cell in my body was hemorrhaging. The physical pain was excruciating but equally the emotional and now the spiritual pain was overwhelming. Luckily, a relief plan was underway.

Paul and his father, Dave, had a friend who was a counselor at an alcohol and drug rehabilitation facility. He was the former pastor of a church in my hometown of Albuquerque, New Mexico. Norm had left the ministry years before and now assisted people struggling with addiction. What I did not know at the time was that Norm was a lifeline to the most important male mentor in my life. He was a close friend of Bob Jefferson. Bob was my spiritual mentor. He was the first adult male in my life I had a relationship with and the father I never had. Bob taught me so many things, and one of the most important was to have balance in life. To have a spiritual, mental, and physical balance and to be cautious of letting one area overwhelm the others.

Bob had passed away in a tragic accident in July of 2002, but this connection with Norm provided the space in my consciousness to help me navigate this critical juncture in life. Higher powers were at work now, and I felt his loving presence. I missed Bob. I missed our talks; I missed the ability to share my heart with another human being. I missed him teaching me, and I missed being able to be honest with him about my struggles with the dark side of my life. I reached out to Norm to start the process for some form of treatment. I called Paul back to let him know about my connection with Norm, and he informed me he was headed out to visit. I was in no physical state for visitors but gladly welcomed Paul, knowing that my solo act needed some support. The convergence of the light in my life was working on all cylinders: Paul and his father, connecting me to Norm, who was connecting me back to Bob Jefferson. Make no mistake—I was still working the dark side of my life at this very moment.

I was hustling up an attorney, working an angle to navigate past number seven without a conviction while also keeping my job. I would adjust my jib and change tack from not being forthcoming with what had happened while in a blackout, to checking into rehab and forcing my employer to keep me employed under the guise I had a health condition needing attention. I would check myself into rehab without their consent and let the cards fall as they may. It's very difficult to fire someone with a medical condition.

The problem was my ego and pride could not take this solution on face value, as another option had to be possible to save my job, get some treatment, and deal with the consequences of number seven without having to sneak away in the middle of the night to find refuge. I find it interesting that the warring factions of my life—light and dark—were working in unison to resolve my dilemma and the common solution would be rehab. The question now was: is it possible to have a life with these two factions working in unison to reconcile the struggle of who I really was—and more importantly—who I wanted to be all along?

Keep in mind that all of this activity—the battle of my will to get past number seven with little or no collateral damage, the waging internal war of being honest with myself about what really happened in my blackout, and the resolution formula being designed by the light and the dark in my life—was all taking place on this Tuesday morning. My perfect storm had picked up speed, reaching hurricane status with flashes of my life blowing past me, and all I was hoping for, all I needed at the moment, was the peace and calm indicative of the eye of the storm. I desperately needed it, as I felt for the first time in life I didn't have what it took to keep fighting. I wanted to give up.

Barely holding on, I found myself standing in my front yard, gazing down the street cascading into the Pacific Ocean, and in a moment of clarity, I made a phone call to Harold, my employer who also was a friend of some ten years. In a rare moment of honesty, I exposed the inner workings of the circus to share the truth as best as I knew it at the time. The bottom line was that I was in a fender bender and had been arrested for number seven while driving a company vehicle. He listened and led with compassion, making sure I wasn't hurt and that no one else was. Our conversation continued, and I communicated my desire: rehab, financial responsibility, and loss of company perks, reassuring him I was willing to do whatever it took to keep my job. He expressed how happy he was with what I had accomplished in the territory over the last year and a half and the relationships I developed. In fact, he would make some phone calls and do whatever he could do to secure my employment. I was relieved.

Essentially, I told the truth as best as I knew it at the time and it seemed like things were going to work out. The assumption was I would be under some new set of guidelines but I would be able to keep my job and the circus of one would have another day. Quickly, unease crept through my bones. Even though I was honest with Harold, I had an overall discomfort with our conversation, since I knew deep down I was still playing with the sanctity of the truth. I was being as honest as I possibly could be, but this was not the difference I felt inside when I woke on the magic couch. Was I only scratching the surface of who I really was and who I really wanted to be? Was the purity of honesty available to me?

It would become apparent that saving my job and my lifestyle would be another attempt at weighing the trivial in my life as more important while altogether ignoring the heart of the matter once again. Half measures followed by success was a cornerstone of my life, and it seemed a similar effort would carry me through again—or would it?

With a new sense of confidence, I proceeded to go to my appointment with an attorney to cover all the possibilities in assuring the continuation of my life, as I had known it. I experienced a brief moment of clarity with Harold, light, following it up with legal maneuverings I deftly used to my full advantage in freeing myself from the consequences of three DUI convictions in the past, dark. The game was on, and I knew the pendulum of me whisking away the consequences was moving in my favor. A new energy and vigor arose in me, enticing me to peek at the light at the end of this tricky tunnel of opportunity, all while still suffering from no sleep, severe delirium tremens, dehydration, and lack of any sustenance.

The counsel this time was an unknown. In the past I had always relied on the counsel of a close personal friend, Jaybird, who was able to secure non-convictions on numbers two, four, and five. The formula was easy when dealing with Jaybird: tell him all the facts, go directly to the Department of Motor Vehicles (DMV) to get another driver's license to replace the one confiscated upon arrest, and bring cash for his services. He would handle all the rest. No paperwork, no showing up for court appointments or DMV hearings, and most importantly assured that full measure would be used to secure my non-conviction. This comfort quickly dissipated when I entered the law offices of CLP.

Upon entering an expansive lobby with an island reception desk, I was greeted and asked to fill out an extensive financial report. My employer, my salary, my bank and checking accounts were the information needed this time around. An uneasy feeling settled in my stomach, but I was driven by my will. My will took all prisoners, including myself. After filling out the paperwork, I was shuffled to another waiting room where a different staff member greeted me. My interview was all of five minutes, and then I sat for the next forty-five minutes while my case was being reviewed.

What in fact was being reviewed was my ability to pay the fee that was being ratcheted up as the minutes passed by. I was greeted by yet another staff member who gave his assessment of the case and what the extreme consequences would be if I was convicted. Then he slid a piece of paper across the table with an amount for their services. A tidy sum of twelve thousand dollars was scribbled across the piece of paper. I felt like I was I buying a used car. We settled on eighty-five hundred dollars in a

11

lump sum payment covering all costs, including a jury trial if necessary. I informed my salesman I would have to come back tomorrow to settle up.

Hurriedly, I drove home to prepare for the appointments for the rest of the week and to return the phone calls I ignored the previous day. I was feeling like things were starting to move in a direction that wasn't ideal for me, since my first thought was to not to have any consequences for number seven. The resolution being played out was looking like some form of rehab, some financial responsibility, expensive attorneys, reduced company perks, and the consequence delivering the heaviest blow to my circus was that everybody knew what was going on with my life and I didn't like that feeling. This was my business, this was my show, a circus of one with only one top hat directing the performers. I was feeling extremely vulnerable at that moment, and what came next was the eye of the storm.

Upon my return from the drug-testing clinic, which was mandatory after an accident in a company car, I placed a call to the human resources department. I was asked to hold for a moment while a conference call with Harold was set up to go over the details of what happened this past weekend. While waiting for our phone call to be connected, I felt a sense of calm come over me. That's an unusual feeling when one is still unsure of what their fate will be. Harold joined the conversation and asked that I restate what I had told him earlier in that day.

After finishing my recorded statement, there was a brief silence, and then the human resources person spoke up to let me know my services were no longer needed. I was fired! I thanked Harold for the opportunity to work for him and let him know how sorry I was to disappoint him with my actions and asked one more time how I could save my job. He let me know that in his thirty-year employment with the company this was one of the hardest decisions he'd had to make. We discussed the close out of my employment and he let me have until the next day to return my computer, BlackBerry, and other company property. He stated that he trusted me and it would be okay to return the items the next business day while I wrapped up loose ends. We said our goodbyes, and I hung up the phone.

What came next was unexpected and the beginning of a series of spiritual experiences unlike anything that I have experienced before no matter how hard I tried to connect with something—anything—beyond myself. To my surprise, a titanic wave of relief and calm rushed through my weary vessel. I was relieved I didn't have to deal with all the games of getting past number seven, realizing that I didn't have what it took to keep the show going. I didn't have the will to carry through on my first thought of how I was going to make number seven go away and continue on with my life as I knew it. The ability to marshal the troops of my circus to continue orchestrating fantasy into reality escaped me altogether. I didn't have one more round of drinks in me; I didn't have one more job, one more city, one more car, one more cell phone, one more woman, one more of anything!

Everything in my life up to this exact moment had been fiction in one form or another, propelled by the ability to turn my first thought into reality. My life was faction. A blending of half fiction and half fact to control the future as desired. Had my whole life been a dream, a life of make-believe?

As far back as I could remember, my brothers and sisters would call me the "Actor." I was the youngest of six. Early on, I realized that I could make things go my way, and this ability resonated in my being. Not only did I believe what was happening was based on the truth, but I was able to make others believe it as well. The kinetic nature of my ability to blend fantasy into reality was astounding. I never planned anything, but the extraordinary always seemed to be the end result. I never knew what was going to come out of my mouth, but the animal in me, the reptile, was never into adulation or wanting to be recognized by what happened, and feedback was not necessary. It was only for my own pleasure. The fine-tuning of my craft was being honed with every breath heaved from my lungs. With every breath, the size of my circus tent of make-believe became larger and larger until the sheer enormity of my life and its utter emptiness consumed me in one short sentence: You're fired!

The collapse of the ego! The inability to keep the circus of one going, the inability to keep the dark in my life chained in the basement, collided on my front lawn in a moment of clarity to tell the truth, as I knew it. I knew full well at that exact moment I would have to deal with the completeness of me. The light and the dark of my life had to be addressed in order to get relief. It was exhausting to keep it all going, and this wearer of the top hat was at the center of the storm and was finally feeling what I had thirsted for, for so long. I had been running from myself for so long, and I couldn't run any longer. The weight on my chest lifted. I could breathe.

I had been alone and isolated in the power of my self-will for the past forty-two years and ten months. It didn't matter who I was within life, I was alone. I was not me, but a menagerie of performers consuming me. I was alone in my own will.

I remember once hearing a young fellow talk about his aloneness, and he said, "I kept the girls around long enough to the point when I made them cry, and the guys long enough until the fun ran out and then I disappeared."

I've experienced my own Vietnam War through my will. The immediacy of my thoughts into action created severe devastation not only in my life but countless others. The "Me," more and now. The "I," self and me. I want what I want when I want it. My reason was tearing me away from having any real spiritual experience in my life. My reason was keeping me from being who I was all along.

The next several days were a blur as Paul came and went and my oldest sister, Maria, came into town to spend the afternoon with me. The conversations with Paul and Maria were important, but not too serious. I was elated that they were here, as I needed to have some family around me—but not for too long. One conversation I had with Paul stood out.

When he was visiting on the weekends during his treatments back in the spring, we would walk down to the beach and sit on the benches perched on the cliff above the shorebreak; there we'd chat about an amazing array of topics. Paul knew me more than most, and I always felt comfortable in sharing the dark side of my life even though I had to water it down for his consumption. And now here we were, several months later, sitting on the same bench, reviewing what had happened and what could have happened. He said something that bounced off me at first but would stick with me and ramble around my head for the next several months.

He said, "You are lucky." The facts were I was alone and didn't have to drag a family through what was to come next, and that I very well could have had a wife or ex-wife and children in this situation.

Paul knew he could pray for me, but also knew he could do nothing to help me. I was alone again, but something in fact had changed in me and it was now up to me to see it through, or not.

2

SUNRISE

It was Saturday morning—one week since the arrest for DUI number seven—and I felt I had been dragged through every emotion and feeling this body could endure. The outpourings of love from those I call family were carrying me through this new set of circumstances. I had never been as vulnerable as I was at this very moment.

My ego and pride were reeling from the past week's episodes, but still intent on sharing their unsolicited advice, advice that had been such a strong vein in my being to this point in life. With reflection, my ego and pride had never given sound counsel on any matter in my life, but it didn't matter because this terrible duo was inducing to me to get back on my feet and promoting a "let's feel better about you" mind-set.

The attorney had been retained, not sure why since I was fired, and the path to some sort of treatment was in the works. The visitors had all come and gone, Paul, Maria, and uncle Rude Dog. The phone calls of support and compassion started to wane. Well, wane was not accurate. I wanted a little time to absorb the past week without a bunch of touchy feely stuff from anyone. This was a change, since earlier in the week I was desperate to answer any phone call, to hear another voice that could possibly quell the pain of the unknown, which was now my reality. Now, I let the calls go to voicemail. I needed some space to devise a new plan. A new act was needed. I was seasoned.

My head was pounding—not so much from the consequences of number seven—but there were some important people, or should I say person, not aware of what happened to me the week before and what my temperature was right now. It was Lisa! Ooh, my heart ached to hear her voice! To reach out to her to let her know that I was okay and that…and that what? Share my feelings and let her know what transpired over the past week? I was incapable of telling the complete truth to the person that had struck such a strong chord deep within my soul, that for this wearer of the top hat was foreign to the human touch.

I met Lisa about a month earlier after a day at the Del Mar racetrack playing the ponies and swashbuckling with the "in crowd" at the Turf Club. The Turf Club is the sports-jacket-required private entrance area of the track that only welcomed the well-to-do and the celebrity crowd for a day of flirting, drinking, betting, and making sure you were noticed by your fellow well-to-doers. The famed million-dollar race, the Pacific Classic, was over, and Larry , my host at the Turf Club, and I headed down to the village of Del Mar for some dinner. The restaurants were bustling with post-race revelry as we settled in to have dinner at Pacifica Grill while sitting at the bar.

At first I didn't notice Lisa and her friend, but soon we were engaged in conversation. The liveliness in her voice and her exuberant personality were breathtaking. She was beautiful and smart and the banter between us flowed effortlessly. I ordered dinner, and we shared a couple glasses of wine, and we in fact shared my dinner off the same plate. She was curious about my heritage, and I told her I was a coyote. A toxic DNA mixture of Mexican, Native American, and an unknown mix of Hillbilly from Tennessee was my formula.

We spent the evening laughing and enjoying each other's company without the uncomfortable expectation our chance meeting was going to go somewhere or mean something. It was simply two people enjoying a moment in time with a genuine ease and comfort. We finished dinner, shared a desert, and then I gave her my business card and we said our goodbyes.

Over the next month, Lisa and I would spend time together, and every time we did, amazing experiences transpired. The settings were romantic, the wine and food were extravagant, and the people we met while together were interesting and not ordinary. It was all so edgy, but at the very same time I was struck by the pure genuineness and honesty of her character. Simply, she was smart, beautiful, and real.

But something much deeper was moving me when touched by her spirit, as I had never had someone pull at my heart like that before in such a short time. It wasn't lust stirring in my being, but what I did know was something was missing inside of me that was so apparent in Lisa. She was so much like the kind of woman I was attracted to in my life: funny, quick witted, confident, smart, independent, and beautiful. In the female form, to me Lisa was a paradox, she was everything I looked for in a woman, but at the same time wasn't like any woman I encountered before.

This paradox was subconsciously tearing me apart and at the same time propelling me forward to get more of what I could not have. You see, Lisa had mentioned on more than one occasion that things were complicated in her life at the moment and she genuinely wished she had met me one year from now. I heard her but wanted more. I was confused, and now with my current situation I was lost in my feelings. How should I proceed?

So many thoughts were running through my head. Should I come clean and let her know what happened, or should I let this play out and tell her only if necessary? A shimmer of light shone through on my dilemma about what to reveal to Lisa, and was this my opportunity to still have her in my life without having to be completely honest? I very well knew I couldn't be honest with her, and with fear the guiding force behind that decision, I had to find another way. I didn't want to lose the magic that was happening between us, and more importantly I wanted to uncover these feelings about Lisa, an inconceivable paradox that had captivated me like no other woman before in my life. What was it about her that made me feel this way? I needed to know.

Would there be a time and place in my life that would allow me the opportunity to uncover this mystery called Lisa? When would we speak again, or would we speak again? I opted for the easy way out and texted her my new phone number, explaining I had quit my job to seek out a new vocational passion in life. Lisa responded as expected with words of encouragement, echoing through her experience, that starting anew was always nice and occasionally necessary.

I had at that moment a feeling of peace with the thought of Lisa, but I knew a time would come, and I hoped it would be sooner rather than later, that we would be able to sit down and speak once again, face to face.

But before anything occurred between the two of us, I had a little business to attend to, an unveiling and uncovering that would possibly change my life forever as I knew it, or alternately might lead me to a place of darkness composed solely of selfishness and self-centeredness from which I would be unable to recover. It was life or death for me now, and the peace and calm represented by the eye of the storm only days before had passed on.

I had always been able to fix the situations in my life that needed fixing, but this time a new dexterity was necessary to extricate me from the perceived bottom that I had reached. *Hitting bottom* is a common human experience, hopefully propelling one to address the obstacles in one's life. A place where, given the current circumstances, it is inconceivable that life could be worse, be less livable. Make no mistake, we are the culprits, having willfully created these circumstances. The fact is you've had this feeling before, but this time you knew it was different.

It was apparent my bottom was not lucky number seven or the direct consequences resulting from it, but rather the pure truth I felt inside of reaching a physical, mental, and spiritual emptiness. Physically I was reeling from the effects of a week's worth of alcohol poisoning and detoxing; mentally I was reeling from the self-inflicted mauling I was taking by not being able to think my way out of my situation. And spiritually, I was completely broken.

The emptiness I was experiencing inside was vast. This low was new. I'd never had thoughts of suicide in my life. The conscious thought of ending my life because the pain was irreversible had never been an option with me. The old formula of using an outside source to cure an inside wound would no longer suffice if I wanted to keep living—and believe me I tried numerous outside sources. But I knew the pain I had been experiencing at such heightened levels recently—the loneliness without being alone, the having a spiritual condition that was healthy in the past but now non-existent, the mental prowess that never failed me but was now paralyzed—had all coalesced into the conscious thought of killing myself without remorse. My mental acuity was tight, and I knew every choice I was making was willful and without a second option. I was aware I pulled the trigger with alcohol being my weapon of choice and survived. I was lucky; more than most one might say.

The course had been charted since the age of eight, and the execution of the plan was being implemented with the skill of a vascular surgeon. If you thought a vascular surgeon was not in my circus of performers, you were wrong. It was neither medical knowledge nor skills I possessed but rather the ability to deftly cut away feelings and emotions necessary for a healthy life. The ability to be fully engaged with another human being was impossible with my tool kit.

Have you ever heard of the saying, "One can be lonely but not alone"? The idea is that though alone physically, you are connected spiritually with your higher power which is always with you. I had experienced "lonely and not alone" before, but this time I was truly alone for the first time in my life.

Extreme measures were necessary, and at the moment I was willing to do anything to not be alone, which in the past I relished and demanded when directing the circus of one. I knew I could seek refuge and comfort and at the very least some warm bodies if I gathered enough courage to attend a meeting. One does not go through six previous DUIs and escape the court-mandated twelve-step meetings. The first meeting I ever attended was with David in the basement of a church in Albuquerque, New Mexico. I went a couple of times and liked them and the spiritual connection enhanced between David and me was an unexpected benefit. I had also attended other meetings in New Mexico and some in Austin, Texas, after number six.

It was in Austin that I had my first willful experience with meetings. I attended *Bridge to Shore* and it changed my perception of what went on in this secret society. The smoke filled rooms with coffee-swilling alcoholics were not my idea of a place where one finds communion with other human beings. I never smoked cigarettes and couldn't stand the effects of coffee. Ironically, I would stuff copious amounts of drugs into my body, inducing the same wide-awake sensation with no side effects. How could I find a place to fit my needs if this is all that was available to me?

Well, what I learned is that there are non-smoking meetings and there were meetings where I felt connected. I likened the meetings to bars. There are hundreds if not thousands of bars in cities as well as an equal amount of meetings. I gladly bellied-up to drink at any bar but eventually I settled in at the places I felt most comfortable. This is true with meetings. If you're not comfortable with the one you're in, keep going until you find the bar/meeting where you can be. At *Bridge to Shore* I learned that alcohol was only a small part of the problem with an equal intent to heal many aspects of life. Being human is complex. I never realized this. How could I? The show clouded my perception. It had always been about me.

It had been seventeen years since my first meeting with David in Albuquerque. I noticed a building on Cass Street in Pacific Beach since my arrival in California in February 2006. The draw was strong. I purposely went out of my way to stay away from the building. The reminder was too painful. My yoke was heavy.

It was Saturday, one week to the day after awakening on the magic couch, and things were starting to change. It was around five o'clock, and my skin was starting to crawl and I knew I needed to go to a meeting. I jumped into the company car and drove down to Pacific Beach to pick up a meeting schedule, donating the fifty cents and quickly returning home to see where I could attend meetings near my cottage. I knew I would be without the company vehicle in the next couple of days, so on the way home I purchased a mountain bike to get around for the next several months, hoping I could find at least one meeting in my neighborhood. My luck ran deep.

A meeting called *Hip, Slick and Sick* was at seven that night and only three blocks away from my cottage. I was relieved and scared at the same time. It was close and that was comforting, but it was close and that was disconcerting. It was looking like I would have no logistical impediments to keep me from going to a meeting.

Without a second thought, I walked down the street to a church and entered a door that led to a stairway to a large room with a fireplace. The room was set up with stackable pews fanned out and facing the fireplace. I was greeted at the door and immediately was handed a ticket with a number on it. I was not sure what this was all about, but I knew I had to share what was going on in my life. I needed to purge.

The format of the meeting was to have the leader share their story and then they would pick out of a bowl the other half of the ticket handed out upon entering the meeting, deciding who else would share. I don't remember the leader's share or if a topic was mentioned, but I was desperate to talk about what was going on inside of me. I had never had that feeling before — the feeling of wanting to share out loud what was going on in my life. I thought back to the meetings in Austin, recalling the relief in people who shared in this way. I prayed that my number would be chosen from the bowl, and I settled in for the duration of the meeting.

My prayer would be answered, as the second ticket pulled from the bowl indicated it was my time to share. With a shaking voice and my face unable to peel itself from staring at the floor, I introduced myself in the customary way when in a meeting:

"Adam…Alcoholic."

It was the first time I actually believed I was an alcoholic, not the first time I had spoken those words. I shared what had happened over the past week and sensed a spackling of relief. It was a little odd in the fact that five days earlier I had been sharing with a few people what had happened to me, the dark, and tonight I was sharing openly with about forty strangers.

With a new sense of freedom and relief found by sharing my story to total strangers, I scurried back to my cottage to find out when the next meeting took place. The significance of storytelling and story listening was always an important part of my learning process in life. I was always drawn to people who were more experienced in years than I, as it was a way for me to absorb their experience and simply learn. But mostly a wonderful friendship was created. I was an old soul.

It dawned on me that the meetings could be a source to relieve the pressure building inside of me and in turn could be a source of enlightenment to the mysteries in my life. And, if nothing else, I could make a few friends who understood my plight.

I quickly returned home after the meeting was over. Pulling out the meeting schedule, I looked to see what meetings were available on Sunday. To my surprise, the next meeting was down the same cascading street I'd gazed down when I had my brief moment of clarity with Harold. It was a beach meeting at nine a.m. called *Pump House.* The exact same pump house made famous in Tom Wolf's novel *The Pump House Gang.*

It was now apparent I had meetings to attend on Saturday and Sunday, but what would I do with the rest of the week? In the front of the scheduler was a section that had daily meetings. I could not believe my eyes, as a meeting was available Monday through Friday at the same church as the *Hip, Slick and Sick* meeting! The meeting was at seven a.m. and was called *Sunrise.*

The irony was funny and not so funny. I was surrounded the whole time while living in Windansea. Three meetings within walking distance from my cottage and all I had to do was step out of my front door to find the opportunity to finally address the battle between the light and dark in my life. It was apparent my move to La Jolla was more than ego driven; knowing I was in the right place at the right time was a relief. But it's not what I had envisioned, what I had hoped for when moving from Austin.

The feeling I felt at that very moment was difficult to describe, but what I did know for sure was my next step. I wasn't sure what direction I was heading, but I knew it was going to be a new road I had not traveled before regardless of the final destination. I was where I needed to be, and I never looked back at the missed opportunity to escape number seven unscathed. It was time to have a plan having nothing to do with fantasy or delusion, or for that matter the first thought entering my mind. It would be a plan that was going to give me the opportunity to address what was really going on in my life. I had one more chance. I felt a shift. Shaky ground.

I guess men in their early forties have what is called a mid-life crisis. That moment in life when we feel the need to recapture our youth before it is too late. The overwhelming fear that if we don't act quickly, the opportunity to experience what has been missing in our life up to this point will have passed. No stone goes unturned. The new sports car, hair implants, tummy tuck or face lift, and the divorce with an impending move-in with the twenty-something girlfriend, all in the guise of finding oneself. How boring!

Well my crisis was not going to resemble any of those attributes. I had a full head of hair, so that was not going to be an issue, and plastic surgery was not needed due to an extra helping of good genes. My current mode of transportation was a twenty-seven-speed mountain bike, so no testosterone booster needed. Lastly, I never found marriage, so any need to disembowel the sanctity of the institution for a weakness in character was unnecessary, and I never had difficulty finding companionship with younger women. My shift would never be normal. The unorthodox was my normal. I was wired that way.

Suddenly, the fast-paced hustle and bustle of my life screeched to a lumbering saunter. I always enjoyed the opportunity to slow down for a bit in life to refuel and recharge for the sole purpose of when it was time to get back to reality I would be ready to attack like never before. The brief reprieve one feels is a delusion since we never really change anything, we just remove ourselves from the arena while all along the planning and plotting is still ruminating in our minds. How can I do the same thing but better this time? I had fallen for these traps in life so many times before, and now by grace, I was conscious of the significance this opportunity was presenting itself to me organically. Change was happening whether I wanted it to or not. This was not my choice, but it was of my doing.

Believe me, it was never a dream of mine to be jobless, carless, and ripped from the stage of life where I alone wore the top hat of what was going to transpire in my life. I was in control and my reason was sovereign. Begrudgingly, I recognized this might be the only opportunity to slow down life for not just a week or two but to see if I could have another way of living this life without the exhaustion and work it took to keep the circus of one going. I had hope. Maybe that's all I had left. Hope.

I made sure not to get to the *Pump House* meeting too early on Sunday morning, having experienced enough meetings to know a lot of connecting with others goes on before the meetings start and after they are finished. I was ready to share and to listen, but I was not ready to make small talk with anyone.

As I made my way slowly and cautiously in the direction of the pump house, I noticed a circle of people forming on the beach below. Some were carrying beach chairs and some were carrying towels and some like me would sit in the sand. It was an interesting meeting, with one person sharing their experience and then proceeding around the circle to the next person. But I was distracted.

I was sitting in the sand with thoughts swirling in my head of what could have been if I made some other choices over the past week, when suddenly my focus shifted to the immediate surroundings, like I was witnessing it for the very first time. In a way I was. The scene was amazing: to my right was the famous Windansea double-breaking surf spot being danced upon by early morning surfers, straight ahead was the pounding shorebreak entangled with bodies of daredevil bodysurfers catching the inside "womp." Far in the distance was the blue sky disappearing until it touched the purple sea, soaring above was the "V" formation of the endangered California brown pelican gently riding the winds to nowhere, and beneath me was the soothing warmth of the sand heated by the early morning sun. Intoxicating.

As the sharing passed from one person to the next, I became amused since I could not hear a damn thing anyone was saying and in time came to realize this was the sole reason why so many loved the meeting. It was not the storytelling or story-hearing drawing one to this venue, but rather it was all the other stuff uniquely present at this meeting of human beings who wanted to be connected to something other than oneself on an early Sunday morning in the greatest cathedral ever created.

I suddenly couldn't remember what I had been doing on Sunday mornings in the past year and a half since moving to Windansea. How had I missed its beauty? There was something magical which now I call a spiritual experience if your receiver is open when experiencing the beach on any early morning. The enormity of God's creation before your eyes and the corollary uniqueness of each part specific to its own purpose, being woven into a fabric of awe for the sole purpose of healing the human soul. The place where time and space disappear and peace and calm are possible if we relinquish the reins of life, as we want it to be.

The *Pump House* meeting would become my house of worship on Sundays that had been missing since my days back at Calvary Chapel, Albuquerque. But it would be the next meeting I would attend on Monday morning that would slowly cast a beam of light on my life, brewing into a new perfect storm since my moment of clarity on my front lawn. It was *Sunrise* and slowly and painfully it would play out as a sunset on my life as I knew it.

It was early Monday morning, one week after my last drink, and my meeting schedule pointed me back to the church up the street. Upon entering the second floor great room, I noticed the setup was different than the Saturday night meeting. Three blue sofas surrounded a fireplace. A lone bookcase to the right of the room held a collage of literature and some inspirational spiritual books set out by the church. To the left of the fireplace was a piano nestled in the corner, and sitting in front of the piano was a small coffee table with a coffee pot brewing along with a pot of hot water for tea. The fireplace was lit with one of those store bought logs that can burn up to three hours if left alone, but who does that when a fire is burning? I came to learn that a three-hour manufactured log has about a good hour of actual burning time after all the poking and prodding it takes to keep a nice flame going. Two folding chairs were strategically positioned along either side of the fireplace for this exact purpose.

It had been two days since the last time I was in this room, and I hadn't noticed any of these things before. I guess the meeting was not expecting a large crowd like the Saturday night meeting, as all the pews that were fanned out before were neatly stacked at the back of the room. A lone foosball table was pushed to the back corner of this now cavernous room. It was looking as if I was going to have to engage with some people at this meeting because of the close quarters and intimate seating arrangement. It was inviting because everybody was facing each other with an added bonus of each seat having an unobstructed view of the fire being poked and prodded into a roaring flame.

I had attended two meetings so far, and it was looking like I would have to share again, having to barf up the same story once again had me questioning if I was doing the right thing. I wanted to jazz up my story. It seemed so boring, the truth; surely I could spice it up a little? But for now I had my story and I was sticking to it, and I wasn't so sure this whole sobriety thing was going to work for me. I was going to give it a shot because at the moment I had little else to do with too much time on my hands.

The atmosphere of this meeting was different. I'm not sure if it was the close quarters, or the fireplace but something set this meeting apart from the others I attended over the years. It wasn't as structured. The person leading the meeting was named Billie. I kept my eye on her as she paraded around the room laughing while handing out some literature to be read aloud. It felt so lighthearted. I was accustomed to the dark, dreary meetings.

The first reading was the preamble, a short reading stating the purpose of the program and who is eligible to enter into the room. A low threshold to ensure entry was the heart of the matter.

"If you have a desire to stop drinking you are welcome."

That's it? Nothing else? I've heard the preamble before, but that portion struck me in a new way. One did not have to already stop drinking to take part in the meeting but only had to have a desire to stop drinking. I guess I fit the category, having announced myself as an alcoholic in the last two meetings I attended. I wasn't totally convinced when I said, "I am an alcoholic," and I was certainly not confident this program would work for me. What I was sure of was I wanted the pain to go away and this place helped ease the pain. I belonged for the moment. Strategic.

Next came the reading of "How It Works." This long reading detailed how the program works for all who are wondering how it works. I always hated this reading in the past on two fronts: It spoke to me directly and I didn't like it, and it went over the twelve steps of the program, which I didn't like either. I think most human beings don't like being told what to do and especially in a defined order, one step after another.

I likened the steps to baking, which I never liked doing and was never good at or had the patience for. Now I love to cook, because it allows for creativity and freelancing in the formulation of the dish that one was making. On the other hand, baking was a disciplined act where every step was measured and in order. In fact, baking one has to let things rise or bake at a set temperature for a set period of time with adjustments for altitude when necessary and then cool for the baked good to be at its potential best.

If one follows the baking process step by step and in order, the probability of success is very high, but that's not always the case when one is concocting a recipe at will, like so many of us do while standing over the pots and pans in the kitchen or in life for that matter. The preparation of slicing and dicing, a measure of undetermined quantity, a pinch of this and a pinch of that all guided by the self-will to make it the best possible tasting meal ever. It was very evident that I preferred cooking versus baking, and it was equally evident that I liked preparing each moment in my life with the same measure, in turn resulting in a wide-range of outcomes. My will was the kitchen in my life, and the next thought that came to mind was the spices, knives, and the uncountable accoutrements tossed in the pots and pans to turn fantasy into reality. My ego was stunted when baking. I lived to cook.

The meat of the meeting was centered on reading the *Daily Reflections*. It is a series of writings for each day of the year, selected from various approved literature with a brief paragraph or two expanding on the topic. It provides the opportunity to hear each step being discussed in depth, allowing one to see that the program is so much more than not drinking. At *Sunrise,* each person was afforded the opportunity to share after the reading, and to my surprise everybody did. When the time came for me to share, I stuck with my story of why I was in the meetings and how I was trying to figure out what to do next. I didn't expect the salve *Sunrise* provided that morning; it quieted my anxious soul.

Sunrise was unique in so many different ways: the fire, the encouraging atmosphere to share, the starting the day out talking about important topics, the spiritual healing aura in the room, but most importantly, the people. Everybody was so interesting and had amazing things to share on the topic being discussed at the break of dawn.

The one thing I noticed early on was no matter the topic, as the baton was passed to the next person to share, never did I hear the same share twice. These people were serious and their viewpoints were thought-provoking and meaningful. There was no blabbering about personal affairs or the ever present drunk-a-log in meetings(that's when someone goes on and on about how they drank and how bad or great it was). *Sunrise* was unique in that the group conscious honored the material and at the same time respected you as an individual and the reason why you chose to be in the room. It was cerebral with a spiritual twist, dripping in humility. I was intrigued. Possibly hooked?

The demographics of the meeting were dynamic as well, comprised mostly of men, with a sprinkling of women, and ranging in age from late twenties to mid-seventies. Trust fund babies, real estate developers, Ivy league graduate, scientists, one helicopter pilot, a big wave surfer, attorneys, a professional beach bum, ex-cons, a male-model-turned-homeless-drunk, a contractor, one astrologist/philosopher, a master sushi chef, an artist, entrepreneurs, consultants, an appearance stylist, fathers, mothers, sons, daughters, and every denomination and religious tradition imaginable—plus atheists.

An uncommon-but-common mix of individuals intent on listening to each other earnestly—and I mean really listening. The kind of listening that happens when you're not thinking about what you want to say while someone else is talking. Now, my high school basketball coach, Jim Hulsman, had a saying that was never quite understood by his audience:

"You look, but you don't see, and you hear, but you don't listen."

It only took twenty-five years, but I finally understood what he was saying. The people in that room were intent on seeing and listening with the purpose of helping and being helped to navigate life.

The whole landscape of God's human creation was in that meeting, and I'd known from the very first day that I'd found a place to uncoil. It dawned on me that *Sunrise* was the first place I had experienced in my life where every person in the room genuinely wanted everyone else to succeed. I'd never experienced that feeling with family, in business, in athletics, in relationships, in friendships, and I'd never experienced it in any of the churches I'd attended over the years. The room teemed with people wanting to help other people without ulterior motives.

The purpose of this room was not so obvious at first. It was a paradox. The finding of a new elixir in life, different from the drink, providing the opportunity to completely transform one's life from within; that was the purpose. The paradox being one can only keep this newfound gift by giving it to another. It's imperative that people be afforded the opportunity to have their own experience to effectively change from within. This all seemed great, but something was going on with me and I could not understand it. Was I losing my mind?

Early on in this journey, I was encouraged by my two sisters, Theri and Maria, to buy a notebook and journal my thoughts and feelings. It had been twenty-three years since the last time I journaled. I had been going to school in London and was required to have a journal for a British Culture class I was taking. The experience was not very memorable and I hadn't done it since. But I guess at this point I was taking suggestions, and if it wasn't too drastic, I would entertain the idea.

I ventured down to the local bookstore and picked up two composition books. Ironically the same composition books that I used while in college. I guessed I would be back in school, learning new things and hoping it would lead to a new way of life. One book was to be for that journal business and the other for the more practical purpose of having a record of the meetings I attended. One of the *Sunrisers* suggested that by keeping a record of the meetings I attended, it could be helpful in the sentencing portion for number seven—if in fact I was convicted. I decided if I attended more than one meeting in a day, I would still have only one entry for that day. I didn't want to stuff the ballot box. This choice was another hint that things were starting to change within me; I wanted to be completely honest with what was being recorded in this book of meetings I attended.

I wanted to be accountable to myself, since that had been the problem all along. But it was a pride issue as well, and documenting every entry in the book would make me feel like I had something really wrong with me. I wasn't that sick, and I surely didn't want a complete record of every single meeting I was to attend. What if this journal landed in the wrong hands someday and came back to haunt me? I hadn't even started to attend multiple meetings in a day, but the planning and plotting inherent in my being of doing whatever it took to lessen the blow of number seven was strong. It would also be easier for me to keep my attendance book secret if I didn't have to pull it out at every meeting I went to. I pre-selected a few people to sign the book, and in fact, the first entry was signed by me. On the other hand, the journaling book would be a problem, and I was struggling how to start.

Logically, I understood why someone would want to write down their thoughts and feelings, but how could I write down feelings I never allowed to surface in the first place? The task seemed daunting. A journey of uncharted waters was under way, surely to be filled with starts and stops, so why not write this stuff down? The reality was my feelings were simply frozen. The desire to lean into this fear was in question, and more importantly I didn't know how to thaw. But something more sinister was going on with my mind, and it was scaring me. You see, I have the curse and blessing of having a photographic memory, and since my last drink I was having a tough time remembering things in the short term. I thought I had done some permanent damage. So my mind drifted to a comforting place, rushing quickly to a solution based on pure nonsense. Drinking again might be the cure to kick-start my memory, I pondered. The absence of alcohol was playing tricks on my reasoning. Delirium.

The amazing stories and suggestions shared at *Sunrise* instigated the recognition of the loss of my short-term memory. The storytelling was filled with crippling honesty of the experiences they had in life in relation to the reflection being discussed and the rising up from the ashes of their experiences to a higher level of understanding. These people had a peace and calm in their life that was mesmerizing. How could they have such serenity after those experiences? There was no soap-boxing or cramming of dogma down another's throat, it was a simple sharing of an experience and how they maneuvered through it. They were sharing the most intimate details of their life with bone chilling honesty, resulting in a life now without limit. It wasn't fantasy anymore as they were now living their dreams, and I desperately wanted what they had.

I realized the significance of what was being shared by all in the meeting in relation to my own feelings, and I wanted to remember what exactly was said and by whom, but I could not. I found myself jumping on my bike after the meeting and quickly going home to write down what I had heard. When I got home my mind was blank. In a few short blocks my memory had failed me, and I was scared. It was the first major decision I faced in whether to drink or not—and it wasn't because I craved alcohol, but rather it was because I could not remember things like I had only one week earlier.

In a panic about what to do next, the answer was right in front of me and the dilemma was solved: I would tote the second composition book intended for my journal to each meeting so I could write down what was said and by whom. If I didn't do this, I would eventually go home and scribble something down resembling what was said but with my own spin and in turn, authorship. Now I didn't know if these things were something they had heard from someone else or their original thoughts and it really didn't matter, but what did matter was the refreshing nature of these thoughts kept me coming back to *Sunrise*.

Now I had a plan and it was in motion: attend meetings and continue on the path to some sort of formal rehabilitation. Unfortunately, logistical and financial obstacles pulled me right back into reality that was far from the calming waters of *Sunrise*.

For the past twenty-five years I had health insurance with supplemental dental and vision, but I can't tell you the last time I used any of those services. Part of my plan was to get a full physical and dental exam and vision care over the next ninety days. I had already experienced the short-term memory lapses, and I was leery of internal damage that had to have taken place with a self-will run riot. My vision was troublesome when trying to read street signs, and I had not been to the dentist to get a cleaning in over a year. I needed a tune-up.

But the main reason to continue my insurance was for the purpose of covering the expenses when I went into treatment. I was spending at least two hours a day scheduling doctor appointments and working with the intake person who handles all the insurance requirements to enroll in a residential treatment program. This was one of the programs Norm suggested, and I was sure it would be safe for me, even though my ego was not happy with this decision.

In one form or another, I was still trying to run the circus of one with an illusion that if I went to a formal rehabilitation program, those who surrounded me would back off and I could eventually resume my life as I had known it. I was going to power through the twenty-eight-day program and check the box for all to see how serious I was about addressing my problem with drinking and driving. The plan was in place. I was confident.

I was enjoying the meetings, and in fact I was attending at least one meeting a day and most days two. My routine would be interrupted with a trip back to New Mexico, planned initially for business but now was going to be the reversal of the intervention my family had attempted back in June of 2000. The attempt back in 2000 was well-intentioned but was not very well thought out, and without the assistance of a professional interventionist (like Norm) who could counsel and convince, was sure to fail. I quickly rebuffed the attempt and further distanced myself from any thoughts of dealing with my habitual drunken driving issues.

My disposition had changed, and this trip back was going to be different. I would approach my family members and a few friends and let them know I was going to finally address my drinking issue with a formal treatment program. In fact, I likened my trip to a reverse intervention. The addict counseling the family on what I was going to do about my problem and making sure everyone was included in my decision. Their reactions ranged from relief to concern to fear.

The fear didn't emanate from my decision to go to formal recovery, as all were ecstatic about this turn of events, but rather that I was going to a Christian-based rehabilitation program. I had converted from Roman Catholicism to Evangelical Christianity back in 1994, and this conversion was always viewed with suspicion, as were those new friendships that I created around my newfound religious tradition. I had weathered these concerns in the past with family members and was resting on the provenance of this rehabilitation program leading back to Bob Jefferson. It was enough for me, and the decision had been made; I was committed to seeing it through no matter what. I now had hope.

The week in New Mexico went quickly, as I was able to spend time with friends and family, and it provided me with the resolve to see this formal rehabilitation through. I had many wonderful conversations and felt things were going to work out for the best. Paul and I were able to navigate our way through my insurance provider and the intake person to place a deposit on a twenty-eight-day stay starting on October twenty-ninth, 2007. Everything was set, and the only thing needing to be completed for the insurance to kick in was an evaluation by a health care professional at time of admittance to confirm the necessity of the treatment.

My week in New Mexico was winding down, and I was going to Sunday services with Paul and his family. What seemed like a normal service quickly turned, and what transpired after church services would challenge my resolve to execute my plan devised only weeks earlier.

Since moving to Texas in February of 2001, when visiting New Mexico I stayed with Paul, Lyn, and their children. Their home was always a refuge from my circus life, as I had to be on my best behavior when around the kids, but more importantly I always felt safe when under their protection in a town and state I could never comfortably call home. I had a feeling of being connected and a part of their family, if only for the brief time I spent when visiting New Mexico.

I met Paul, Lyn, and the kids at Hoffmantown Church that morning. A lot of my life's memories were rushing through my mind at that moment, and I was distracted enough not to get much out of the sermon. Thoughts of Bob Jefferson were overwhelming me, and I wanted to hear his voice and take his counsel on what I should do in the weeks and months ahead. His voice provided comfort, especially when he had to clear his throat, because something powerful was always forthcoming when he did. His spirit would be all I would need to make it through the next thirty days, or so I kept telling myself over and over. I thought of Norm, who I hadn't yet met in person but was calmed by his peace and sound counsel. His presence over the last thirty days was no coincidence, since Norm taught this very same congregation years ago. I was where I was supposed to be. I felt Bob close.

The service was over, and we headed out to have breakfast with Paul's mother, father, and sister and her two daughters. As we separated, Lyn asked the kids to go with Paul, as she wanted to walk me to my car. Over the years, Lyn and I have had some thoughtful conversations, but the energy was different this time, and I'm not sure which one of us was more nervous about what was to come next.

We small talked while walking, and when we reached my car, she gently hit me with a blow to my ego and pride, encroaching on a place deep within my soul never touched by words from another human being before. She let me know her deep concern for me, that I was not just another one of Paul's friends, but that I was a part of her family and she cared for me and loved me and wanted to see me get better. She told me she was aware of my DUI in Texas and had "written me off," thinking I was no longer a positive influence on the children. In fact, she had shared with Sara and Emily what had happened to result in me losing my job. She wished I could have seen the look on the girls' faces when she tried to explain what was going on in my life, and she could only describe their expressions as "confused and painful." Tough love. I needed it.

My first reaction was to let her know how I thankful I was for her concern and that I was serious about my plan of addressing my problem, at least this time I told myself. The conversation was fast-paced as I let her know how much her family meant to me and my intent to get better. We hugged and went our separate ways to meet at brunch. I jumped into my car and started to cry for the first time since my perfect storm collapsed upon me. I had not cried in years. I was hurt, mad, destroyed, and exhausted. I could not believe she had shared my situation with Sara and Emily! The perception I wanted people to see was crumbing. I felt like I was losing control of the circus.

It was at that moment I realized Paul was wrong when he said I was lucky by not having a family. The irony was it was his wife Lyn who revealed it to me. I had believed him when he said it and I took it literally, but that was my mistake. My actions or inactions in life had affected others. Stunned. I was not alone in the circus of one, and even though my will was directing a path that would resemble being alone my life and how I led it was impacting others directly and indirectly. My body went numb.

It took everything I had to drive to brunch and sit at the same table with Paul and his family. I was crushed beyond belief and sat quietly while eating an assortment of fruits and sausages, cringing at the fact I had indeed affected other people.

My only thought was that in a few short hours I was getting on a plane and out of this place I never called home to return to Windansea to be alone...once again.

3
CLOWN REHAB

Arriving back at Windansea, I safely made it through the airport without having to wrestle with the comforts available to my circus performers while traveling. Did I mention how much I treasure airports, train stations, bus depots, and embarcaderos?

The ability to shape-shift and be whoever I wanted to be was enhanced in these venues; honing my craft in these environments allowing me to connect the first thought entering my mind with people from other cities, countries, and every imaginable walk of life. The next patron of my circus was being placed at my feet for me to entertain as they flowed down the escalator like water from a waterfall. It felt so electric. I was alive.

The airport was the ultimate fantasyland for adults when transporting themselves from one locale to the next. We lay out the new dress or the perfect suit and tie, the tightly coiffed hairdos are planned well ahead of departure, cloaking oneself for the opportunity to be a little more or less than who you really are. A place where the ability to create another reality, even if it is only for a short while, providing one a safe space to exercise the boundaries of fantasy.

The questions we ask each other in these environments can easily lead one to freely juggle the truth. How often do you travel? Where is your destination? Is this business or personal travel? Are you single or married? Can I buy you a cocktail? What do you do? The imagination churns;

the body is toned even if it actually isn't. The shell has been dressed-up, touched-up, and the odors emanating from one perfumed body to the next intoxicate our decision-making.

If you can at all relate to the possibility of hedging the truth in one form or another in these settings, then at the very least you are being honest with yourself. The transporting of our physical bodies from one locale to another seems to inject a dose of the suspension of reality until suddenly the screeching of the wheels on the tarmac jolts us back to reality. The hustle and bustle to get off the plane to retrieve who you really are is imminent.

The carousels go round and round with every imaginable shape and size of luggage, all looking like the one containing our real identity. Cautiously, we watch the luggage tumble down the ramp containing the trinkets and clothing that has become who we are in our modern world. A world where having the next best thing is only surpassed by having the next best thing.

Horror jumps to the forefront of our consciousness if our luggage doesn't descend. What will we do? Then, out of nowhere, it appears through the chaos of the other lost souls scrambling for the same inanimate object containing our masked identities. Clearing a space in front of the carousel, I gathered my balance in anticipation of steer wrestling my life away from the other thespians. The anxiety dissipates when the luggage is secured as you head out the automatic doors to step back into your life as it started out earlier that day. Aren't we all actors in one form or another?

Unfortunately for me, the luggage of my life never left the carousel as it continually went round and round, playing to untold numbers of unsuspecting patrons. But things were starting to change in the subtlest ways; as I lifted what represented me off the carousel, I symbolically tossed the top hat of controlling what happened next in my life aside for the moment. Maybe I could let what should happen next, happen?

I was back in the safety of Windansea for now, unsure of what resolve was needed to stay the course while still feeling the effects of my talk with Lyn that seemed so long ago, but in fact was this morning.

Awaking before dawn, I rumbled around my cottage until it was time to go to *Sunrise*. I'm not sure why I was going, but the pain resonating inside my vessel after my chat with Lyn needed to come out and this sharing out loud with a bunch of strangers seemed to work in accomplishing that very goal.

The cast of characters at *Sunrise* seemed to always be suited for what was needed at the time, and I was starting to trust this newfound refuge, the light. At the very same moment I was calculating the flight time to

South America—Chile in particular—and the amount of resources I had available to start the winery with attached boutique hotel, which happened to be my first thought when feeling the pain I was feeling inside, the dark. I liked this newfound refuge *Sunrise*, but the draw to the formula of connecting my first thought to a new reality was overwhelming. But a shift had occurred in how I was navigating life, finding myself desperately holding on to the shimmer of light slowly growing at *Sunrise*. Simply, I felt like I had no other choice at the moment. Uncomfortable relief.

The light and dark were dancing to their own tune, carving out space in my life on their own terms, again. I'd been a complete mess since awakening on the magic couch some three and a half weeks ago, and this new battle racing in my head on what to do next was exhausting an already taxed system. Go to *Sunrise* or implement what had already entered my mind, Chile? I didn't realize it at the moment, but I was having more than one thought at a time, a troubling unfamiliar territory for a self-will toned at executing only one thought at a time before exercising the next thought. Thankfully *Sunrise* was only minutes away.

Sunrise's general lack of formality did have a daily structure starting with the prerequisite readings and then a share by the meeting leader to eventually proceed around the room until it was your time to share.

I needed to share this morning. Taking a deep breath, with eyes still fixed to the ground, I shared how I had reverse interventioned my friends and family, and how I had made everybody feel better about what was going on in my life for the next ninety days or so. As I rambled on about me, again, a hint of the truth crept past my lips, sharing my conversation with Lyn and how it had devastated me in ways I failed to fully comprehend. I was finally sharing some feelings and emotions, and most importantly, I was finally being honest to the best of my ability.

As much as I clung to the delusion that my circus was composed of one, it was now uncomfortably apparent to me I had affected others with my actions or inactions in life. I had never cared what people thought of me—a vital character attribute when living your life implementing into action one thought to the next. Unknowingly, what was really going on in the unfiltered caverns of my mind was starting flow out in the form of words to my new patrons. I even surprised myself, as I shared my thoughts of running to South America to ensure I would never willfully hurt another again. My intent was to make sure those who still cared would never be burdened again, providing the space for them and more importantly, for me to move on with life without the tether of relationships—regardless of their frayed condition. I finished my share and passed to the next person, losing myself in the flickering of the fireplace flames as the meeting was near its end when the poking of the fire was reaching its climax.

As was customary after the reading of the *Promises*, a short reading detailing the benefits afforded when one vigorously works the program, all the *Sunrisers* stood to join hands and recited the *Serenity Prayer*:

"God, Grant me the serenity to accept the things I cannot change,
the courage to change the things I can,
and the wisdom to know the difference."

I've ritualized this prayer but never really understood its significance or cared for it because I didn't want to change anything in my life. Suddenly, the significance of the prayer illuminated those dark caverns I hid so well, and I understood it could help me as I walked through my day. The first line exposes the people, places, and things I cannot change. The second line confirms I can be changed by me. The last line takes the issue to a power greater than oneself for the "wisdom" to know the difference. I acknowledged its significance, but it was a little early to start taking new ideas and implementing them into my life. I wanted the pain to stop, that's it!

Meanwhile, as the prayer was being recited I had the feeling someone was looking right through me, so I quickly scanned the room to identify the source of this heat when I locked eyes with Franz and his piercing bloodshot tear filled eyes. I was hoping he was eyeballing the coffee pot for the last drops coveted after the meeting is finished, or maybe he was lusting over the day old pastries sitting on the table adjacent to the coffee pot. Lady Luck was not in my corner as he made a beeline for my personal space.

I noticed Franz several weeks earlier and was struck by his story and the depth of his honesty. Ten months earlier Franz had been three years sober, but now he was unable to put the bottle down when the desire arose or when the pain was too much to bear. According to others, he worked a great program of helping those who suffered from the disease of alcoholism. He was a testimony to the paradox inherent in finding a new way to live a life without an outside source: alcohol, sex, money, power, gluttony, sloth, and any number of other human addictions. The paradox of the program was simple. To keep this new way of living one must freely give it to another so they can have life anew as well. But it was during this process of giving away his sobriety in the form of service to another when he stumbled and was now unable to unlock the shackle of the drink from his life.

One of the young men he was helping came to a standstill in his life, resulting in the only imaginable resolution to the dilemma of living a life without the aid of an outside source to subdue his pain. Suicide. He would ramble on about the desperate act his friend had taken and how he failed his friend. The pain Franz harbored inside was unfathomable, and the only remedy possible in his mind to quell his pain was to pour obscene amounts of alcohol down his gullet. The way he saw it, he didn't have the guts to take the quick path to a painless existence like his friend had chosen, but rather he was making the same choice of suicide only in slow motion, one drink at a time. Drinking yourself to death was like being kicked to death by rabbits. Why was he still showing up to these meetings? He was drinking again with no intention to stop, but he kept coming back. I was intrigued and scared. He was making his way toward me. I wanted him to stop. Please not me!

I had, at this point, attended at least a meeting a day, including my week back in New Mexico, and was lucky enough not to have had any real engagement with another before or after a meeting. My plan of slipping into a meeting and getting what I wanted — suppression of the pain — and then slipping out without connecting to another was about to end. He couldn't stop himself if he tried; I only wish he could.

Franz lumbered across the room, wearing his adult, two-piece pajamas, cloaked in a satin smoking jacket and house slippers, and reeking of scotch. I felt as if time had slowed down to a point where every breath I was taking was exaggerated and every heartbeat he was having thundered in my ears as the distance between us diminished. I wanted to run, but my flip-flops were encased in concrete. I was frozen and shackled to this moment in time, and I wanted nothing to do with what he had to say or share. I was going to have to converse with Franz whether I liked it or not. Please stop!

Who in my cast of performers could save me now? I think we're all familiar with the feeling when you sense something important and even life-changing is about to happen right before it happens and you want to run like hell. I had that feeling, and the reason why I wanted to run is because I didn't know the outcome before it had a chance to happen. I wanted to know what was going to happen before I committed to this interlude and concrete laden flip-flops were my only faith at the moment. God help me!

As Franz moved closer, I could see the tears welling in his eyes. He greeted me with a hug lasting way too long for my goal of not wanting to connect with these people. I needed to ease the pain dwelling in my soul, not make friends, especially not with the likes that roamed the rooms of sobriety. He thanked me for my share, and what then rolled out of his lips was truly manna from heaven.

He told me I didn't have to run and hide, and I could be an example to those two young girls. I could be an example of transformation. A life that stands up and takes responsibility for my actions or inactions in life, rising above the wreckage I created in my life, willfully.

It was if I could see the words literally moving past his lips through the air into my ears and, for the first time in my life that I could consciously remember, to my heart. I was having one of those spiritual experiences again where one person shares their heart and experience for no other reason than to help another. He moved me deeply. My armor was pierced.

With reflection, it was apparent Franz didn't want me to feel the same pain he was feeling inside, and he was accomplishing this by sharing with me the pain he was feeling inside. He wanted to make sure I uncovered all the stumbling blocks he felt he hadn't uncovered for his friend who committed suicide. He didn't want me to fail as he felt he had. I was connected to another human being for the first time in my life, and it was amazing! Connected mystically, since he knew exactly how I was feeling inside without me saying a word.

The tears started to freely flow from my eyes as the shackles that had constricted me from the age of eight started to relinquish their death grip on my being. It was the tears Franz willfully spilled at my feet that allowed me the freedom to meet him in a place of complete honesty and openness, stripping away our protective shells to reveal what was really going on inside, so that the potentiality of healing could take place in both of our lives. We hugged once more and I thanked him for talking to me as I scurried down the stairwell to hop on my bike for the short ride home.

It was at that moment, while peddling down Nautilus Street toward Windansea Beach, that I felt my head tilt back and felt the Kool-Aid of sobriety trickling past my lips in the form of another human being. An elixir not man made, but made of man. A new resolve was instilled in my heart, and it was not my idea, but one freely shared by another human suffering from our shared humanness. I was not going to act upon the South American extravaganza for now, which would be an amazing experience for all my performers. I decided to set it aside while I trudged a new path not of my own will.

At Sunrise there is a saying, "contempt before investigation," meaning we disregard something or the value of that thing before being fully investigated. I had dabbled in trying to fix the emptiness in my life for so long and had wrestled with many options but with limited and temporary results. My experience at *Sunrise* was revolutionizing my perception of the program and the steps one works through to change their life from the inside out. I had tried various religious traditions, with limited results, and now was resolved to give this program an honest effort. So many things were organically happening in my life, and one of those was this newfound realization that if I was going to have a chance at this peace and calm my fellow *Sunrisers* lived under, I was going to have to work at it. It was going to be the fight of my life. The stakes were higher than ever before.

As far back as I can remember, everything in life came easy to me and had no meaning. I never applied full measure to anything or anyone, nor had I devised a plan and executed it in my entire life. I would have an idea and then use my circus of one and my growing cast of performers to implement the next thought that came to mind. The only thing left to do was to watch, without a care in the world, the fruits of my will pour through the door of life. It was that easy. In reality it was an illusion.

Ironically, I didn't have the same comfort when devising my new plan for the next ninety days. The plan was to attend at least ninety meetings in ninety days as recommended when attempting sobriety—I had thirty meetings under my belt so far. I was going to rehab for twenty-eight days at the end of October—only ten short days away. I would get out of rehab and go spend the Christmas holiday with my sister Theri and her family in Chicago, like I had done for the past several years. Upon my return from Chicago, I would resume the revenue-raising activities of my life that always seemed fruitful: I would find new work. I had a new resolve and a plan that was achievable—though I'd been unsure of what that meant because I'd never had a plan before in my life—but the new course was dialed in and I was ready to do what was necessary to execute the plan.

I heard a share in my first couple of weeks of sobriety and wrote it down, but was not sure why it resonated: "If you're a newcomer to the program and you have a plan, it's wrong." How funny. I recently developed a new plan for the next ninety days. My ego was resilient. It never lacked confidence.

With a life never navigated by plan before and now having one for the next several months, it seemed my course was set in stone; if executed willfully I could possibly be the example of transformation Franz talked about that morning at *Sunrise*.

The time leading up to my departure to rehab was filled with meetings and visits to the doctor, dentist, and optometrist. But what took precedence was the spinning of my mind to figure out what was going to happen after I returned from Chicago. I signed up to several job-recruiting sites and was scouring the local listing for what to do next, career-wise. I knew my options would be limited, what with driving privileges suspended for up to nine months and only a bike for transportation.

I looked for opportunities daily, conscious of the fact I couldn't seriously look until I returned from rehab, but this didn't stop me from spending hours a day plotting my rise back to something that provided the outside comfort I was accustomed to in life. Although empty, it did provide comfort. What I didn't realize was how isolated I had become until I started to plan being away from my home for the next thirty days. No one would miss me while I was away. Not a soul.

In one form or another, I contacted all the people who would know I would be gone for the next month, and this included Lisa. Via e-mail, I shared with her that I would be gone for a while to do some cleansing work, both physically and spiritually. At least I was moving in the direction of telling the truth, even if it wasn't even close to the whole truth.

Why was I holding onto someone or something that was a brief moment of time in my life up to this point? Was Lisa another one of my fantasies, the sinister willful act of doing all this life-changing stuff over the next ninety days so I could have the chance of being with Lisa once again? Would I be going through the motions to check all the required boxes just so I could get what I wanted with her? The separation from Lisa was painful.

The thirst I had for this connection was unquenchable. It drained me. Why had she touched me so deeply, and why could I not shake her from my mind and heart? I ended my e-mail with "love you." Lisa responded with understanding and compassion and shared that she intuitively knew I was struggling with something and would pray for me. How could she know that I was struggling? Was it that obvious? Had I revealed, without intention, the pain I was feeling inside? She closed her e-mail with a simple—but for me, life-changing—word: "Love."

Unfortunately for me, fear and love were so interconnected in my life that sharing those words and feelings with another was paralyzing. The fear of it not being returned was the heart of the matter. It didn't feel that way this time. I just wanted to let it out. We had not spoken since the week before my perfect storm and had never spoken those words to each other back then, but we had now done so in writing.

All the boxes were checked. I was now ready to go to rehab, even though it was not my idea and not of my will.

It was the twenty-eighth of October, and my sister Theri was in La Jolla for a medical conference furthering her certification as a practitioner of integrative medicine. Theri was the Director and Founder of The Raby Institute of Integrative Medicine in Chicago, and she was the only sibling I had developed a relationship with as an adult. I had reached out to her after number six, wanting to get my physical life back in order, and she was able to connect me with some amazing people in Austin. It was a healing process for me in so many ways and the beginning of the foundation of a relationship I had desired as a child with my brothers and sisters but was not possible. The conference had been planned months ahead of time, and her arrival happened to be the day before I went into rehab.

I was committed to the process of checking in to rehab and staying the twenty-eight days—which, by the way, had me staying through Thanksgiving. I was at peace with this decision. I just wasn't sure this was going to help me. A feeling stirring deep inside me about my true intent with this rehab stint was a constant over the past several weeks. It was becoming very apparent that my run-ins with the law were always associated with drinking, the trivial, but the heart of the matter for me was never, ever addressed. I was hoping the providential nature of the connection between Bob Jefferson and Norm was going to be enough to see me through the next twenty-eight days. It was comforting to have Theri so near, and in retrospect, it was perfect because she would be in La Jolla for the next several days.

Early the next morning, Theri left for her conference and I was off to *Sunrise* for the last time before rehab. My bag was packed and I said goodbye to my new friends and hurried home to wait for the driver to pick me up. It was too late to back out now—but let me tell you, South America was sure sounding ideal at the moment. I was reflecting back to when I was a child and had attended summer camp for the first time, and I hoped this experience didn't mirror the experience at camp, where I had been dismissed for not following the rules. Apparently I only liked the walls *I* constructed.

It's tough to follow rules when you live your life guided by the next thought entering your mind. I was relieved that a driver was going to go pick me up, since I wasn't sure I would make the sixty-mile trip north without assistance. I assume that's why they have someone shuttle you to the final destination—because let me tell you, the anxiety and the mind-scrambling that happens when you know you are only minutes away from the rehab facility is intense. Within seconds, doubt was creating some space in my mind; it happens that quickly. How could I have let outside influences direct my reality? Rehab wasn't in the cards for my life. The mind does tricks on you when fear and doubt settle in and jostle for position in the process of deciphering the truth. It becomes confusing and the clarity is muddled, at best.

In a whisper of a moment, all of the resolve to be an example to others by transforming my life from the inside out was not even on the first page of why I was trying to make myself better. My life was great, and having

41

multiple DUIs was no big deal because everything else in my life seemed admirable and enviable. Right?

I had money, freedom, no attachments, and health, with the ability to move halfway across the globe at the drop of the hat, and now I found myself sitting in the back seat of a four-door, black sedan, heading up Interstate 5 to the unknown. This was all wrong, and I felt shackled once more—shackled to reality and not fantasy, and it was a strange turn of events. I was truly in the wrong circus ring, no performer devised for this act.

Ironically, it was the two of us: me and my lone piece of luggage that never made its way off the carousel of life, now tightly nestled right next to me. I was clinging to me like never before, and what truly represented me was packed away in that lone piece of luggage. I could not run or hide from me anymore, and would rehab be the answer to helping me reconcile the light and dark of my life? I needed this to work out; I was not sure what that meant, but certainly was desperate for something to happen.

I was rolling the dice and expecting miracles and curiously craving a little banter from my driver while on the ride to rehab, but the unusual always played out in my circus. The driver was disconnected from my experience, taking one phone call after another, furthering my feelings of being all alone. My circus meant nothing to him. My act was boring in his eyes. The mind-scrambling intensified. What was it going to be like for the next twenty-eight days? Was it going to be like *Sunrise?* Would I have to tell my story again? Would I have another gut wrenching, uncomfortable feeling and experience like I had with Franz that turned out wonderful, or would it fall short at rehab and sour my short but sweet experience with honesty?

My resolve at the moment was to make this happen, and if it failed it was not of my own doing, releasing me to resume my circus act with full measure, without fear of disappointing anyone with my actions or inactions. The table would be set and everyone would know the score, and I would drift off to another place, ready to resume the ending of my life. The car reached our destination, and I slithered from the back seat, ready to face my new reality…rehab.

The two-storied, U-shaped building was tightly positioned halfway down a residential street that resembled any middle class neighborhood in southern California. The telltale sign was the uncountable number of cars parked in every possible nook and cranny. An unbalanced ratio of cars to people was evident. My vision of a beachfront house with grand gardens and a swimming pool the kind displayed on television by news helicopters trying to get a glimpse of the newly crowned celebrity rehab victim, was crushed. This courtyard was of concrete with a picnic table and a few round tables in one corner and to the other side, a ping-pong table with an assortment of tattered and under-used exercise equipment. My ego needed more.

As I entered the courtyard, a half dozen people were milling around the tables, chatting and smoking cigarettes. I was experiencing the uncomfortable feeling when you enter a room and everybody knows each other except you and all eyes are upon you but no one will acknowledge you. It's almost like they were scared to talk to me or even greet me — like some kind of code is established when you enter rehab for the first time. Disheartening.

Quickly, I was whisked behind closed doors to an office doubling as the dispensary for the medicine residents were prescribed while in the facility. Medicine, doling out drugs, locked cabinets for personal items such as cell phones and money. What the fuck did I get myself into?

Mike, my intake counselor, greeted me and we settled in to fill out some paperwork so I could be one of the fellows sitting in the courtyard smoking cigarettes. It was really quite comical as the phone rang incessantly. Adding to the chaos, the room we were sitting in was being painted. As soon as we would resume the intake process, a patient needing his medicine or access to his personal items interrupted the flow. It was a mad house, and with each pause in the process, fear and a mounting dose of anxiety was building inside me. It took two hours to fill out two pages of the intake form, and we still had several more to go when everything came to a halt because it was lunchtime. Apparently, in rehab, when it's time to eat, you eat.

Mike escorted me to the second floor dining room kitchen but not until we locked down the valuables, drugs, and medicine, which in my wildest imagination would be a vital necessity in rehab. It makes sense now, but at the time it didn't, especially when you are in the process of checking into rehab. Drinking was my poison and occasionally drugs would be a compliment, but this place was a fucking pharmacy and not the ideal place to be checking a patient into rehab. A serene environment to give one the sense of safety and comfort was far from my experience. The dark side of me liked the haphazardness and recklessness of my check-in, but the light that had guided me here was wrestling with the idea of being compliant in my stay and this was not looking like an ideal place for me at the moment. But none of that mattered when it was time to eat.

Taking a deep breath, I opened the door to the long rectangular room that contained five large round tables seating up to eight people each. On the left side of the room was a kitchen with a serving line. Apparently, it was a good day in the mess hall. Excitement was brewing with a menu of sliced beef, salad, and canned fruit.

The patrons of this eating establishment had served themselves and were situated at four of the tables. I nervously picked up a plate and served myself, turning to scan the room for an empty seat with the hope of acknowledgement and some conversation to change the way I was feeling. This was easy, I thought. I had the skills to create a connection in any situation. Not a seat was available except for the open arms of the lone empty table. I would be conversing alone this afternoon. I was the pariah, the leper, and the one who hadn't been officially tagged as one of them and accordingly I was shunned. Not a nod to acknowledge my presence or even a glance in my direction. My gut twisted another knot.

Hunger was driving me now, so I settled in to eat while gazing around the room to see if I could connect with my fellow inmates from afar, knowing full well I could with my circus of performers. I wanted — or better yet, needed — to know what performers were necessary to pull from my archives to make the next twenty-eight days palatable. As you can imagine, in this environment water seeks its own level, and the individuals clinging to each other for safety were obvious in one quick snapshot of the room.

In the human experience, we seek our own kind in strange and uncomfortable environments, if only to make small talk until the uneasiness wears off. The young surfer dudes were grinding at one table, the middle-aged, Midwest cats joshing each other at another, the loud-talking East Coast cats bullshitting at the third, and last but not least a table of fat guys. I could easily make it here for the next twenty-eight days if I could only get one person other than Mike to acknowledge my presence. Lunch was coming to a close, and as quickly as the room had filled with hungry bodies, it emptied.

Was this the place for me? My mind was on hyper-drive and my casts of performers were all elbowing each other to get to the front of the line so they could get some face time in this new venue called rehab. It was a first for all the performers in my circus. We had never worked this circuit before and believe me, the casting couch was full of salivating actors ready for an opportunity.

This could be fun! The rehab gig was going to be kindergarten for this wearer of the top hat, and I was feeling confident that I had the necessary performers to make the next twenty-eight days a successful run. The kind of runs that washed up and no longer relevant entertainers accomplish in Las Vegas today. This was another show for me, and I wanted the curtain to rise with an eventual bow at the end of my stay so I could move on to returning from the holidays in Chicago and getting on with life. But the paperwork had not been completed and more importantly I had not been interviewed by a healthcare professional to get my final approval by my insurance provider to approve my treatment and their obligation to pay. Details.

The chaos making up my intake earlier had subsided, allowing Mike and I to move through the remainder of the paperwork fairly quickly. I was ready to sign the documents. The only thing standing between me and my stay at rehab was my signature and the evaluation.

The nurse was busy at the moment, and I would have to wait till about two thirty to get evaluated as per the insurance requirements. At this point I was getting a little nervous because my insurance provider was on east coast time and would be closing at six thirty. It was cutting it close to get evaluated, processed, and approved in about an hour's time if the nurse showed up at two thirty like they said she would. I had been at rehab for about five hours now, and all I had to show for it was some sliced beef, a dose of fumes from the newly painted dispensary, a lot of blank stares but no real contact from my fellow inmates, and the uncertainty about checking into rehab for the next twenty-eight days.

The fear and anxiety that had been in a lull earlier in the day was starting to crescendo into panic as I sensed my plan was starting to unravel. The rehab stint was a big part of the plan on my personal road to a new way of dealing with the heart of the matter in my life, me. I reached out to Paul and let him know what was going on and that the intake process had come to a halt. We laughed and injected some humor into the situation when he suggested a quick plane trip to pick me up to get hammered, so that the evaluation of my physical condition wouldn't be in question. It would be the first time I actually counted the time since my last cocktail: minutes rolling into hours, hours adding up to days, culminating in a whopping thirty-six days. As fun and ridiculous as it sounded, the option of getting hammered so I would be a viable candidate for rehab in the eyes of my insurance provider was absurd.

I couldn't help feeling like this process was leaking out of my control, so with some seriousness, we agreed that signing the intake paperwork without the authorization from the insurance company was not an option. The insurance company made it clear weeks ago that an evaluation would need to be done and the rehab center made it clear that signing the paperwork was no big deal. The fact was, if I signed the paperwork without authorization, I would be personally responsible for the entire amount. I was currently paying the five hundred dollars a month premium to my insurance company to have coverage, and I was not going to pay twenty-three thousand dollars more for twenty-eight days in rehab when I had already been sober for thirty-six days. So I waited for the nurse to show up. What I really needed was a shot of Jaeger and a blast of cocaine. This concoction never failed. The red flag was raised.

It was becoming very apparent I would have to lie to the nurse during my evaluation so that I would be able to enter rehab with authorization from the insurance provider. Would I have to stretch the truth? Let's not forget my method of manipulating the truth did not include lying for the most part. And since the spiritual experience I had with Harold on my front lawn, I had in fact been honest with pretty much everything as best I could over the last thirty-six days. Starting to drink again to get into rehab was as absurd as starting to play footloose and fancy free with the truth to secure my spot in rehab. I was starting to change. Baby steps.

Lauren arrived at two forty-five to evaluate my physical and presumably psychological condition, leaving forty-five minutes to finish the evaluation and report back to the insurance company for final approval. We danced around the medical and family history questions and determined a genetic link to my predisposition for the love of the drink. I let her know I had ruined relationships and my own recent job situation as well as a history of driving while under the influence. With seven DUIs under my belt, one would surmise that even an insurance company would recognize that I was in need of some assistance. Or maybe in their eyes I didn't meet the criteria for someone who needed help. Maybe I wasn't in bad enough shape to get the help I desperately needed in the eyes of the insurance world and their secret formulas for approval.

The game the nurse was playing was poetic in the sense that she added to my truth to make it sound better — or worse, depending on how you looked at it. The funny thing was, I had no part in making the "truth" sound more dramatic than the truth. Lauren was doing a fine job all by herself. We ended the interview after about fifteen minutes, and she pranced off to make the phone call for the expected final approval. I was relieved to know the process was over and rehab was only minutes away.

I had a few minutes to burn, not tobacco at least not until I was admitted, while Lauren was away doing the dance providers do with insurance companies to get the dead presidents flowing. It was about this time that one of the inmates, Sammy, made his way over to ask how my intake was coming along. We chatted up the usual topics, and he mentioned that he was from Farmington, New Mexico. Small world, but the big shocker was the reason why he was here specifically was because of Norm.

As a child, Sammy's foundation for church on Sunday commenced by flicking on the television and dialing to the station that beamed Pastor Norm presiding from the pulpit. This early life experience provided the faith he needed to try this rehab stuff someone else's way, raving how amazing Norm was at helping all the patients get to the heart of their matter. He had experienced a difference this time, pinpointing that if it weren't for Norm's presence, this place would be like the other six rehab facilities he had tried but eventually failed to secure long-term sobriety. A spiritual awakening was the difference this time, guided by the steady hand of a man he trusted when he turned on the television as a child. The connection started long ago, culminating in a life-changing arrangement benefiting both human souls. Nothing is by chance.

Was this the affirmation I was looking for to comfort me while my admittance was in question? I was only hoping! I had not spoken to Norm for about a week and at this point trusted the process. I was at peace. I had done all I could do to get into rehab and now the result was in the hands of God. I think? Who knows? My faith was weak.

It was chow time, and Sammy was off to the mess hall to get his grub on while I patiently waited for Lauren to bring me the good news. Lauren exited the office and sat down and calmly explained my insurance provider had not approved my stay because I was not in a chronic state; I was not in the need of medical care. Lauren had asked to speak to a supervisor to override the initial decision, but there was no guarantee it would be reversed. She suggested I stay the night to see if the insurance company was going to change their decision. The hook was I had to sign the paperwork.

What? If I stayed to eat some fish sticks and mashed potatoes out of a box I would be responsible for the twenty-three-thousand-dollar fee. That's pretty expensive lodging and I loved staying at expensive hotels with top-notch services. My favorite local sleeping establishment was the Bel Air Hotel, and if I did it right I could stretch those funds for a month of lounging, fine vittles, booze, and women to cure my desire to change everything. I decided staying the night with the uncertainty of the insurance company reversing their decision in the morning was more comical than drinking to ensure my admittance.

The bottom line was, I was being denied coverage to enter rehab because I was sober for thirty-six days. I grabbed my life, luggage on wheels, and waited for the cab to pick me up to take me to San Juan Capistrano to catch the train back to San Diego. I caught the last train back and departed at Solana Beach to hail a cab to my final destination, Windansea.

It was past midnight and I was exhausted. I was tired of all this up and down emotional stuff that was easily fixed in the past by my circus of thoughts implemented into reality. But for the moment, I had abandoned this comfort in search of a new way of life. I was naked. I liked being naked, but this was different.

This new course was proving to be less than comforting as I dragged myself into my cottage, placing my luggage safely in my bedroom for safekeeping while I made my way over to the safety and comfort that only the magic couch provided. I powered up my late night friend, never changing the channel, as I needed some noise to keep me company. I was numb, empty and without emotion, gently gazing in the direction of the noise while trying to figure out: What went wrong with my plan?

I didn't like the pain I was feeling without the elixir allowing me to knock off the edges in life. I had tried to go to rehab, but that didn't seem to be in the cards. I needed something to knock off the edge, and I was pretty sure drinking was not going to be an option, at least tonight. Maybe my life had a few bumps and all this rehab and changing my life was just too much? I had no idea what to do next, but strangely I was comforted by what I did know: *Sunrise* was a few hours away.

4
LIONS, TIGERS, AND SEALS

I love waking up on my two-piece green- and rust-colored sectional couch. It can easily fit two large adults comfortably or a gaggle of smaller human beings with room to spare. It has big pillows and small pillows that can be positioned in a thousand different ways to achieve your desired level of comfort.

For the past ten years when sleeping alone, I have chosen the magic couch to rest my frame, rather than my extremely comfortable and equally gargantuan four-post with hand-carved headboard king-sized bed. I loved being alone, but I hated sleeping in my bed alone, so I sprawled on the magic, aided by the comfort of the television and its cast of all-night thespians that never rested, not unlike the cast of thespians in me unable to find a restful place of their own. My mind continually churned, and even in those few hours where I was able to sleep per night, my mind had something to keep it company as my body desperately drifted to sleep. An uncomfortable alliance—dependency with compassion.

This was my routine for the last ten years, and the loneliness consuming me with a thousand moving parts and performers rambling around in this box of rocks hoisted above my shoulders desperately needed relief. The alcohol and occasional drugs saved my life up to the point when they stopped working. It had been years since the snake oil was effective.

The alcohol business was a young man's game, and I had already passed my fortieth birthday when all the debauchery of my life was going to end by one willful act. No more drinking. The setting of an arbitrary date to pinpoint a monumental change in the type of life I had led up to this point without some type of internal transformation was bizarre. I had relied upon my will for so long. It was the two of us slicing and dicing our way through the world, all while seeming logical and plausible that within a day's time, I could unravel my circus and walk away without any attachments. Attachments? I didn't have any attachments—or did I?

I always considered attachments were of the material nature, and my personal belongings were consciously kept to a minimum for a variety of reasons. The most important one being if I ever had to move quickly for whatever reason, I would be able to do it in a half day's time. I don't have photo albums, rock collections, or an animal furthering my ability to change directions or locations on a moment's thought. As I pat myself on the back for not having physical attachments, my reality that I've been attached to every single outcome in life somehow escapes me. I had a boatload of attachments and the necessary and essential performers in my circus to ensure every single desired outcome. What a complicated mess!

The plan of having a new life at forty comes in many forms. The desire to be physically fit is a common theme in the human experience, presuming one has gotten a little soft over the past decade trying to raise a family, amass a nest egg, or in my case, debauchery gone awry. Pushing the extremes of time management by waking up at ungodly hours and getting in the cardio and weight training to recapture the physique of our past takes time and dedication. One has to weave not only physical activity, but also eating habits have to be changed to achieve the desired results. The most critical of all the elements in changing our physical look is the time commitment. Patience surely is in short supply when vanity is the end game.

Not only does life speed up as we get older, it takes longer for things to change as old habits and ego push their way to the forefront of our lives. But for this crafty thespian of the big tent, time was not a consideration. When you're always getting what you want and keeping what you have, then you find little time to complain about time. Interestingly enough, I was in tiptop shape when I turned forty, hoping a physical change would instigate an internal one as well. Physically, I was fit, but spiritually and mentally, I was a mess. No balance.

My plan to flick the switch to a new way of living only worked for as long as the next thought came to mind, as I willfully jetted off to San Pedro, Belize, for my self-celebration of scuba diving, partying, and hunting up the next warm body to keep me company for the week. I was post forty and not sober. Oh well…

In my mind's eye, I got kicked out of rehab and was now experiencing a feeling of failure, knowing full well that trying to get what I wanted with a plan had failed me once again. Living a life with a plan was too static for my nature, regardless of my desire to get to the heart of the matter. Somehow, I had to reconcile the loneliness I was feeling and the corresponding pain it was inflicting on my mind, body, and spirit, as well as the haphazard "fly by the seat of my pants" lifestyle. The rehab stint with honest intentions and perceived providential nature emanating from Bob Jefferson had derailed right in front of me, and now the dark in my life was pushing me out the door down the street to *Sunrise* to see who in fact I really was and wanted to be. My plan would no longer be my plan, as I was starting to move ever so slowly, and one might say organically, toward God's will not mine.

What is God's will for me, or for that matter anyone, trying to live a life based on spiritual principles? Honestly, I don't believe I struggled with this thought consciously in my life, and that would be buttressed by how I lived my life so wantonly. Continually chasing the next thought consuming my mind can only be accurately coined in lay terms as selfish and self-centered. My mental prowess in cahoots with my circus performers was responsible for my stellar résumé. Or was it?

Was it possible something other than my own will could be at the helm guiding my rudderless ship? If I really thought about it, making a thought come to fruition had to entail some type of planning or non-planning. Not making a plan is like making a plan as is not making a decision making a decision.

It was time to really start slowing down my life to a pace that would allow me to gather my thoughts and move through the day taking small bites out the debacle my life had become, which I desperately needed to expose and unravel if serenity was the end game.

If I was going to earnestly and honestly move past the trivial matters in my life and get to the heart of the matter, I was going to have to slow down and let go and let God. Not only had I heard the term before, but I'd graciously offered its healing advice to countless others without the experience of actually making it a part of my daily actions. In other words, I did the exact opposite, unable to let go of the reins on my life, no matter what. If the details of life became unbearable, the only possible entity capable of helping me was me.

I once heard in a meeting this little gem of advice: Let go, let God, or get dragged. I loved being dragged around by my will and the ensuing depression that followed, but my saving grace was I didn't like depression, and that's where the next thought entering my mind worked so well. My next thought was the active ingredient, and when exercised, the immediate emotional lift was produced and instantly the depression was vaporized.

With reflection, my life was a never-ending cycle of anxiety, excitement, and then depression. Anxiety in the form of what thought was going to come next, excitement at implementing the thought into reality, and depression resulting from the implementation of the thought which I experienced and now the ensuing boredom of needing more and now something different. The cyclical nature of my reason and its associated insanity of doing the same thing and expecting different results were equally exhilarating and exhausting. If you have the will, the stamina, and the ever-growing cast of performers in which to keep the show going, then this lifestyle is sustainable. But if one of the pieces to the puzzle was weakened, then a perfect storm can crumble a highly engineered man-made structure. I was my own man-made structure and my perfect storm crumbled me into submission and humility. I was now going to have to find this peace and calm I wanted so badly in my life one moment at time, without a plan.

No plans, wake up in the morning, get cleaned up, and start my day off with *Sunrise* and see what happens next. That was it? This didn't sound very promising, and now I really had a lot of free time on my hands. No rehab, no job, no friends to speak of that lived locally, and an uneasiness in what tomorrow would hold for me. I called Theri and let her know I had been denied entry into rehab and asked if she wanted to get together for dinner. How perfect was it that she was in town not for seeing me off to rehab, but rather to be there for me when I was kicked out? Apparently, I don't do well in controlled environments, and Manzano Day School summer camp as a child and rehab as an adult were testimonies to that fact.

Theri was staying at a resort in Mission Bay, and after *Sunrise,* I jumped on the bus to be near her, enjoying the amenities while she took classes and studied for her exam. It felt like a distant memory, but in all reality, it was only a few hours ago when my experience at rehab consisted of paint fumes, fruit out of a can, concrete, cigarette smoke, and unfriendly and poor customer service. And now I magically landed ass first into my new rehab oasis composed of wonderfully manicured gardens, crystal clear pool, state-of-the-art athletic center, freshly picked fruit, water with lemon, and four-star services. I was living my celebrity rehab, and it didn't cost a dime and it didn't have to involve insurance companies and my current alcohol content. I rested, exercised, ate well, and had time to be quiet. These accommodations and Theri's presence only lasted a couple of days, but the imprint the experience had upon me would be the start to a new way of navigating my way around my new home, Windansea.

On first thought, it seemed obvious that Theri's presence was critical for me to actually go through with the rehab experience, knowing full well in my heart I would only be continuing my circus within the walls of rehab.

It would have been another show, another town, and another box to check in life. I always performed with passion for my patrons. It laminated my loneliness with connection. It would no longer suffice.

What I desperately needed was to find a way to heal my heart and cure my inability to have and keep relationships with other human beings. But higher powers were at work now, and it was the quiet time I experienced those few days after my departure from rehab and the luxury to have Theri so near in a time when my compass was clearly looking for the path of least resistance. It was the real reason God had her so close, and the timing could not be more brilliant. The long road would be my path. What I could not fathom was how difficult it was going to be to meander my way around on my bike, waiting for the next thing to happen in life. Troubling.

I was completely dependent on being the active ingredient in my life, and taking a back seat to my reason was a scary proposition. If you ever are taking any type of medication, read on the back of the bottle and it will tell you what the active ingredient is in the medicine you are taking. It's the ingredient in the medicine making you feel different, and if I wasn't going to make me feel different, who was? I never had any luck relying on other people, and maybe it was that love/fear combination that inhibited me from having a healthy experience with human connection.

Now, places were always fun for me and I moved around often in life, but I never stayed long enough to outlast the boredom that set in to see if, in fact, there was something beyond that feeling. Material things were never a hook for me in life. I loved to do nice things and go to nice places and enjoy nice food and drink, but I never had the desire to accumulate things or money.

It was natural to be generous, and I always enjoyed spending more than I liked making money, witnessed by thousands of waiters, waitresses, bartenders, bellhops, valets, car wash attendants, shoe shine personnel, strippers, and countless others who could testify that I was one hell of a tipper. If you were in the service industry and you were aware I was in the room, you wanted me to be at your table or nestled up to your bar. Rent was on its way, my friend.

But things were different now, and my old way of filling the space of loneliness by capturing acquaintances in every environment I entered was in my past. I had my bike, I had *Sunrise* and the other meetings I attended, and now I had to find a way to integrate myself into my new home at least for the time being while number seven worked its way through the legal system in California.

Kicked out of rehab? What the hell happened? I shared my experience at *Sunrise,* and all had a hearty laugh. The laughter at *Sunrise* was also very intoxicating in this supposedly dreary, sullen, and destitute environment. It was a different kind of laughter — one that came from the belly. It wasn't a laughter based on vulgarity, mean-spiritedness, or making light of another's situation, but rather, it was the identification of a shared experience and the exuberance of not having to experience it again. It was a comforting laughter based on a common experience called being human. I was eager to learn more as my journal was being filled up with insightful thoughts:

Alcoholism is the only disease you have to catch in order to get better, and if you insert life in for alcoholism it applies equally well...Franz.

The hidden inner cleansing is profound in the example we set for others...Deborah.

Happiness is right here right now, If I want for it I will not find it...Ricky.

If you're kind and gentle you give a person chances to experience love...Mark Scientist.

The journey for me is that I get confused, and don't want to ask for help. But when I do things get better...Nina - Chicago.

What comes out of my mouth hasn't been a big seller. Being true to who I am, rather than whom I want you to see me as, is the ultimate show...Deborah.

I keep coming back to meetings not for what I have done, but rather for the things I haven't done... Barry.

There is no such thing as a bad prayer or meditation, the act of surrender is the significant act... Laura — Bermuda.

Underneath these white socks and white tennis shoes are dirty feet. My face is shaved but my armpits stink. I might look good but I am not taking care of myself. I have problems and I have to share them with you...Jeffrey.

It was a great meeting, and my usual dashing back to my cottage for some job hunting was going to take a back seat today. In the rooms, the meeting before the meeting and the meeting after the meeting are the pillars to healing. It's the time when you get to know people on a not so personal level—if you know what I mean. A time to find out a little less about each other and more about having a bit of time to exhale and enjoy some food, drink, and small talk. I was invited by Billie, Joseph, and Chopper to go to the Windansea Café to grab breakfast and hang out. Hang out? I was having mixed emotions because I needed to get my life back on track, and then it hit me—I just needed to relax and see what happened next. New tricks and tracks were needed.

This sitting back and letting something else guide my life might in fact be more difficult than trying to stop the drink and, more importantly, discover who I am and who I want to be. Jetting off to Chile, not knowing a soul, and trying to put together a life and business would definitely be the easier, softer way for me. Funny thing is, I haven't had the desire to have a drink since awakening from my perfect storm, and I'm not sure I really want to find out what lies within. I've been able to orchestrate an entire circus with all the performers, props, and guest appearance flawlessly for so many years, and now the decision has been made to sit back and see what God has in store for my circus and me? Let's say I was more than a little uncomfortable with these coordinates.

Chopper, a nickname since he was in helicopter flight school, mentioned this was the place where Eddy worked and wondered if had I met him yet. I had not.

He continued, "Eddy could do these crazy Chinese push-ups."

Chinese push-up? Apparently, it is when someone lies face down, arms stretched out above the head, palms down and legs together with toes pointed, and they do a push-up. Try it. I did, and it's impossible. I was a little nervous and uncomfortable without my ensemble of thespians to accompany me to the café to meet this Eddy character, but hunger was the deciding factor and I agreed to go along. My belly always leads me into new experiences. We were cohorts.

Apparently, Eddy had been back in Florida for the last several weeks visiting his mother and pops and would be back at work today. Upon entering the café, I scanned the room to familiarize myself with the layout and to catch a glimpse of this Eddy fellow. It was an odd-shaped room with bench seating, a few round tables, and two very low sofas. The room was painted a stark blue. Emanating from the walls was the thumping sound of European house music. I looked behind the counter and didn't see anybody tending the saloon, and before I could glance back to my new friends, a character bounced up from one of the tables and greeted Billie, Joseph, and Chopper.

I love when we picture someone in our mind before we have physically met that person, and when we do, he or she generally looks nothing like we envisioned, but my vision of Eddy was spot on. Eddy was wearing some board shorts, a wife beater, flip-flops, and an apron, which was the only outward sign that he was in fact working today. He was of medium height and was in extremely fit condition. His muscles rippled, stretching the cotton fabric of his wife beater to its limit. For the next several minutes, he shared about his trip back home to spend time with his parents and his desire to return to help his mom care for his pops, who was experiencing some health problems. He mentioned that with his newfound sobriety, he was now available and capable to set aside his selfishness for his aging parents.

Instantly, I felt his warmth and authentic nature. I think we are all familiar with people who have a high energy and zest for life, making one wonder if it's possible to be happy all the time. Well, Eddy is that person, and he's genuine and not a front. I watched him scurry behind the counter to take our orders while Billie took the opportunity to formally make an introduction. I thought to myself that Tony Robbins had nothing on this cat as he greeted me like we were old friends that hadn't seen each other in years. We all settled in as Eddy made our bagel sandwiches and brewed our lattes and teas.

It was comforting and uncomfortable at the same time. Comforting that I had some new potential friends to hang out with that, on face value, seemed interesting, and uncomfortable finding myself hanging out at a coffee shop with my new friends when I should be making something, anything happen. I was having an out-of-body experience, desiring to be someplace else. I was stuck for now. It was a blessing—or maybe a curse.

After a couple of hours of silly banter, storytelling by Billie, and belly laughing, it was time to say our farewells until tomorrow morning. As we were all making our way out the door, Eddy walked from around the counter and hugged everybody, thanking us for coming in and hanging out. When he approached me, I was expecting a handshake. Instead, he hugged me as well, holding me tightly he whispered in my ear, "Love you, bro." Shocked, I didn't know how to respond, but it sounded so genuine,

I responded in kind: "Love you, too." It was a first for me when meeting someone for the first time. What I've come to understand about Eddy is that he leads with his heart, and that can be a very excruciating way to maneuver your way through life. Well, at least from my point of view it did, for the simple fact that I never lead from my heart. I always lead with my head. We exchanged phone numbers as I looked forward to my next encounter with my new friend Eddy.

Eddy leading with his heart! This is what I have in store as I am trying to find out who I am and who I want to be? Who was this Eddy character?

Eddy was born in Bethesda, Maryland, and quickly moved with his family to Miami, Florida, where he spent the next eighteen years of his life before moving to Columbia, Missouri, to play baseball at the University of Missouri. He loved baseball and college life, but it was the snow and the classroom that didn't sit well in his soul. He wanted to do the right thing and push through the experience, but one thing he couldn't do was be something he was not. The funny thing was that like most of us at the age of nineteen, he didn't really know what that was. He lasted all of one year till the snow and classroom repositioned him back in Miami and smack dab in the middle of a pizza joint, where disillusionment filled his being like an overstuffed calzone.

In an effort to redeem his perceived misstep in Missouri, he joined the Navy to be close to the surf and sand. He knew he wanted to be close to the water, but he was unsure of his role in the Navy, so to right his ship, he felt the need to stretch his abilities to overcome his failures, culminating in the decision to see if he had what it took to be a Navy Seal. With a three-phase training regime totaling twenty-six weeks, including the mind, body, and soul-crushing fourth week called hell week in his rear view mirror, Eddy had become one of the most highly trained fighting machines to walk the planet. A Navy Seal.

Graduating second in his class, he optioned San Diego as his home base, allowing him the comfort to someday realize his childhood dream of only needing a surfboard, bike, and a beach to be who he really was. The uneasiness of abandonment that had welled in his belly since birth had calmed under the safety of his fellows Seals, and he knew this to be true, as the command to never leave your buddy no matter what was the active ingredient that separated the Seals from all the rest. He had finally found home. It was a long, painful journey. Biology does not necessarily ensure a sense of family. Eddy doesn't exactly remember when his biological father left the family as he was growing up, but he does share a story that represents who Eddy is on so many different levels. He remembers going down to the beach during the summer while his father tended to his bar business that coincidentally was located in a part of Miami where the black community was heavily populated. With no one to monitor his wanderings, Eddy would play with the neighborhood kids from sun up till sun down. The thumping of the boom boxes on the boardwalk tapped his love for music. This love was woven into his being so that today, if you care to challenge Eddy to a "Name that Tune" game, you are sure to lose. He truly has his funk on.

In fact, Eddy didn't notice he was different from all the other kids he played with during the long hot Miami summers, where the culture of food and music flowed so easily in this energetic neighborhood. It wasn't until third grade, when the teacher passed around the room a Christmas card with Santa Claus on the front and asked the class what's wrong with the card. The card made its way around the room, with no one telling the teacher what was wrong with the card. She pointed out that there was no such thing as a black Santa Claus.

Eddy loved Santa Claus and he loved everybody equally. He loved being at the beach with his friends. He loved being in the mix of everything: dancing, running, swimming, singing, laughing, and being a part of the fun and simplicity of life. He speaks fondly of this gargantuan of a man called Butterball, who wielded a crafty tong at the barbecue pit, drawing his moniker from the amount of butter he slathered on his chicken wings. He would run from one event to the next, stopping for a moment to nibble on some chicken wings, preferring them crispy and even more so when they were burnt. This simple story says so little in detail, but says volumes about the character of his character.

First and foremost, he very rarely shares any stories about his childhood, and if he does, it is always shared in all seriousness, and Eddy, for the most part, would rather not be serious. He never mentions his biological father. I guess the pain, disappointment, and anger are too deep and probably not far enough in the past. Secondly, music and its nourishing properties have the ability to break down barriers that our human nature builds up from a lack of understanding and compassion for those who are different. Eddy has this gift of attaching music to a place and time in his life that invigorates those same feelings in you, and before you know it, you're singing and doing a little dance to a song you haven't heard in twenty-plus years. And food! Even though he eats like a bird, he enjoys the companionship a meal can afford. Eating for Eddy is a community project involving as many as possible, not unlike the community eating taking place on those long hot Miami summers as a child.

Finally, it's the blindness Eddy has for the human shell, allowing him to quickly embrace strangers like family. The family he felt he never had was only a handshake away. Eddy has the largest sense of community and family of any person I have ever met in my life. No one is a stranger and no one is treated any different. Eddy knows you even when he has never met you, and everybody that has met Eddy has a friend for life. He is the kind of cat that if you don't like Eddy, something is wrong with you. His heart is huge and his compassion for the human experience is immense. His mind is sharp and his sense of humor is perfectly suited for my ear.

He was another paradox in a seemingly growing cast of paradoxes in my life: a rough-and-tumble, physically imposing Navy Seal on the outside, and on the inside, the most caring and sensitive person you'll ever meet, a sort of mama seal. Eddy would share two things with me when I asked him about his walk through the program, finding myself holding onto these two things with everything I had to make it through the next ninety days.

First, "the only thing I needed to change was everything," and second, "I had to do this someone else's way." The first was daunting and the second was foreign territory. I was glad to have Eddy as my new friend, and as it turned out, our friendship and the time we would spend together every day over the next five months would be happening much quicker that we both could have anticipated.

The meeting after the meeting moved to The Living Room when he was fired the very next day, serving as the venue where I would build my relationship with Eddy and a host of other people, both in and out of the meetings.

Eddy didn't attend *Sunrise* often, but he did command center stage after the meeting. Arriving with jeans, T-shirt, hat, sunglasses, work boots, and a pack of cloves to smoke was all he needed except for the seemingly gallons of coffee he swilled, laden with mounds of brown sugar and crème. It was neither really hot coffee nor cold ice cream for sure. You see, Eddy wasn't going to work. He wanted his girlfriend, whom he lived with, to think he was going to work so he could be by himself, wanting to be alone, but not completely alone. All those that communed after *Sunrise* felt the exact same way. We all cherished and needed our early morning sessions of clever banter, belly laughing, storytelling, and shedding our layers of pain, but most importantly, trying to hold on to each other for our own selfish reasons.

The pain was deep for those who attended the meeting after the meeting on a daily basis. Soothing this wound of not wanting to be alone at this juncture in early sobriety was what was binding us together. Eddy, George, Joseph, Billie, Chopper, Val, and I all had less than a year of sobriety, and the newness to a different way of living our lives was a hot topic.

59

What would we do next? When to go back to work? Should we go back to work? Should we get a sponsor to lead us through the steps? How do we communicate what's going on in our lives with our significant others, who cannot understand what it's like to be like us?

The honesty and openness of the challenges they were experiencing in their personal relationships was strange to my ears, as I would never share what was going on in a personal relationship with another person, and especially not at a group level. I guess I was lucky not to have to explain all this to another while trying to figure it out at the same time. Maybe Paul was half right?

The room would fill with laughter, but I couldn't keep from feeling the intense uncertainty, pain, and desperation we all were experiencing while we tried to find some relief in our lives. This was uncharted territory for most of us as we navigated directly into a new storm, consciously knowing we no longer had the luxury to control our lives if sobriety was the desired result—and for me, the higher purpose of finding out who I really was and, more importantly, wanted to be.

On occasion, another *Sunriser,* Tony, would join us for coffee, and I could tell you my first thought was that this guy was a real jerk. Tony was five years sober. When he attended the meeting after the meeting, he announced when sitting down that he only had a few minutes to spend with us. I didn't really notice at first, but what would come out of his mouth was negative and condescending to whomever or whatever the topic was going around the table. I didn't like this guy. He rubbed me the wrong way, and it was messing with my experience of how we were helping each other. Tony pushed people away with sarcasm and a sense of humor directed at your expense. It didn't take me long to speak up and let Tony know his time had expired and it was now time for him to leave. He would linger on for a little while longer and then depart, and civility was restored to the group.

Tony owned a business down the street—I liked to call it the Saloon—and it so happened to be on my way back from The Living Room to the public library. Out in front of the Saloon was a park bench facing his entrance, and on occasion, I would stop to say hi to this person I didn't care for at all. At first, our conversations were brief, centered on the topic discussed at *Sunrise* and its relevance to our own condition. In time, Tony grew on me. He lowered the barriers he'd created to keep away people who might inflict pain on him, or maybe it was that he became less suspicious that he would inflict pain on another. Slowly but surely, Tony was moving away from the condescending humor and mean-spiritedness as a mechanism to keep people at a safe distance and moving toward a trusted friend who was in pain and trying to figure out how to do the next right thing.

But it was the extreme isolation that Tony had perfected out of sobriety that was the most intriguing and frightening to me. The similarities were shocking. Tony standing behind the safety of his work was full of life and conversation, but without this safety and comfort, he would retreat to his seaside condo and commence to check in with his warden, himself, and lock himself into the safety of himself. We laughed about his willful condition, but it was not funny.

This topic uncovered and stirred my own experience with this type of pain over the last year and a half of working to be successful in my job and coming home and never leaving. The only remedy I knew was to lean on old tracks, lifting myself out of isolation to settle in at a bar/restaurant to start making acquaintances, with the elixir of alcohol being the lubricant. Although alcohol was no longer in my formula, I surely didn't want to end up like Tony, and at the same time, I wanted to be his friend so we wouldn't be so lonely. Funny how things work out if you reach out beyond your first thought. We needed each other. We became close friends.

My days started to have a flow, and it wasn't always centered on my newly created friends at *Sunrise*. I would go to the community center every day and lift weights and then the library for job hunting, reading, and to eat up time so my mind didn't have time to reanalyze my situation. The community center was my first foray outside of *Sunrise* where I began to slowly start expanding my sense of community and family. Jake and his dog Margarita, who rode along in the saddlebag on his bike; Diane, a mother of two; Axel, a German expat; and Cathleen, a wonderful soul who peddled her bike named Betty to the gym, wearing a hat that resembled a beekeeper's head shield to block the sun. It was essential for me to start building relationships outside the meetings, since I was sure that this would be a short-term experience as soon as the pain drifted away. I was relying on this hope.

The organic nature of waking, suiting up, and showing up and letting what was going to happen next was exciting for now. But the old tracks were strong as I found myself desperately trying to figure out what was going to happen next in my life. What would be my legal consequences? Would I be able to find a job in January after returning from Chicago? What would the job look like, because I didn't want to do what I was doing before. Would I still feel alone? Who, in fact, was behind the circus tent was the bigger question. How did I allow this to happen?

I didn't want to let go of my ability to control what was going to happen next, a uniquely western trait to look beyond things rather than to address the here-and-now, moment-to-moment lifestyle indicative of the rest of the world. I didn't like the idea of staying in the moment, as it seemed more fruitful to imagine what it could be like, rather than what in fact I was feeling and experiencing at the moment. The better question for me was, was it possible for me to let happen next what was going to happen next? Maybe it was happening and I didn't recognize it?

What I really wanted, what I thirsted for, was the human connection.

A new character at *Sunrise* emerged. Her name was Deborah, and she was now attending the meetings several days a week. There was something unique about Deborah as she sat in the back row of the outer circle with a stack of books and a notebook, which she rummaged through when something in the dialogue of a share aroused her interest. When it was time for her to share, she would almost certainly pass to the next person without sharing. But on the rare occasion when she did share, my pen was scribbling as quickly as possible, filling up my notebook with deep thoughtful insights of not only recovery, but also how one maneuvered through the minefield of our humanness.

It was as if she was speaking directly to me in a language perfectly suited for my ears. She was smart, mystical, and thought provoking. She quoted great thinkers and really challenged the group to think about the provenance of the traditions and steps of the program. I was hooked because she was speaking my language, the language of reason, and I needed it so much right now.

All this touchy-feely, emotional "one day at a time" shit was getting old, and my mind needed some stimuli and I needed to trust this step stuff before I tried it. Where did it come from? Who were these Bill W. and Dr. Bob characters the literature was referencing all the time? Was this the foundation of a new religious tradition that I had already tried before in life with short-term results? I knew one thing for sure—I was not going to work the steps and I was not going to get a sponsor until I was able to wrap my mind around this program with some facts.

It became quite obvious that Deborah had facts and she spoke in a way that was confusing to the untrained ear. When she did speak, I would look around the room to see the delight I was feeling inside for what I just heard on the faces of the other *Sunrisers,* and what I mostly witnessed was confusion and bewilderment. I would hunt up Deborah after the meeting to get a little more of what she was serving, and shyly, she spoon-fed me a little more. I asked her if she would like to join us after the meeting, and she declined, saying, "I don't do coffee shops." If I wanted to talk, we could do so by phone. I told her I hated talking on the phone, a sure latent effect of living a salesman's life. She wanted to know if I would be at the meeting on Friday, as she had a book I might be interested in reading. I was drawn to her quickly, and nothing was going to get in my way of getting what I wanted.

I wanted to study and interact with her, I wanted the ability to pick her brain, and I wanted to know why she kept coming back to these meetings after being sober for twenty-six years I wanted to know if I did this shit, the steps and sponsor stuff, would it work?

Let's say I suffered from that all too common human experience of having little faith. Faith in the form of not wanting to commence on a path unless I knew what the end result was going to look like. A path never at issue before, when you're implementing the next thought that comes to mind, turning that thought into reality, and then moving on to the next thought. But my coordinates had changed since making the decision to travel this new road of doing my part and then seeing what was in store for me next, at least for the time being. The only problem with my new navigational settings was that the insatiable desire to know what was going to happen next had not been removed. This feeling was a roadblock and needed to be resolved if peace and calm was going to be a possibility in my future. Many roadblocks lay ahead.

Friday came quickly, and I was eager to see what Deborah had in store for me that would be helpful on my potential journey in the program. The book was Ernest Kurtz's *Not-God*. The title itself was a little unnerving, as I believed in God, but didn't trust him with guiding my life. Was this program another religious tradition, or worse—a cult? I was intrigued by Deborah and her thoughts and wanted more of what she had as I hurriedly moved my way through the day until I arrived at the library, nestling in a quiet distant corner to see what this *Not-God* was all about. I quickly realized the book was a look back at the foundations and history of the program and the development of the steps and traditions that gave it life.

My curious nature was a strong theme in my life, represented in my voracious reading habits of non-fiction, history, current events, and anything to do with social, political, and economic conditions and their effects on the human condition. It was perfect for my nature, as I always wanted to know where things came from. As a child, I humored my brother Ralph-David for taking perfectly working stuff around the house like a clock radio and taking it apart and putting it back together again. The problem was that I was mechanically inept and parts were always left over. Needless to say, the radio never worked again. My curiosity was more of wondering *why* something worked than *how* it worked.

Somehow, my reason came to the conclusion that unless all the pertinent information of why something worked was crammed into my brain, allowing me to create a space within my being to have faith in something, only then would I believe in said thing. Isn't that an oxymoron? I have to understand something and where it's going before I can have faith in it. Isn't faith the opposite of that? At an elementary level, I believe in the wind, but I cannot see it, and that's faith!

I gladly consumed this manna represented in black and white as it leapt from the pages, filling me with hope I could possibly do some business with this bunch. Over the next two days, I absorbed the provenance of the program and how it developed its traditions and the twelve steps, but it was the title that had provided discomfort since the day Deborah handed me the book, which ironically was the punch to the groin I needed to propel me forward one day at a time. It was I that was *Not-God,* and this truly was a new revelation.

I wanted to shout out and share this newfound source of inspiration with all who would listen, but more importantly, I knew I had found my muse in Deborah. Had I found her, or was she brought to me? This I was not sure of, but what I was sure of was I found someone who I could study with in my recovery process.

Could Deborah be the person I was comfortable enough with to share the deep thoughts and questions mulling incessantly in my mind since my perfect storm sixty-four days ago? Maybe I could go deeper with her to my unshared past? I needed to connect with her. I wasn't sure how this was going to happen, as she didn't like meeting with people and I didn't like talking on the phone. I did know that she went to several meetings a week at *Sunrise,* and my plan would be to stalk her for the insights she might have on the questions that were keeping me from jumping in the water, so to speak. I mentioned to her that I'd read *Not-God,* and she responded with a smile and a giggle.

"I have given that book to twenty-plus people, and you are the first person who actually has read it."

I quickly thought, *Why would someone hand out a book that no one ever read?* I presumed Deborah never gave up on faith and practiced it without expectation. We exchanged e-mail accounts, and I hoped this would be the medium we could both work with for the time being.

Who was this Deborah character that was now a part of my new and growing sense of family and community in Windansea? Deborah was born in Kansas City, Missouri, to a privileged family whose business interests were wide, the source of its wealth coming from the construction business. She had older siblings, but the years between them and her birth was ten. She tells a story we can all relate to as children of being on one side of the door or the other.

As the youngest of six, like myself, she felt like she was always trying to push on a door to get into the room her older siblings were in and that they were on the other side, pushing back to keep her out. A [illegible] struggle arose to gain access to a place in which she thought she [illegible] be, but was in fact kept out by other forces—sometimes that f[illegible] from within her. The force of not wanting to conform to what is [illegible] against us in life can be the impetus needed to push back. At a young age for Deborah, it was the conformity of formal schooling she pushed against, being kicked out of one prep school or Catholic school after another.

It was at an all girls' boarding school she attended in Connecticut and how her lack of conformity, pushing back, arose in the subtlest of ways. With a uniform dress code to adhere to, the only real garments one had to manage were undergarments: panties, bras, and socks. Deborah didn't like cleaning, and washing clothes was out of the question. She had the financial means to buy new undergarments if the old ones became dirty, but a more sinister solution was at hand.

"When my panties became soiled, I'd go and get another pair from one of the other girls' laundry and throw the dirty pair away."

Color was not a concern. It was simple. Her panties were soiled and needed removing.

This folly went on for months until it came to the attention of the administration that a lot of panties were missing and there must be a male rummaging around the dormitory stealing panties. The panty caper became such a big deal, an assembly was called to address the potential danger brewing and to report any suspicious activity at once. All while, little Debbie was sitting in the crowd donning freshly cleansed panties.

It wasn't long after the great panty caper that Deborah was found with cannabis seeds, prompting her parents' decision that the only remedy for this door pusher was to remove her from school altogether. The constant pushing and pulling in a young life coupled with a family demanding intense psychotherapy to remedy this behavior luckily never materialized. Deborah exited her early teens to a ripened opportunity to really exercise the boundaries of the mind-altering substances so common in the late seventies. At the age of eighteen, she got sober at a group home in Las Vegas, Nevada, of all places. Sobriety was a lonely path in this era, especially for a teenager.

I was grateful for my newfound friends and was wondering how all this was going to weave itself into my plan of coming back from Chicago after Christmas to jump back on the horse of life...Again.

...ne people presenting themselves to me during the past several months were quite glorious and would fit perfectly in my circus of one if I had made them up like all the rest. But I had not made any of these people up, and they were perfect. My mind's muscle was extremely creative, but some of these people would have tested the limits of my creativity. A gem of a human being was on its way, which, in hindsight, was critical for me to take the next step.

One day, Eddy and I were the only two left at The Living Room, waiting patiently for the noon hour to arrive to watch the newly inducted cast of language school students emerge from their first day of classes, when a character came a peddling up Girard Boulevard.

It was a friend of Eddy's, and his name was Michael. He was short in stature, with a funky style consisting of a strange pair of sneakers and a hooded jacket framed by a pair of dark sunglasses. Michael was gifted with a wonderful Irish accent. He sat down and ordered a cup of tea as we all gaggled and goggled over the new class of foreign students milling around the front of The Living Room, as they had nowhere to go—not unlike our current situation.

Michael was quick-witted, with a beautiful Irish sense of humor, as we spent the next hour or so laughing about everything, which meant nothing. Michael was in the program, had been friends with Eddy for a year or so, and in fact used to attend the *Sunrise* meeting every day before I arrived. Michael knew all the characters I had met over the past several months, and he lived a half block from me. Our time together was coming to an end, and before we all peddled away to varying destinations with no real purpose, Michael and I exchanged phone numbers.

Maybe it was the vulnerability I was experiencing in my new method of making, or should I say not making decisions that had me feeling feelings. Eddy, Deborah, and now Michael was someone I could trust while I maneuvered my way past the holidays with the idea that the new year would be the ideal time to start making life happen again.

I was quickly approaching ninety days sober and was doing all the things I was expected to do except for getting a sponsor and doing the steps, the vital ingredients to the program. I was only writing one meeting a day attended in my book but was attending multiple meetings a day, not including the meetings after the meetings. I calculated that in the first ninety days, I had attended two hundred eighteen meetings. I wasn't sure if the sheer volume of meetings was significant in maintaining sobriety for me personally or if it was a way for me to make up for not being admitted to rehab. In retrospect, I believe it was a way for me to not be alone, realizing I was in fact all alone for the first time in my life without the comfort of my circus performers. Michael was ideal and he was available and he could help me. I knew this.

Michael was born in Belfast, northeast occupied Ireland, and was second in line to five boys, with the three younger ones being stepbrothers. His biological father was sentenced to life in prison for killing a British policeman when Michael was still in his mother's womb. His dad's life was consumed by the plight of his fellow man in the Irish struggle for independence and in the struggle with the drink, leaving little time to raise or be a part of a growing family.

It's uncertain when the struggle in life begins, and for Michael and not unlike any of us in the human condition, it might have begun when the amniotic fluid was the breath that sustained his life. The brokenness that surrounded his mum during the pregnancy surely affected her chemistry, as the sharing of her nutrients that gave life to young Michael might be the imprint stamping him for life. We truly don't know when it all starts. No one does.

Michael speaks of the unspoken acknowledgement of his biological father's existence between himself and his older brother and mother. Keeping this secret stuffed deep down amongst the three of them to keep the safety of the family intact from retribution was the concern. The confusion and secretive nature of the household was the beginning of the inability to share what was welling in his heart. He remembers being so unhappy at the age of eight that he ran away from home to a field with the intention of getting some attention. This attempt failed, as no one came to look for him, and after a while, he became scared and returned home, his absence going unnoticed.

The battle raged within young Michael until he found the saving medicinal salve of the drink, drug, and fight. I'm not sure whether it was his smallish stature that instigated the fight or the psychological enhancement of his stature by the drink and drug that propelled young Michael to have the desire to fight anyone, no matter how small the disagreement or the size of the opponent.

Michael tells a story of being in the wrong bar in the wrong part of Brooklyn, New York, and needing to get to the bathroom to get high when he realized he was going to have to fight his way out of the bathroom and bar. Michael found himself outnumbered in a Puerto Rican establishment, as his mouth and ethnicity had, in a few short minutes, worn out his welcome. He was strangled by the desire to drop into one establishment after another to wet the whistle. More importantly was the necessity to partake in the drug of choice to keep the high going in order to not feel the effects of coming down.

It was shortly after Michael announced his presence in this establishment that he hurriedly exited to the bathroom to get high, when a bottle came crashing over his head. Blood pouring down his face and highly outnumbered, he instinctively fought for his life, as he knew if he didn't make it out of the bathroom and the bar, he would be dead. The drinking, fighting, and the drugging continued on saving his life, as no other remedy was in sight or plausible in those rare and brief moments of clarity in between the drinking, drugging, and fighting.

I heard early on in a meeting that if you cannot remember your last drink or drug, you haven't had it yet. The idea being if the experience wasn't memorable and life changing, it was like any other experience. If so, then you haven't had your last drink, and if that's the case, keep drinking until you're ready—with most never being ready.

Michael talked about the end of his days under the curse as being dreary and without hope because the drugs and drink had stopped working, but his mind kept on clicking away thought after thought after thought. He found himself in a strange apartment in New York City, isolated and hungry for the touch of another human being. A foreign feeling when we have our best friend always by our side, the drink and drug; the collateral damage being that the desire for the human touch is vanquished by the desire to push more alcohol and drugs into our bodies.

The drug and drink for Michael was no longer a trusted lover, and the desire to have intimacy with another human was the only plausible replacement. The hole left behind was vast. But the last thing we actually want is to have another human being at our side during these darkest of moments, as the desire to keep the secret of our true desire is equally immense. Sadly, it's no secret. He clearly remembers looking around the apartment for anything that resembled the human form, and the only thing fitting the bill was a gangly object pushed into a corner of the massive loft space, a ten-speed Schwinn bicycle.

He laughs when he says he tried to have sex with the bike, and it really doesn't matter if he petted the bike or lay next to it, but what does matter is that Michael is able to share from his heart the pain he was experiencing in this lonely and dark moment in life. No one wants to share this stuff or actually admit they had the thought of having companionship with a bike, but Michael has this uncanny ability to share his thoughts and feelings in a way that makes you want to share in the same genuine way. Through Michael's example, I was starting to share what was really going on inside, rather than what I wanted you to see or hear that was a fraction of what was really going on inside the circus of me.

Michael was teaching me to reach deep in my heart and talk about feelings and thoughts that, up until this point in my life, were off limits and would easily be excused by the next thought entering my mind. Life was slowing down, and the cast of characters I was meeting outside of my circus was transforming me in unexpected ways. I was finding myself taking bits and pieces of the people God was surrounding me with and starting to build upon a mosaic that would hopefully lead me in a direction to uncover and eventually reveal the completeness of me.

It was interesting and honestly a bit uncomfortable that the cast of characters I was building my foundation of transformation on were as broken as I seemed to be. In a word...Perfect!

5

A MONKEY WRENCH AND WD-40

Thanksgiving came and went without the traditional fixings. However I, had been absorbing and then storing a lot of nutrients over the last sixty days from my fellow *Sunrisers*: Eddy, Joseph, George, Chopper, Billie, Deborah, Daniel, Jim, Val, Franz, Tony, Erik, Ricky, Taco Tray Tom, and now Michael.

I would have been back from rehab by now, and my mind was drifting to an all too familiar place of "what if." The thoughts of what I would have done or not done, this or that, were running rampant in my mind, trying to free me from my feelings and my current situation. The group of people currently touching my life would surely be different. To be honest, I wasn't too concerned with those who were surrounding me; I just wanted what was currently transpiring in my life to be different. Oh so human.

The inability to manipulate my environment retroactively didn't stop me from mulling over my recent decisions to see how I could change my present situation. What if I had stayed at rehab? Would I be better off than I was now? What if I had never revealed number seven to Harold? What if I got up tomorrow and bolted off to Chile for some real fun and adventure? What if this whole "finding who I really am and who I really want to be is" another form—the most extreme attempt up to this point—of getting what I want and keeping what I have? Staying alive!

It was evident to me now, with some clarity and time under my belt without the drink, that I was killing myself with intention, and the scary revelation was I didn't even care. It was a precarious union between my will and the drink. I was lonely without my trusted friend and the performers I created along the way. How would I navigate? Was this all worth it?

Was it possible my new path was to uncover the real me without my cast of performers? If I wasn't all these things I developed over my lifetime, then who was I? And could the battle between the dark and light in my life be uncovered and exercised to create a new me? Maybe my entire circus was, in fact, just me with the inability to navigate my way through my own selfishness and self-centeredness, leading me to a premature death by my own hand. Was it presumptuous to think I could be the author of my own transformation when the facts proved my director's abilities were elementary at best? I had been in charge of me for the past forty-three years, and this was what I had to show for all the effort and energy exerted to keep what I have and get what I wanted. Wasted energy…or was it?

My mind was spinning quite early on the fourth of December, and those were just a few of the thoughts absorbing my energy before I commenced to leave my cottage for my daily dose of *Sunrise*.

I hopped on my bike and headed up the alley when I realized my handlebars were coming loose and it would be difficult to keep a steady course for the next several blocks until I arrived at *Sunrise*. I thought of turning back and retrieving my newly acquired tool to tighten my handlebars, but I was running late and wanted to be on time. It was an all too familiar feeling of heading out on a path or decision in life and knowing full well it is futile. Then the knight in shining armor arrives in the disguise of the ego and self-will, pushing one deeper into the delusion of "I can make this happen" even though the end result is inevitable.

I arrived at my destination with my handlebars only being held up by my own power, knowing if I released my grip, they would swing down below the bike frame, leaving me unable to guide my way safely to the meeting. Finding myself standing next to my bike on the patio, I noticed Taco Tray Tom approaching me to see what happened to my bike. Tom was a beautiful soul, tortured by his past but always greeting you with a huge smile and a hearty laugh. Taco Tray Tom was a moniker he earned for his body surfing prowess he perfected with the aid of a taco tray from the local taco shop. He was a local legend, honing his craft no matter the water temperature. Now it was obvious to the both of us that my handlebars needed to be tightened to fix my problem of guiding my bike safely from place to place. What I was oblivious to was how vital this morning would be to me loosening the grip on how I lived my life going forward. A turning point for sure — if I would only listen.

It was early in the morning, and my bike needed a special size wrench to tighten the handlebars, and out of nowhere, this man approached us, riding a bike and wearing a backpack. Noticing my problem, he mumbled something while sifting through his backpack, and lo and behold, he pulled out a wrench that perfectly fit my handlebars. As I was tightening them, the stranger suggested I might need some lubricant for my chain as it was starting to rust. It was as if he knew everything that was going on with me that morning before he arrived on the scene. He rambled on about how the moisture and salt in the air exacerbated the rusting process and it would be a good idea to address the rusting of my chain before it became a problem. Before I could respond, I noticed him digging in his backpack and pulling out a can of WD-40. I thanked the stranger for his help and pushed my bike to the foyer of the church to make it to *Sunrise* on time.

The meeting was being held this week in the library of the church on the first floor. Missing was the coffee pot and hot water for tea, the openness of the second floor great room, the comfort of the blue sofas, and most importantly, the roaring fire. The library was a small, cramped fifteen-foot by twenty-five-foot room with a rectangular table that seated ten. It had a wall-to-wall bookcase at one end of the room with a stately portrait of Martin Luther hanging on the opposite wall.

Sunrise was attracting about eight to ten people per meeting, and in the large upstairs room, this number of *Sunrisers* was dwarfed by the space, but the small library would be bursting at the seams with this many people. It was the regular cast today, mixed in with a few visitors and not enough chairs available, so I gave up my chair and sat on the stairs next to a door that opened to the church altar. It brought back the memory of being an altar boy when I was given access to the sacred areas only granted to a few. This included drinking the sacramental wine when no one was looking. My senses were heightened. I was in the spotlight. My blood was curdling; it was happening again.

I was drifting off in isolated thought when the meeting began. The stairs provided an elevated viewpoint, allowing me to see the entire cast of *Sunrisers* surrounding the table, and out of nowhere I started to get that funny feeling again, when time slows down considerably and something important is about to happen.

It was the same feeling I'd had before about calling Harold and when watching Franz walk across the room. This time I knew something important was about to happen — the difference being I didn't want to run this time; I wanted to feel and experience what was going to happen next. It was a new feeling of allowing what was going to happen next, happen next. In the past, I constantly changed my feelings and present experience by my next thought, so I didn't have to experience something not of my own will. That had been the navigational coordinates guiding my entire life no matter the circumstance. Suddenly, a sense of peace and clarity rushed through my veins as I settled in to watch the show.

The earlier activities of the morning flashed quickly through my mind. How I left my cottage with a bike with no usable steering mechanism only tethered together by my will to arrive at *Sunrise*. I was greeted by a stranger who had the specific tool to fix my handle bars and in addition he suggested some lubricant to fix something on my bike that had gone unnoticed since it wasn't impeding my trip to the meeting, but in due time it would be a problem.

The lesson went deep to my core as all I had to do was to get to *Sunrise* and I too could be fixed in the same way the stranger fixed my bike. He had the necessary tool to fix my noticeable problem, handlebars, and the necessary tool to fix my unnoticed one as well, rusty bike chain. I knew the foundation of the program was to address the desire to stop drinking, and with lucky number seven dancing in my reality, this place made sense. What needed attention was the unnoticed rusty links to the chain of my life, and if I continued to show up to these meetings and really listen when someone was speaking, then I could learn by another's experience what links of my own needed attention.

If this healing process of learning through the people God was placing in my life was to be possible, I had to consciously vanquish the desire I had to be the author of my healing process, since the legacy I was writing up to this point in my life was neither noteworthy nor desirable. The me, more and now, the I, self, and me were wasteful and now boring.

Creating fantasy and implementing it in my life was elementary compared to living life as it happened organically. The greatest show on earth is living life on life's terms, realized through self-examination. I was missing the real show the entire time. I was recognizing, for the first time in my life, I needed others not to be just voyeurs of my circus but rather to be the source illuminating the unnoticed issues that needed to be addressed for sustainable healing to be possible. I needed to push the restart button on life.

I had been writing so many great quotes in my journal over the last several months, but had I really listened to what was being said? Up to this point I don't think I can honestly say I listened to what my fellow *Sunrisers* were saying when they were speaking from the heart. It was like I was back in college, voraciously taking notes when the professor was speaking. I would write everything down and then memorize it all so that when test time came, I was prepared for whatever was to be tested. The thought was that if I crammed all the information in my head, this act alone would be sufficient enough to prove to others I knew the material by regurgitating it *ad nauseum* whether you wanted to hear it or not. It was half measures refined.

The process of cramming and regurgitating never allowed for the opportunity to relax and really learn in college, and unfortunately this process carried on to my personal life as well. The paradigm was simple: acquire all the necessary information in my head to sufficiently navigate my way through life; coupled with my ability to implement the first thought into reality and this tragic duo was off and running. Reason manipulated with action. I was dead set on you noticing I was thoughtful and relevant to any topic possible. With a little time, life experience, and an ever-growing cast of performers, I was able to weave the information I gathered to get the desired response from my audience. I was building a tool set for life that didn't have the capability of fixing anything including me. I was an automaton to my own will.

I realized I was being controlled by my desire to represent myself in a meaningful way to the group rather than being honest the way Michael was when he spoke from the heart. At each meeting I was preparing for the test of when it was my turn to share, to show everyone I knew the material being discussed and could offer some insight with the goal of being helpful to another. It so happened that today I would be the last to share, which worked perfectly according to my plan of creating perception rather than being honest about what was really going on inside of me. My internal honesty was on the line.

The all too common human experience of wanting to address someone else's problem rather than the gut-wrenching task of looking inward and tackling your own demons takes precedence.

In the program, newcomers are advised not to get into a relationship for at least the first year of sobriety. The rehab romance is a quick way to lean into the comfort of another rather than addressing the pain of self-examination that arises when one digs with full measure to unravel who they really are. I wasn't interested in a relationship. I wanted to get back from Chicago so I could resume my life again, but since I was here at these meetings, I might as well help somebody. Right?

The *Sunrisers* were helping me so much. I misguidedly directed my energy in wanting to help them with my mental prowess while altogether missing out on the opportunity to share what was really going on inside of me in the here and now.

As my mind was spinning with all these thoughts, I found myself laying my pen and notebook down and intently listening to each and every person who shared that day. Each share was building a foundation for me to stand upon, chipping off a little rust of my chain called Me. The love and honesty they shared became the human salve I needed for so long, lubricating each and every link in my chain of life which had been strangling me since birth.

Some of my links needed to be removed and discarded, while others needed adjusting. But most importantly, all of my links needed to be healed by the intimacy of the human connection. A connection that in my past I would never allow too close for fear of it being taken away. I desired it now. It was critical to my survival.

I was being cleansed and healed by all that surrounded me inside and outside the rooms. Now all I had to do was to wake up, jump on my bike, and see what was going to happen next. Unbelievable.

I arrived in Chicago the day before I would have received my ninety-day token for being sober, feeling exhausted and grateful to be with my sister Theri for the holidays and equally relieved I would not be getting recognized for having been sober for the past ninety days. In the past I was able, through self-will, to go years without drinking, and I didn't see ninety days sober as a notable milestone for myself; I found no sense of personal accomplishment in its recognition.

In preparing for my arrival, Theri asked several of her patients who were in the program if they knew of any meetings in close proximity to her neighborhood. With rave recommendations, the *Mustard Seed* meeting on the north end of Michigan Avenue was high on the list. I thanked her for the information but was equally bothered she would share my private life. My prideful nature wanted to keep my current situation a secret. Secrecy was one of my issues all along.

My desire for secrecy was currently being trumped by a hunger for normalcy. That had never been what I thirsted for, and I was unsure what it really meant, since I'd never experienced *normal* in my life. At least that's how I viewed myself. I felt like I was in a new environment and didn't want the reminder of what happened over the last three months to dampen my experience while in Chicago. I needed a break, a mental and emotional vacation.

On my third day of vacation from Me, I was ready to go to a meeting, and I set out to attend *Mustard Seed*, walking from my sister's house on South Michigan Avenue on a cold and blustery day.

The change in weather and the wonderful time of the year collided with the storefronts gussied up for the holiday season. I snuggled close to the Windy City's bosom, hoping to nourish my famished circus. She was up to the task. My favorite part of being in a big city was the incredible people-watching. Chicago's energy made me feel alive without the constant reminder of my current situation. I wanted to engage life for a little while, and this was accomplished by mixing it up with folks parading themselves up and down Michigan Avenue.

The provocative glance of a beautiful woman, the smell and sounds of the city at work, the chatting up of all the people crossing my path, all were critically needed for my battered self-esteem. Even though my meanderings caused me to miss *Mustard Seed,* in due time the long tentacles of the *Mustard Seed* meeting would present itself in a much grander way than I could ever imagine. But it was the meeting composed uniquely in front of me on the streets of Chicago that was the remedy I desperately desired.

I thirsted for its nutrients with gratitude, swilling to my heart's content. I walked for hours, darting in and out of stores to feel the energy the city was giving me at that moment in time. It was the right tool for the right situation. At the moment, Chicago was allowing me to breathe and reflect on what had happened over the last ninety days. I had not noticed I was holding my breath the whole time.

It had only taken three months to realize alcohol was the least of my problems, the trivial, and that an unraveling and uncovering of me — the chain of my life with the individual links needing to be inspected and individually diagnosed with a corresponding treatment — was the heart of my matter. I was making some progress.

In retrospect, I maneuvered my way through the past ninety days of my life accomplishing the following deeds: I had survived my first week after waking on the magic couch; I had reached out to friends and family to share what was going on in my life as best I could with what I knew at the time; I had recognized the battle between the light and dark of my life and my inability to live peacefully with these polar opposites and the incompleteness of me; I had made plans to devise my own triumphant return to my life as I had known it and watched it crumble in front of me and survived; I had allowed myself to recognize the healing properties of the meetings; I had relinquished some of my will over to God and let what was going to happen next, happen next; I had allowed people into my life that I would have otherwise not had the time for while enacting the next thought that came to mind.

Regardless of this progress I knew I was fighting this transformation with everything I could muster. I didn't see all of my life experiences up to this point in time as wasteful, to be slashed and burned from my life going forward.

One would think that anybody with a half a brain would see the fortunate nature of my recent path and would gladly hand over the reins of life to a power greater than oneself, but not I. I was still interested in crafting this three-month sabbatical as something other than what it was, disguising it as an extended vacation I had not taken since my last one year sabbatical from life in 2000.

This current reprieve was an opportunity to quit drinking, and I didn't have the desire anymore, so mission accomplished. Equally it became a launching point to put my professional career in the past, one that was financially prosperous, although unfulfilling and boring, and this created the perfect opportunity to start anew. I would now seek passion, having no idea what it actually was.

I wanted to use the next ten days or so to relax and to let my mind, body, and spirit rest…not a chance.

My relationship with Theri started to bear fruit back when I lived in Austin, when I reached out to her after number six to address my physical state. When growing up, I never felt close to any of my siblings, and it was Theri I felt the most distance from personally. Slowly we would build on our relationship through phone conversations centered on the healing methodology of Integrative Medicine.

The approach is to maintain and prevent health issues by addressing the wholeness of our being: mind, body, and spirit. When we treat them separately, these human elements have their own healing merits, but when woven together into a fabric of addressing all of our daily encumbrances in life, not only is the squeaky wheel benefited, but our whole being as well.

The difference is that our modern western medical methodology wants to dissect our woes down to the cell level so that a manmade healing ointment or pill can instantaneously remedy our current pain, jettisoning one to a new way of feeling. The quick fix mentality of our modern medicine misses the opportunity to create a learning environment for the patient, allowing one to participate in our own health. The integrative process provides the patient an opportunity to learn about all the elements of their being, applying those experiences to a future experience, empowering themselves in taking ownership of their whole health.

Unless the health practitioner can link all the areas of one's life affecting the others — mind, body, and spirit — how can a remedy or plan of action be devised to treat our unique individual conditions? We all are in pain, in one form or another, but the pain one feels is uniquely our own when taking into account our whole being. The Integrative approach melds together the ancient practices of Eastern medicine along with and when necessary the advances Western medicine can provide. We are all suffering, in one way or another in the human condition, linking us all in the largest of families. I was learning I was responsible for my own well-being. In my past I was irresponsible.

Theri and I were able to connect through this healing process, and our connection grew into a friendship based on trust. I didn't realize it at the time, but Theri and I were opening up to each other, starting to share the hidden dark shadows of our lives with one another, allowing room for a trust to develop that was impossible before in our lives. She wasn't my older sister who was a doctor in Chicago anymore; she was a human being with pain in her life—which I had been oblivious to, never knowing the depths of her struggles. She hid them well. We all do.

It might be obvious to others, but for one who had the inability to create intimate relationships with anyone in my life, this was a hidden breakthrough going unnoticed for years. She shared a long held secret: I had been in my early teens and had stolen liquor from the house to take down the street to drink with my friends. She had stayed up for hours that night, waiting patiently for me to return home to make sure I was safe and then listened in silence as I slithered in and out of the bathroom to throw up what I had swilled only hours before. Theri never said anything to me; she prayed for me and listened and watched as I slowly built the foundations of my circus of one.

What I've come understand is that her pain and confusion was as deep and complex as my demons seemed to be, and now I was relieved to be in her home for the holidays to laugh, eat, rest, and share with her what had gone on in my life over the last ninety days. We were in pain, hoping and trusting we could help each other.

With my short term memory still in question and the ability to sleep more than a few hours a night still absent, the only tangible improvements over the last few months were freshly cleaned teeth and a pair of glasses I could wear while driving at night, but for all intents and purposes I did not have a grasp on what actually occurred in my life over the past ninety days. I knew what happened chronologically but was unable to connect feelings and emotions to the experiences.

What I did have was this emerging gem I toted around from meeting to meeting in the form of my journal describing in detail what I was experiencing at *Sunrise*. I didn't have my own words to describe what was going on in my life but rather the words of my fellow *Sunrisers* on what was going on in their lives and how they had navigated through the ebb and flow of their daily lives.

I sat down with Theri, opened up my book, and read aloud the quotes I had written down when hoping I could connect my experience with feelings. I wanted to feel something. Anything…

Sometimes it is really hard to do the right thing… Ralph.

Definition of Humility: It's not about being less selfish, It's about thinking about me less…Anonymous.

Before I make decisions I should be spiritually sound. If I am spiritually sound I will make better decisions…Ricky.

There are only two directions: Going toward or away from. And it's not important how far down the road you are just that you are on the road…Ricky.

It's none of my business what people think of me… Joseph.

If you have one foot in yesterday and one foot in tomorrow you will be pissing on today…midget girl.

Do something for another every day and don't tell anyone that you did it. Big or small just do it…Franz.

I treat loneliness with isolation…Joe – Boston.

I am better at critiquing than doing my part…Ricky.

God of my Misunderstanding…girl from New York.

The focal point in life is our feelings not our thinking. Lead with your feelings not your thoughts. One cannot out think what God has put in your heart…Deborah.

I was right on time, but you were early...Tripp.

The wisdom to know the difference. Serenity happens when I can practice this subtle understanding...Jim.

We get sick alone and we get better together... Brian — Toronto.

The Addiction to self makes drugs and alcohol look lightweight...Deborah.

The need to find the right size for me, too much ego not good, not enough ego not good. Finding the right size for me is critical in having a peaceful life...Rebecca.

The idea that the wounded can be the healer is the gift of life. We (Humans) are all wounded uniquely...Deborah.

We nested on her red leather sofa for hours, discussing how these statements and many more shaped our thoughts and how in fact they touched our own lives deeply. It was the first time I had read what I had written in my journal since taking it to the meetings back in October. It allowed for some reflection on what really had gone in my life over the past ninety days or so.

What it wasn't was making it through the first week, or being honest what was really going on in my life with others, or recognizing my inability to navigate my way through the dark and light in my life. It was the shattered life I had lived and the interesting mosaic being revealed to me through those who surrounded me once I surrendered to it.

My inability to have feelings of my own was being replaced by the feelings of others I could relate to when they shared their experiences. What I could not consciously grasp as feelings for the experiences I experienced in life up to this point in time was being exposed by the thoughts and feelings from my fellow *Sunrisers*. On the outside we were all different, but on the inside we were all the same. Complete differences with no differences.

In the rooms, the word "acceptance" was highly valued for a shared character trait amongst the members of always trying to change our reality or feelings through an outside source i.e., alcohol. In a word: denial. If you can imagine living your life directed by the first thought entering your mind, you can see the troubling patterns one develops and later refines for survival. In the rooms, it is determined if one can accept their drinking issue along with their individual character flaws then the answer to their problems is at hand. All one has to do is to accept the concern and then actively work on addressing what was once denied and now undeniable.

This acceptance stuff was not the answer to all my problems as it had been for so many in the rooms and in the human condition in general. The strain of my disease was immune to acceptance, and my sound reason assured me of this calamity. The side effects of this immunity were extensive: the inability to have any kind of real relationship with God, family, friends or the opposite sex was recognized and accepted long ago; the alcohol issue was accepted long ago; the juggling of the simplest of truths was accepted long ago; the fear of love was accepted long ago; the thought I could live this life alone without being lonely protected by my circus was accepted as foolish long ago.

Acceptance wasn't the answer for me because if it had been, then maybe, just maybe, I wouldn't have found myself in the situation I was currently in. My problem all along was my inability to take acceptance of these issues and untold others in my life and surrender to them completely. What was missing was complete SURRENDER!

To actively put down the weapons in my arsenal of living a selfish and self-centered existence was keeping me from having life for the very first time in my own skin. Eddy had shared with me only two months ago, "The only thing I had to change in life was everything." At the time that seemed daunting, but now it was plausible in my mind. Unless I surrendered to how I really was, and in turn wanted to be, I wouldn't have a chance of having peace and calm in my life.

I'd wished I'd had what it took to surrender my life and will over to something, allowing me the time and space to not have to make life happen one moment to the next. My life as I lived it was too much work!

My trip to Chicago was much needed. I returned to Windansea to get back to being serious about finding a job and resuming my life as I had intended three months ago. My plan had experienced some ups and downs, but for the most part I'd accomplished what I had set out to do and was ready to move forward with life without the drink.

Honestly, I had not thought much of the drink since my perfect storm back in September, and that sounds kind of funny from someone who had attended hundreds of meetings with people who were fighting for their lives because of alcohol. The romancing of the drink one struggles with early on can be overwhelming. In early sobriety, the warmth a drink delivers to the shattered alcoholic can easily remedy the crushed self-esteem, which is weighted with the heavy burden of guilt over those one has hurt along the way. The drink is a subtle, yet clever foe.

Over the past several months, I've witnessed people with twenty plus years of sobriety share that a day doesn't go by without the lure of the drink being present. I can't imagine being continually drawn to the elixir that ruined your life and those surrounding you. The facts are exposed and undeniable and you still can't shake the thought that a drink sure sounds like a good idea today. This is a pain and struggle, and since my perfect storm it had been lifted from me, and I am grateful.

Even though I couldn't remember what I drank and where I drank over that three-day period. I've been able to piece together enough of the story, with the number forty forever reminding me of my last drink. I find it funny and equally sad that I had tried willfully to stop my drinking and destructive lifestyle at the age of forty, which lasted all of a week and now it was my blood alcohol content of 0.40 — the reminder never allowing me to forget my last drink. I was lucky to be alive.

Currently, I was looking to get back into the job market and the only hindrance was the looming revocation of my driver's license. Magic was in the air, and possibly all this legal maneuvering would pay off. My attorney happily delivered the news with a phone call and commented that his firm had never had a client with that high of a blood alcohol content result win a hearing to retain a driver's license — and they represented thousands of DUI cases a year. In fact, my attorney was now some sort of hero at the firm just for being able to pull off this non-conviction.

A discrepancy was found in the police report, as the arresting officer knew arresting me off my couch would be problematic, so he claimed he arrested me on my back porch. The legal technicality was that no one could confirm if I had been drinking in my home when the police officers finally arrived at my cottage, thus it couldn't be proved that I was over the legal limit of 0.08 blood alcohol content when driving. The arresting officer had stretched the truth to get his desired conviction. It was the reason I retained my license and might be the difference I needed to be cleared of good ol' lucky number seven. We all juggle the truth.

My hearing for the DUI would not be for several more months, but the good news was that my driving status was intact for now and would not hinder me from getting a job.

83

During the last week of January, I was handed a key to open the church for *Sunrise*, saddling me twice a week with the responsibility of unlocking the door, preparing the coffee, and lighting the fire. One of the tenets of the program is built upon the service component when in the early stages of sobriety, giving the wavering patient the added incentive to get to a meeting. This would be the surface reason with the real intention being to distract the newcomer from their own situation and feelings, harnessing the "poor me" attitude and diverting that energy to help another.

The service work comes in many forms, consisting of, but not limited to: greeting people at the door, making coffee, setting up the meeting, breaking down the meeting, cleaning up in and outside of the meeting, leading the meeting, outside visitations to hospitals and institutions, dispensing literature, and most importantly and easily forgotten, showing up.

My outlook had changed with my recent legal victory, causing me to hesitate accepting the service work, since it was now plausible I could be completely absolved from the legal consequences for lucky number seven. I had every intention of being cleared and if somehow the consequences were removed, I would be free to get on with life, wherever that may occur. At the same time, I was deeply grateful for all the help and companionship showered upon me by my fellow *Sunrisers*, and I wanted to return the hospitality in some way. I was thinking of others first. A new track.

I accepted the service work with one caveat: if my legal troubles were vanquished, it would free me to easily return the keys and move out of my cottage in a few short hours so that I could head to South America with no strings attached. Things were coming together without my constant fidgeting with what was going to play out next. I was ready for anything. At least I thought I was. The unexplainable was about to happen.

On a fairly consistent basis, *Sunrise* would be the destination for visitors from out of town, adding a nice mix of people, perspectives, and life experiences to the growing numbers of attendees over the last month or so. The early morning meeting allowed for people visiting on vacation, business, conferences, and weddings to reach out and be touched by the welcoming arms of the burning fire provided by *Sunrise*. The sofas and assorted folding chairs that once contained our patrons were no longer sufficient, and the unused pews stacked at the back of the room were needed to meet the growing demand. A mystical give and take was taking place as the growing numbers were sharing the gifts of life and the harrowing dance with death. Magic was happening, and you could literally feel it upon entering the room.

It was the first Tuesday of February when I heard a voice from downstairs inquiring about where the meeting was located. I directed the visitor to make her way up the stairwell to the second floor. She was from out of town, and her name was Nina. It is customary, when you are visiting, to share where you're from and the name of your home meeting. Nina was a spitfire, standing about five feet tall, with a presence and energy that filled the room. She was visiting from Chicago, and her home group was *Mustard Seed*. I froze. My mind quickly flashed back to when my mother and I would be in some sort of disagreement, resulting in a standoff of not seeing one another, and then she would reach out and say, "Since Moses will not come to the mountain, I guess the mountain will come to Moses." Lo and behold, *Mustard Seed* was coming to *Sunrise*.

Nina was a bright light at *Sunrise* for the two weeks she graced us with her presence. Her humor was infectious, her ability to share what was going on in her life breathtaking, and her quips were sizzling and gut wrenching. But the proverbial penny dropped for me when it was time for her to share on her last day before going back to Chicago.

The discussion was centered on the topic of the depth of bottom one has to descend to in order to finally surrender to the idea that something beyond oneself could be capable of quelling the insane behavior indicative of an alcoholic and eventually restoring them back to sanity. A common phrase is "it takes what it takes." Hitting bottom provides one the opportunity to look up, pause, and hope things cannot get any worse. At a meeting, this would be the time one would hear all the gory details of the depths of bottom, how we allowed ourselves to be taken to this place and the destructive nature of those depths inflicted on family, friends, spouses, children, employers, and society as a whole.

Now Nina had a take on the whole hitting bottom issue, which for many upon entering the rooms is a gargantuan stumbling block when struggling with the idea of accepting whether they are stricken with the disease. The immediate natural human response when listening to these stories is to account for the differences we all tend to lean on when being compared to one group or another, providing the shield from being labeled like those people even when they are singing our song. It is so much easier to point out the differences we have with others—especially when discussing topics such as religious tradition, political view, racial make-up, and economic policy—than it is to see the shared resemblance. It's very easy to defend a separateness, but it is extremely difficult to see the similarities because it takes two vital ingredients for those walls to be broken down: time and respect.

It takes time to get to know somebody, and in that time we invariably find a lot of shared qualities, opening up new unthought-of possibilities, and suddenly the unthinkable act of respecting the differences we in fact do have is welcomed in a healthy way. The need to defend your way or my way falls by the wayside and we find common ground.

Let me tell you—no one wants to be an alcoholic, just like no one wants to have cancer. Having cancer is deemed regal when compared to having alcoholism, but the bottom line is that either one is beyond the control of the recipient of the disease. One doesn't have a choice about having alcoholism, but we do have a choice in accepting its unmanageability in our life and seeking help to get better.

Personally, I didn't want to be in these rooms. I didn't want to be labeled an alcoholic. I didn't drink like some of these people did. I didn't want to get a sponsor and do the steps. I wanted to stop getting DUIs, and that was going to happen anyway since I no longer had the desire to drink. So why do all this other unnecessary stuff? All this work smelled of overkill!

Then, out of the mouth of this tiny angel in the form of a woman from Chicago, would be the "Atom Bomb" to my ego I would need to take the next step in life. Nina said:

You don't hit bottom by what happens to you in life, you hit bottom when you stop digging...Nina — Chicago.

Instantly, I understood the essence of her share, and it rattled me back to reality. In order for me to really have a shot at finding out who I was in this long and exhausting life of mine, I had to actively, through conscious choice, participate in digging through my life experiences to uncover why I do what I do. It was the freedom I needed, working so well within my willful nature of keeping what I had or getting what I wanted. I didn't like the idea of having to do the steps because someone said I had to, but I did like the idea of moving through these steps with a sponsor so I could find my own bottom in life, and in turn, possible growth. It was about me. I was relieved.

Over the past several months, I not only realized I was a patient in the rooms but that I was also a student. I was interested in not only how it worked, but also why it worked for so many different people with different backgrounds and life experiences. What I had experienced by coming to the rooms and listening—and I mean really listening—when people shared their bottom stories is that it didn't matter how they reached bottom; a freedom arose, allowing one to push the restart button in their lives. It dawned on me that I could have the same experience if I choose to dig as deep as I wanted, and this intrigued me to my core.

Selfishly, I wanted to know how in the hell had I gotten to this point in life, so empty and so alone on the inside but full and surrounded by others on the outside. Bottom line, I wanted to have a life, any life, except for the one I'd had for the past forty-three years. Doing the steps with a sponsor worked for others so why not me?

On the intellectual side, I was always curious why things worked, not just how they worked, and I was simply amazed at why this worked for so many who had everything in common and nothing in common at the same time. In the human experience, we all share in the commonality of pain in one form or another, and on the other hand we are individually unique in our creation and experience.

I was ready to be the patient/student, as this would be the only plausible way to keep my interest long enough so I didn't fall back to the old shoe of acting on the next thought that came to mind. This was my golden parachute. It was time to select a sponsor.

My decision on who to ask to be my sponsor would be an easy one, as my fellow *Sunriser* Joseph had been encouraging me for several months and on many occasions had offered his services. Joseph was one year sober this time around, with three years under his belt before he'd decided one evening that a glass of wine would be great with dinner. All it had taken was a few months after that first glass and he'd been ready to throw his life and family away, one glass of expensive wine at a time.

Joseph and I were connected in so many ways. We talked politics, economics, social change, sports, and we loved to read newspapers. I always thought I was peculiar in this way, but for the past ten years at least, I have read about seven newspapers per day. I devoured the rags from front to back, and soon realized Joseph had the same affliction. We didn't always agree on everything when discussing a given topic, but I honored his intellect and loved working my brain's muscles on a daily basis with Joseph. We shared similar backgrounds, both growing up in Hispanic families and playing high school basketball. Joseph had also lived in Austin for some ten years, and even though he had moved back to California before I arrived in Austin, our paths and watering holes were mirror images.

Joseph was perfect for me, and I trusted him completely. But it was one statement in particular that Joseph shared, reassuring me he understood the parts of me that even I didn't fully understand. Joseph had come from a family of six, and he mentioned he never felt a part of his biological family. He knew how I felt inside, even though I didn't really know what that was. I was ready to uncover with his help.

It was the end of February. It took all of five months from awaking on the magic couch to accumulate hundreds of meetings under my belt and numerous spiritual experiences all propelling me to this point in time. I surrendered my will, summoning up the courage to ask Joseph to be my sponsor. Every experience since my awakening was vital for me to completely surrender for the first time in my life. I willfully turned my life over to a process and a person who would allow me to dig until I hit bottom. You see, bottom couldn't be number seven and the ensuing consequences. It had to be something else; at least that's what my ego and pride were telling me. I couldn't go down like that. I made the decision to do the twelve steps in order and to follow the suggestions of my sponsor.

This was in no way an easy decision for me, and I had to make one other very critical decision. For the very first time in my life, my intention was to do the steps with full measure. I'd never done anything with full measure, not even my drinking, which I had done with half measure as well—only drinking on weekends and holidays to ensure it wouldn't interfere with the other portions of my life. This decision was critical.

Life is tricky since short-term success while giving half measures was in fact short term and never really worked for me, or anyone else for that matter, in the long term. My way of doing things with half measure and reaping the short-term benefits until the next thought came to mind was over for now. I realized the peace and calm my fellow *Sunrisers* exhibited was what I wanted, and I was willing to be willing for the very first time.

6

ELEPHANTS?

I wish I had a better setting to remember the moment when I met with Joseph for the very first time as my official sponsor. A place that would signify the extreme risk I was taking and the union of healing I was hoping for with higher powers guiding this occasion, but tranquility was never a part of my journey. Instead we met in front of the Vons supermarket in the village, nestling on one of those round, plastic outdoor tables with attached umbrellas that are always filthy no matter how often someone tries to keep them clean. Joseph's demeanor was different. He was all business. This was sacred ground. No drum roll.

Joseph quickly set the ground rules by sharing his experience of how he chose a sponsor during his second attempt to complete the steps and his decision to switch sponsors midstream, feeling he needed a stronger hand to guide his willful nature. He reminded me I had the very same discretion to make a change if needed. No offense would be taken since this was my journey, not his. He spoke about his failed first attempt to do the steps by not being honest with himself. His new sponsor had reminded him he didn't care if he wasn't honest but the end result would be failure in every aspect of his life, including not drinking. "So, don't waste my time or yours," Joseph insisted. We discussed at length the inability to be honest and how this had affected our lives and those who surrounded us—not to mention those impacted going unnoticed.

Joseph knew me without knowing me because he was beginning to understand himself as he humbly shared his experience of trying to paint a picture for his sponsor that was not reality. A common human response when fear gets in the way, so you start self-editing your experience on the fly to make it sound better or not as bad as what really happened. Deceit comes in many forms; it seems when it's all tight and neat and easily recognizable we think it holds some lofty position as being more acceptable to a broader section of voyeurs. In the past I never struggled painting pictures for my voyeurs, as it came out in the performers I built around me to support my circus of one. Painting pictures was easy and the ability to come up with new performers was limitless, but the energy it took to keep it going was finite and now exhausted. I was tired of painting, and I wanted to be who I really was without an audience to perform for and with a new resolve to see what happens next.

My experience of doing life alone and my current exhausted state I likened to the elephant story I heard in a meeting one day from my male model turned homeless drunk friend named Jeffrey. Now homeless would be inaccurate; living on the streets where he was more comfortable was a better way to describe his living conditions. Not unlike Taco Tray Tom, who lived on the stoop at *Sunrise* for the past twelve years, Jeffrey was equally uncomfortable with the security that four walls bring to most people. Tom's and Jeffrey's sense of home was different, and if you really thought about it, was much grander than any manmade structure could ever emulate. The four walls consisted of the night sky, the earth beneath them, and the ocean to the west, and Mt. Soledad to the east. A grand abode on any standard and then throw in the personal landscape hand-painted by God and it makes you want to curl up outside and soak up what they already knew…Home!

My connection to Jeffrey was special. We were introduced to each other on my first day at *Sunrise* and he had been one week sober. We shared the same sobriety date. He was a tall man, wearing white slacks, white tennis shoes, and a polo shirt, and he sported a slick hair do and a tennis tan. A young George Hamilton comes to mind. This cat was handsome, and he was well-versed in the recovery speak. It seemed like he knew what was going on with all this code talk being spilled around the room, and his presence gave me comfort. He was cool with an old Hollywood vibe. I liked that.

After attending the meeting for several days, I noticed a new attendee at *Sunrise* with a scruffy beard, dirty clothes, and reeking of booze and vomit. When it was time to for this man to share, I recognized the voice, not the vehicle carrying the voice. It was shocking. It was Jeffrey. No one ever sees the transformation one physically undergoes when burdened with the yoke of the drink. In three short days it was mind scrambling to see a human being go from one extreme to the other, and as I came to know Jeffrey, the ebb and flow of his outward appearance and sobriety was as unpredictably predictable. Jeffrey suffered from chronic relapses, but would always come back to the meetings no matter what his condition, and sometimes it was necessary to swill drinks of beer stashed outside so that he could make it through the meeting.

At first I found his behavior disruptive to the learning and healing environment provided at *Sunrise,* but what I came to learn is what better place for an alcoholic to be when drinking than with those who can understand. I had been to meetings where the idea of letting someone in this condition participate with a share would be frowned upon and quickly squashed as to not negatively influence the newly sober. But *Sunrise* was open to all and in any condition as we actually practiced compassion for all who suffer when entering the door, regardless of how long it's been since their last drink, which for Jeffrey meant drinking while at the meeting.

The commonality we shared at *Sunrise* was we were all in pain in varying degrees, regardless of how long it had been since our last drink and how we could as individuals or as a group determine who is less sick or in less pain than the other. The thought of being better than another because one has linked together days and for some decades of sobriety, allowing one the space to start building back the ego by exercising the differences we once shared but now don't. Seeking growth is the desire—not how many days one's been without the drink.

There is a saying in the rooms, "Stick with the winners." What is a winner? Who determines what that looks like? Is it presumptuous to think through my brokenness I can decipher what is winning and what is not? One of the amazing attributes of *Sunrise* is the space we gave each other to find our own way through this torturous and dangerous path to serenity. How we came into the room was unique, and how we make it out of the room was equally unique. Sounds a lot like life to me when we honor the individual journey.

Well, Jeffrey certainly stretched the boundaries on more than one occasion, and his shares would range from barely coherent to extremely insightful and revealing, to the thoughts we all internalized but were afraid to share out loud. Jeffery had no filter and we were all the better for it. He would share about the responsibility that elephants innately have for one another when one of them is injured or sick.

The jungle or plain is a very dangerous place, and if you're not careful, severe harm and possible death is lurking around every bush, hill, or watering hole. In the animal kingdom, the top predators come out at night to prey on the weak and young to sustain themselves. This is where the instincts of shared responsibility come into play for the elephants. When one of the elephants is sick or injured, all the other elephants are aware of this distress and tightly surround the ailing elephant to keep it from lying down at night. The elephant in distress would be a perfect target for the roaming predators but with the assistance of its brothers and sisters it is supported from lying down where imminent danger waits.

Jeffery likened the *Sunrise* meeting to the elephants as he felt he could come to the meeting and find refuge no matter what his condition was physically, emotionally, and spiritually. We could keep him upright when all he wanted to do was lie down and give up, and this is why he kept coming back specifically to *Sunrise*.

It suddenly clicked for me, and once again my perception was askew. Jeffrey was spot on when describing the shared responsibility we had for each other and the strength it gave us when we relied on another and equally when another relied on us. I couldn't and didn't rely on others, and thus I created my circus of performers to keep me from falling to the ground to be consumed by the dark shadows of my life. It was all too evident now my circus could no longer sustain me if I wanted to have life for the very first time, as I was ready to forsake the company of my performers for the presence of real human contact and support, Joseph.

The sun was shining on my face as I nervously awaited Joseph to unveil some strict guidelines on how we were to interact and what was expected of me as his sponsored. I was willing to do whatever he wanted me to do, I constantly kept reminding myself. This deference would stretch me. The fight for change had begun. My will was strong and my ego was lurking over my shoulder.

Joseph cautiously unveiled details of his experiences that he didn't feel comfortable sharing at a group level while navigating through the steps. His legal mind was double-checking his freedom every step of the way. He insisted on one vital action as I moved forward: honesty. It would be the key to my uncovering and a foretelling of how successful the quest for peace in my life would be for me. The all too common first glance reflection where we are confident honesty is being tapped, but with some deeper reflection through meditation and prayer and the assistance of others you come to realize you've never really gone past the illusion you created for yourself to see what lies beyond the perceived truth…the truth. We quickly went over the first three steps:

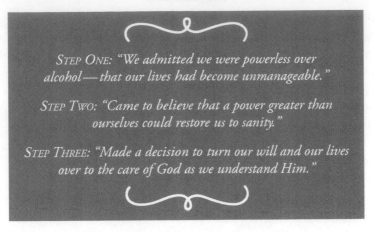

STEP ONE: "We admitted we were powerless over alcohol—that our lives had become unmanageable."

STEP TWO: "Came to believe that a power greater than ourselves could restore us to sanity."

STEP THREE: "Made a decision to turn our will and our lives over to the care of God as we understand Him."

He felt it unnecessary to go over these steps methodically. If I was comfortable, we could press on. He had been observing me over the last five months, seeing the changes in me, and was confident I was ready to move toward the fourth step to start uncovering my life. I had changed? That definitely went unnoticed for sure. If Joseph said I was okay to move forward then I was going to move forward. I was trusting, with hesitation, for now.

Over the past five months I came to realize the first three steps of the program are huge stumbling blocks for most who gather up enough stones to make it to a meeting. The decision to even attempt to shake the monkey off their back by moving through the steps with a final result of attaining serenity is mind-boggling at the very least. I had to make peace with the first three steps before moving on. No half-measures.

Step One: I was powerless over everything in my life even though I thought I was in complete control, so number one was a no brainier. The illusion that one can effectively control all the outcomes in one's life is a sure sign of unmanageability. Box checked.

Step Two: I believed in God, just didn't trust him, but I was willing to be restored to sanity—whatever that meant. Number two down the hatch.

Step Three: I made the decision to turn my will and life over to God, it just didn't mean I had done it yet and that was cool by me in case this step and sponsor stuff didn't work out. The thought being I could go back to my circus and me and that was a relief.

In a half hour, I moved through the first three steps and the fear and anxiety of this process quickly vanished into a sense of accomplishment.

But this third step is tricky business, and a real deal breaker for most who don't believe in God or have had a salty experience with religious tradition. The fact is, most never move beyond this step with the cycle of self-inflicted pain continuing, not to mention the inability to stop drinking. A fellow *Sunriser* called "Pockets" talked passionately about his meanderings in and out of the rooms for twenty-eight years and never getting past the third step. He would share the bone chilling experience of grabbing a fifth of vodka to crawl into a rabbit hole to subdue his pain of not being able to sustain sobriety centered on this spiritual dilemma. It was the cross he could not carry.

This step is often misunderstood or altogether not clearly explained. It centered on a single word: decision. One has to make a decision to venture down this road to see what may occur not to actually know who or what the god of your own understanding actually is. One doesn't have to know how to pray or meditate or whatever it takes to commune with their higher power or more importantly to identify what that actually is to move past this step. Not knowing this nuance can paralyze decision-making and continue the reliance upon the drink.

Simply, it's a decision to move to the next step, knowing something might develop in this untapped area of your life. It's kind of like a keg of beer without the tap. The third step is the acknowledgement you might need the tap to get to the beer so you might as well put the deposit on the tap so you can haul the keg and ice to your vehicle to get to where you're going to open the keg which is under great pressure. The keg is you and the tap is the higher power that if exercised, will relieve the pressure in your life. It's really that simple in comparison to the next step.

STEP FOUR: *"Made a searching and fearless moral inventory of ourselves."*

I was aware of the significance of the fourth step and the work it entailed to thoroughly and methodically uncover the liabilities and assets in a life. This is the writing step where pen and paper meet and the miracle that happens when one writes about their life experiences. There is something restorative when one writes, making it more real in a surreal way. Not only does it give clarity to the actions or inactions in life, but it also allows for the freedom to express, in a safe way, those secrets or unshared thoughts pressed deep down within our beings.

The keg (you) has been rustled from the liquor store (life), tossed in the back of the vehicle (experiences), sloshed around until the destination of choice, and now is expected on demand when tapped to pour a crystal clear river of beer (honesty). If you have ever tapped a keg, you know it makes sense to let it rest or at least not to have the expectation the beer would flow freely and without foam (dishonesty). But it never fails, as a lot of foam comes pouring out of the pressurized keg until you get the pressure right, and then and only then does the beer flow freely.

The fourth step allows one to carve past the trivial and not so trivial matters in a life and get to the source of what keeps one from having peace in life. I was excited at this point to get past the foam in my life and move past all that liquid to get to the bottom of my barrel. I could dig till I hit bottom, and I was going to give this the full measure I had not given to anything in my life.

Until I uncovered and disrobed the veils I purposely hoisted in my life to not deal with the completeness of "Me," I would not be able to have the peace so apparent in my fellow *Sunrisers*. I had no idea what Joseph had in store, but I was ready to do whatever he asked of me. I waited patiently with a busy mind.

With heightened anticipation, I watched Joseph dig through his pockets to pull out a wadded up piece of paper with writing scribbled in all directions. I guess I was expecting some glorious magical document that would save me from death by my own hand, but it was perfect because it was not. It was written on this mangled mess needing to be unraveled and deciphered for its content. Oddly enough I was a tightly wadded up piece of human flesh wrapped around bones, and the answers to my story lay beyond the scribbled writing of Joseph. The only question now was the depth to which I was willing to go in order to clean out this vessel that had become me but wasn't me. I was seasoned enough to pull off the impossible due to years of performances under my belt, but this effort would be the most difficult of my life.

It took a while to decipher his chicken scratch, but within an hour I had transferred the formula to my five-section notebook with instructions on each section. It was the last bit of advice he shared with me that made all the difference. He reiterated his failed attempt to paint a fourth step which in no way resembled the truth—his intention being not to reveal to his sponsor what really went on in his life and how he missed the whole honesty component of the exercise.

Could this be another turning point for me? I would be wasting my time and his if I wasn't going to be honest with my feelings and what really transpired in my life. He suggested I find a quiet place outside of my home to sit down for a least an hour to write as much as I remembered and then put the pen and paper down until the next time. But most importantly, he wanted me to pray before writing that God would guide my pen, keeping me on a path of honesty no matter how uncomfortable the topics and the truth became.

With formula in hand, I guess I had only one big question that pertained to the fourth step and another question that had to deal with my current work situation, or lack thereof. I felt a little funny asking Joseph's advice, and this was a momentous occasion for me with my life only guided by the next thought that came to mind. I needed no filters or advice on how to run my circus, and unlike my drinking with a pack habit, this circus could only be led by me. Now I was reaching out with caution, but reaching out nonetheless.

First, I needed to address my job situation. I had not been working since my perfect storm back in September, and my cash flow had dried up, but I did have some resources and could use them until I found a buyer for my house in New Mexico. With no tenant, if my house didn't sell in nine months, debt would crush me. My bleak financial fate was staring me in my face, and I had an innate desire to generate funds to keep the show going. I truly wanted to make something happen on the work front, but I had promised myself to give this step stuff full measure and to rely upon Joseph when I had to make some decisions—at least in the short term.

I took my dilemma to Joseph and asked him if I should go back to work, and without hesitation, unconditional love came pouting from his lips. He told me that I could choose to go back to work or not and the beauty of having some sobriety was I now had choices. But with choice comes consequences, and even if I avoided major negative ones, I should think through those possibilities and then make my decision.

I'd always thought I had choices before, but when you act on the first thought that comes to mind, only one choice is genuinely available until that cycle is finished; then, and only then, would I move to the next thought. I didn't know it at the time—and Joseph surely didn't intend to teach me this lesson—but funny things happen when you enter the foreign territory of doing things differently in life without the security of "this is how I've always done it."

With all that being said, Joseph shared one last suggestion harvested from his own experience. He himself had not worked in over a year and had mounting pressure from his family to find employment. In fact, he had taken this very same question to his sponsor some time ago. With a peace and calm I envied, he shared the advice his sponsor had given him: "This might be the only chance you will have in your life to take the time and get your life right because you know what is awaiting you if you don't!"

I pondered his suggestion, with my first thought being South America-boutique hotel / wine making-here-we-come, and then something funny happened: I had a second thought, a recollection of my last drink and the pain of it all. I quickly shook off the first thought and decided to gamble the money I could borrow with my credit and hope my home would sell in the next nine months before my funds would be exhausted. This would allow me the time necessary to get this process right and not worry about finding and keeping a job, at least in the short-term.

The work portion of my life that I despised but was crucial in allowing me the freedom to exercise the first thought that came to mind, would come to an end. Now the only thing between me and how I got to be this illusion of me was the twelve steps and a gargantuan dose of honesty.

I guess I genuinely trusted Joseph. I hadn't really trusted anyone since Bob Jefferson, and even though I had been truthful with Bob, I had a feeling this fourth step stuff would uncover some truths I wasn't aware of or had created as a truth but in fact was fantasy turned into reality a long, long time ago. How far back did my gift of turning fantasy into reality go? I needed to know where I should start, and therefore my next question to Joseph was: "Where do I start this uncovering?"

He replied, "How far back can you remember?"

I quickly thought of how my photographic memory had served my circus of one so purposefully. Would all this exercising serve me in this most vital task of my life of finding out why I became who I was? At first I thought he was joking around as we always did, but quickly I realized he was not. He strongly suggested that if I thoroughly and honestly addressed my past in writing, a life would await me that would not forget the past but would allow me to use my past experiences as a new way of making decisions. I would be able to see the ebb and flow of life and the meanderings of my experiences with clarity not possible before without this gut-wrenching honesty.

In essence, I could use these life experiences to chart a new journey one moment at a time, allowing not only myself but also those surrounding me to consume the fruits of a thoughtful, self-cleansing, self-examining, compassionate, unconditional loving life guided by a strengthened spiritual condition. My experiences would no longer be put into categories of good and bad, but rather would be transformed into the jewel box of my life. I could now source these jewels for the benefit of guiding my own choices going forward, and when not applicable for Me, I could share with another for their benefit when asked.

Wow! I thought I wanted to stop getting DUIs and the pain associated with them, but Joseph was passing on a tradition that had been with mankind since the onset of time: the unconditional sharing of the gifts of life as viewed through our experiences to help another human being. The old tradition of uplifting another without motive had been consumed by our modern, consumerist world. The hustle and bustle to carve out your own space in the world for your own needs without concern for others along the way, highlighted by having the next best thing, can lead to being consumed by the self. I had been consumed. I justified this behavior by helping others along the way, with the rationalization that when I really made it, I would be able to do more.

It is important to help others, but what Joseph was exposing to me through his experience was his newfound, albeit somewhat uncomfortable, ability to be there for another by sharing your brokenness and how you moved past the fear of that brokenness to have a deeper, more meaningful life with others. This was foreign territory for Joseph; he was just as uncomfortable sharing it with me as I was receiving it. Not because he didn't know it was the right thing to do, but because it was a new way of living life. We were in this together, and I hoped his experience of being my sponsor would be equally powerful and life-changing as I hoped it would be for me. Who was helping whom? Another paradox!

The addiction to self reigns king over the countless addictions available in the human condition, and I was stricken. I was the king of my castle, and it was time to start dismantling my edifice one stone at time to get to the foundation of my life that was a blurry mess at best. After all the rubble (the fantasy turned into reality) was hauled off, I would be able to dig past the surface, down to the roots of my life to find who I was and who I really wanted to be. I was always trying to build this image from which when I reached its height I would be able to look down and see the wonderful life I had built on my own. A model of living that is not unique in its infinite paths, but common in its singular outcome of isolation in the self-will.

I'd fallen victim to the worldly thought that by amassing and building things a comfort and peace in life would be assured. I thought it wasn't possible any other way! Ascending to new heights would be my drug of choice, but something was never quite right with me all along as I practiced this me, more and now philosophy but at the same time despised the taste it left on my soul. I was never quite comfortable in my own skin, so I would create another skin which to wear until it, too, became uncomfortable and then another was created and adorned till its demise. I loved and hated these skins so much, but they were never discarded. The skins evolved into the performers for which my circus tent gave cover until the time when they became useful at getting what I wanted and keeping what I had.

It became excruciatingly apparent that I would have to dig past my adult life, past my teens and childhood, into the far reaching roots of my being if I desired to find the essence of me. I would not be building *up* to find who I was—a common theme in many religious traditions—but rather I would be digging *down* to find who I had been all along. In an uncomfortable way, this was comforting. Uncomfortable in that I would have to go back and with clarity and honestly scroll back my life to see in fact how my life unfolded to the point of when I awoke upon my magic couch five months earlier. Comfortable in that I would not be doing this alone and I could trust another.

There is a saying in the rooms: you're as sick as your secrets. I now willfully wanted to expose my secrets as far back as I could remember.

My five-section notebook was ready for some writing. The question now: was I ready? Who really is when radically changing life is the task confronting us? Full measure is a must.

> SECTION 1. MY RESENTMENT LIST: *People, places, and things, including institutions and principles. What was I resentful toward, what was the cause of this resentment, and how did this affect me personally?*

One definition of resentment is to re-feel something when it comes to mind. I guess I had resentments and this would be revealing in some aspects, but you have to remember my inability to have feelings and emotions served me well in this area of my life. If you can't really feel anything then how can you be resentful toward someone or something about how it affected you? In the past, I didn't have time to wrestle with this stuff while enacting the next thought that came to mind. I needed to dig past the surface for sure in this area, as I'm positive events along the way changed my course.

> SECTION 2. MY FEAR LIST: *What was I fearful of? What is the source of this fear? Where was I at fault? Whom do I fear? What would God have me do instead?*

With this new source of honesty, I was realizing I had a lot of fears and this source of honesty was being revealed through the experiences my fellow *Sunrisers* were sharing so openly at the group level. I most assuredly had some work to do in this area.

> SECTION 3. SEXUAL INVENTORY: *Who and what happened? When had I been dishonest and inconsiderate? When did I arouse feelings of jealously, bitterness, or suspicion?*

You've got to be kidding me! How does my sexual life have anything to do with my drinking? The answer is it might or might not have anything to do with it, but had everything to do with who I am and how I treat others. This was not going to be fun and my honesty was going to be tested for sure.

SECTION 4. SEXUAL RELATIONSHIP IDEAL LIST: *What would I like my personal relationship to ideally look like? What do I want in my partner? What do I have to offer?*

Each question had to have at least ten responses. I found this line of questioning odd, but I couldn't achieve what I couldn't envision, and my inability to have a long-term relationship was evident, so at least this portion sounded helpful in that regard.

SECTION 5. SECRETS: *Things that I need to write down but are between my maker and me and shouldn't be revealed to anyone.*

I found this troublesome, since wasn't the whole process of achieving a sense of peace and calm a direct result of being honest about everything in my life? Joseph quickly explained sometimes people do things against the law and there could be dire consequences, including prison time, if they were revealed to anyone. These were the things we must write down and be honest about but not necessarily share with another human being.

This section baffled me, and then I remembered a conversation with my friend Naomi in Austin that shed some light on my confusion. We had been talking about the topic of unconditional love when she shared a conversation she'd had with her father, as he reminded her that actions have consequences and with that said he would love her just shy of triple homicide. Now Naomi was angelic in my eyes, but it was the reminder I needed. Our actions or inaction in life do have consequences, challenging the ideal of unconditional love. I understood and was glad that I would have nothing to share in this section.

It took several days for me to gather the courage to move from the safe confines of the open reading area of the village library with its comfortable seating and prime people watching, to the cubicles sequestered in the nooks and crannies of the book stack areas of the library where solitude and quiet were at a premium. With a short prayer asking God to direct my pen for insurance purposes only because this human shape-shifter of the big tent was incapable of doing this honesty trip alone, I commenced to sit in solitude while going back through my life to reach my first memory.

It was a really interesting exercise, as I can best describe it like those little books you would make as a kid where you drew stick figures and on the next page repositioned the figure and so on and so on until the point when you could rapidly flip through the pages, giving the figure the illusion of movement. The cool part was that you could flip through and see the figure go in reverse back to where you originally started, and that's exactly how it felt. I must have sat there for hours without picking up the pen, sifting through a mountain of experiences, some of which brought great sadness and regret and some which brought great joy and laughter.

I was not lacking in the experience department, for sure, and one could surmise not only did I have my fair share of experiences, but gluttony would be a good word to describe the results of a life guided by the enactment of the first thought that came to mind. I did a lot of stuff, and I find it kind of surprising even to myself how many diverse experiences my human frame was able to stuff down in a relatively short period of time.

It was as if I was standing at the end of the buffet line, glancing down at my plate and having a representation of each and every item available and the first thought would be: "What am I missing? I need more. I don't have enough." And don't forget I did everything half-assed, so with that restraint in tow, things could have been even grander—or for that matter worse—on the experience front. I didn't make a single mark on paper the first day when attempting to answers the questions Joseph had posed. But what did happen was a realization that all of these experiences flashing through my mind all had purpose in shaping the man I had become, not necessarily the man I wanted to be.

This retrospect stuff can be a dangerous exercise, especially when one is trying to decipher the truth, challenging an already fear-ridden undertaking when through this uncovering process, one inevitably feels regret for what we have or have not done. Regret can skew the ability to dig deeper to the source of our authentic self, due to the sheer uncomfortable nature of the feelings and emotions that arise. But I was blessed with a gift that my friend George had so graciously and unknowingly given me one day at *Sunrise*.

George was a tall slender gentleman of sound reason with a bevy of life experiences and a Harvard MBA to boot. You see, George gave me a gift no other person could have as he himself had been consumed by the drink for fifty-three years, achieving sobriety at the tender age of seventy-four. It was not George's idea to get sober, as he had been the recipient of unconditional love from his immediate family and was coerced into rehab by intervention.

His will and reason was strong, as not only did he have to be convinced to go to detox, the first step to be completed before one enters rehab, but then had to have a second intervention after detoxing to be convinced rehab would be a good idea as well. His ego and pride fought valiantly for the first week in rehab until that moment when he had his spiritual experience allowing him to lay down his armament of reason and separateness from those whom he was surrounded by, succumbing to the fact he was withering away physically and had more in common with these people at rehab than he realized…an issue with the drink.

The gift George unknowingly bestowed upon me was the gift of having no regrets. George wasted little time rehashing the past and what could have or should have been but rather he used it like "a screen door to keep the bugs out." He relished in his sobriety and what he had at this very moment, and I was grateful for his honesty with his experience.

George allowed me the freedom to go back in life and experience it for what it was, not what it could or should have been. I was free now to document my past without letting the bugs in, so to speak. The bug of regret can sap desire, energy, and full measure, disallowing one to purposefully move through one's past to a point where the fruit of life is attainable and serenity possible. I was relieved! George coincidently debunked the "old dogs can't learn new tricks" adage, as he was slowly changing everything in his life—I, too, could do the same. I love George and our friendship is amazing.

I returned to the library the next day, hoping I could retrieve my first memory, and it came to me: it was Easter Sunday, and I was two years old. This memory wasn't a new revelation for me, as I had shared this story with a few people in my life when asked what was it like growing up not having a father. In fact, in elementary school this was a common question children asked, and I'm not sure whether there was ill will behind the question, but I would like to think it was a question children like to ask when they don't understand something or are just curious.

My stock answer was: "I don't know what it's like to have a father because I've never had one."

From an early age, I knew that this type of response would squash any further questions on the topic, and in fact, this statement was true for the most part, except for that one single moment in time…my first memory. My first memory preceded this line of questioning and my stock response, becoming the mortar to the cornerstone of my castle of self-reliance and isolation…my circus of one. It was the only memory I have of my biological father living in the same house when growing up.

It was Easter morning. I was excited to see what the Easter Bunny had left for me, but more importantly I wanted to do this Easter egg hunting business that had been built up over the past few weeks. The tradition of coloring the eggs fueled my anxiety as I clearly remember wanting my father to come with me to do this egg hunting. I desperately wanted to go hunting for the eggs and I clearly wanted my father to come with me, but all I remember is that I ran back and forth and back and forth to get him out of bed to do this damn egg hunt and he wouldn't get up. I'm sure with some psychotherapy I would be able to pinpoint the effect this episode had on my development or lack thereof, but I am certain that would be a waste of time at this point. It wasn't my first experience in this vessel I call Me; it was just the first one I could remember.

I believe that more often than not in the human experience, we want to pinpoint a moment in time as the turning point that caused the joy or strife in our life. Weighing a moment in time in a special way as the reason we became this way or that way takes precedence. We all want to know why, don't we?

What I've come to learn is this: each of our experiences is like hundreds we've had before and countless others we will have in the future. The significance is that each experience affords the powerful opportunity to choose how that experience will impact our decisions going forward. The desperation I felt of wanting my father to come with me and not getting that immediate response struck a deep chord within my being, this I'm sure of. It's my first memory of my being in this vessel, and I don't need psychotherapy to tell me it's important. What I do need to recognize is I am responsible for my decisions going forward in life and no one is to blame for the construction of my life, no matter how tenuous its foundation. I, and I alone, placed one stone after another, with the mortar being my will, resulting in a life foreign even to myself.

What I didn't like was this feeling of having to rely upon someone for anything. This self-reliance stuff would prove to be a theme in my life and in all of my siblings in our childhood and into adulthood. The race for I, self and me was on!

7
FEED THE ANIMAL

I love to eat!! I will eat anything, try anything, and I can honestly say the only food I don't particularly care for is the Pacific Islander staple Poi. The taste and texture reminds me of art class, when you would make a concoction of flour and water to dip newspaper in to cover objects like balloons. Now, I love Hawaiian food, with my favorites being Pipikaula short ribs, Lau Lau, Lomi salmon, Kuala pig, and Poke. My summer stints living in the forty-second story of a Waikiki tower would be the introduction to this wonderful culture that resembled my Indian heritage, honoring the gifts from Mother Earth and, in the Hawaiian culture, a sourcing of the sea for nourishment. I welcomed this new twist as my taste buds salivated in these delights.

The cultural backbone of capturing and gathering foodstuffs to be brought back and prepared by all, eventually to be consumed family-style, gave life to their spiritual and physical well-being. Taking care of each other without condition was the real staple being served. It was the same communal eating in childhood with my five brothers and sisters that might have been the experience I drew upon when not wanting to drink alone. I preferred the banter and liveliness of food sharing and how it enriched me personally and the voyeurs of my circus. A unique phenomenon when nurtured.

My childhood memories of sitting on the counter while my mother made breakfast, lunch, or dinner and my desire to help stir the pot or pour the pancakes was insatiable. I watched her make it up as she went along, with an occasional glance at a recipe for assurance, but with a confidence that a little more of this or that would be better. I loved when it was time to eat, but I loved more the preparation it took to make what was to be broken to fuel our beings. The essence, beauty, and art of food runs deep within my being, and nothing pleasures me more than the romance of breaking bread with others and, if necessary, alone.

This insatiable thirst with food in the spiritual sense for me was being quenched while going to school in London. I ventured out of the core courses offered in traditional school, dipping into the well in the form of cooking classes at the famous Harrods Department Store, which, by the way, has one of the most amazing food markets you will ever encounter — thousands of food items honoring every culture imaginable, all eloquently performing together like a well-tuned and seasoned orchestra. Every item in its place, playing a note of gastronomical excellence that by itself would be another item in a highly polished high-end market, but together was pure magic to the senses.

It wasn't a typical cooking class where you learned to make a sauce or bake a pastry, and the focus wasn't on learning to cook a particular type of cuisine, but rather to honor the ingredients one chooses to cook with and to be playful with the paring of seemingly improbable companions in the concoction of a meal. The simplicity yet complexity of picking the best possible vegetables, fruits, meats, legumes, herbs, and seafood available were taught. The varied preparations available for each ingredient enhancing and changing its taste and texture were exposed. The idea being one would shop for the meal you are making, rather than the western standard of hoarding a month's worth of food in multiple refrigerators/freezers to unthaw for those we love. I don't see a whole lot of romance in that, do you?

Now, I haven't cooked a meal in my home for another or myself in the last decade, but I still love to walk through markets, seeing what is available and what might make a wonderful meal. It's fantasy for me, as invariably, I walk out of the market empty-handed in the physical sense, but my mind has developed a menu for the evening and all that is waiting is my inability to share my hidden passion with another, my inability to be who I really am.

It was survival of the fittest in my childhood household, and this learned behavior of maneuvering through life can be represented in the simplest and unnoticed habits of life, like driving a car or in the way one consumes food when eating. It's comical when observing one of my siblings eating, but not so comical when you are sitting across from one of us, trying to enjoy your meal. These same learned habits are present to this day in our eating habits, the trivial, and in how we do life alone, the heart of the matter.

As a family, we always sat down together to eat dinner at this hand-carved table with benches purchased at a commune outside of Santa Fe, New Mexico, in the early seventies. With six hungry mouths to feed along with the always-present neighborhood kids, everyone gathered was assured of at least a single full plate. But when it came to a second helping of food, if available, one had to have had completely finished their first plate in order to get another with permission. With that being the guidelines of getting a second helping, an unspoken race commenced to finish the first plate to see if a second helping was possible.

To this day, my siblings and I are some of the fastest eaters I have ever witnessed wolfing down whatever is in front of them, even when sitting alone. Even though we were all imprinted by this experience at an early age, and in turn, chose our paths going forward uniquely, the me, more and now were cast deep into our beings.

At first glance, this story revolving around the eating habits of my childhood household seems innocuous for me, but it created the perfect atmosphere, allowing for the building of my circus of one to go unimpeded. We were all fighting for our survival, and the thought of another was not possible, even when sitting together to have a meal. I'm not sure why we all felt this "I'm all alone" feeling when surrounded by so many siblings, neighbors, misfits, and throwaway kids from the neighborhood. And I cannot fully explain their individual experience, but what I can do is explain through my experience how and when my perfect storm had its birth and the experiences in between that led to the formulation of the performers in my circus of one and the death of this way of living my life that took its last breath on the magic couch some forty-two years later.

What I did know, regardless of the circumstances and the means it took to get what I wanted or keep what I had, my first memory would be the onset of how I would maneuver through the light and dark of my life going forward.

The light and dark of life. What does that mean? It even sounds a bit odd to me. Light, dark, shadow material, enlightenment, life and death. I still don't have a good definition of what those things are, but what I do know is the feeling one experience provides versus the other is drastically different. What I've learned through other people's experiences is the light in one's life can be the dark in another person's life. It's really difficult to put your finger on why it means one thing to one person and the very same experience means the complete opposite to another.

Our experiences are uniquely our own, even though we all have similar experiences in life. Only the person feeling those feelings when experiencing the experience really knows what is going on inside of them, thus, it's unique while at the same time being shared through its likeness.

My problem all along, my self-inflicted disease, was the inability to navigate my way through the light and dark feelings in my life. My road map was my self-reliance buttressed by my will and carried out by the first thought that entered my mind, resulting in getting what I wanted and keeping what I had. An extreme form of selfishness all disguised in a package so well thought out and orchestrated that its cloaking mechanism could not be cracked for what really laid within by using old patterns of problem solving.

I once heard in a meeting that, to get something you've never had, one has to do something they've never done.

It was impossible for me, the creator of this circus of one, to unravel the code to who I really was unless I was willing to look into the past and see why I clung to the dark experiences in life as if they were the light. But what I do know is the dark—or shall I say what I deemed as the dark—in my life had such a strong presence in my life at such an early age. Its germination was unknown.

The mystical side of life in the eyes of our modern world has been relinquished to a status of fortunetellers and all-night infomercials toting psychic readings of love, wealth, and what will or will not be happening next in our lives. With a quick swipe of a credit card, our lives could be unfolded before our eyes, setting in motion a series of expectations that may or may not come to fruition. In no way am I saying these forms of communication are wrong, but what I am saying is our modern world seems to be leaving less and less space for the areas of life that cannot be explained any other way. The modern world of scientific reasoning to prove or disprove phenomena cannot neatly find a welcoming place for the side of life where words or conscious thought is unable to explain.

In particular, I'm speaking of the dream life we all experience, with some having a special gift in deciphering and explaining what cannot be explained in any other way. All of the major religious traditions in their ancient's texts describe in vivid detail how certain characters possessing this gift of the subconscious would be able to communicate with their higher power through their dream life, enabling the followers to seek a certain path versus another. Sometimes, these revelations lead them to a promised land, and at other times, forewarn of drought and famine for past transgressions. I guess what I'm trying to explain here is that I don't have the gift of being able through dream life to see what is being communicated to me through higher sources of understanding, but what I do know is I have to unravel the dark dream life I experienced as a child and, if possible, to see the meandering of my path toward my perfect storm.

I know I'm not unique in this experience, but my dream life as a child was extremely vivid, terrifying, and dark. The themes of death, vampires, and Satan consumed my sleep life, and I found myself running with desperation from one or, when it really became torturous, all of these characters as they played in my subconscious over and over in my head night after night after night. The fear of sleeping at any time whether, it was dark outside or not, was extreme, and when I did sleep, the cold feeling of bedwetting always awakened me.

I was embarrassed by the bedwetting, and that seemed to override the cause—horrifying dreams—which I effortlessly chained to the basement of my life, for fear of letting another know these thoughts consumed me in my sleep. My dream life consumed my nights, when I would drift to sleep only through pure exhaustion to an awaiting torture chamber of thoughts, and my days, trying to push down these thoughts so I could just play. All while knowing nighttime would be approaching and the cycle of fear, then exhaustion, then sleep, then dreams and finally awakening by bedwetting.

My reasoning was being honed early on, as I gathered my siblings didn't have this bedwetting problem, which assured they didn't experience dark scary dreams as well. I was positive they were connected. It was embarrassing enough to wet the bed, and this set in stone the decision not to reveal to anyone what was actually going on in my subconscious at night.

The ability to create a skin for myself had its awakening as a result of these horrific dreams that I wouldn't and couldn't share with another. Hence, I pushed down what was really going on inside of me, creating an exuberance for life and willing to do anything, all centered on the fear I might be consumed by these dark vivid images haunting me throughout my nights. In my mind, I wanted to overload on experiences, as I was confident I wouldn't be able to escape these dark images, with the end result being an abbreviated existence on this earth.

My daily meanderings as a child, which became the birthing canal of my circus, was a result of my dream life, as I slowly befriended the dark dreams in the same way when someone hugs you in an uncomfortable way. I love hugging, and we all need a daily dose of great hugs. Luckily, I had a hug mentor.

My dear friend in Austin, Kimberly, my acupuncturist/herbalist/spiritual healer, whom I met after number six while I was seeking out changes in my life physically and spiritually, is one of the all-time best huggers.

When she hugs you, you can feel her energy moving through you like when a beam of sunlight pokes its way through the clouds, illuminating a spot on Earth below, healing not solely your physical being, but also the essence of your soul. She was a true healer in her ancient practice of the mind, body, and spirit.

I think we all have the experience of getting a hug from someone and it makes you feel connected to something other than yourself with its amazing healing properties, but on the other hand, there are those times when you sense a bad energy emanating from a potential hugger who might have ulterior motives insisting on getting some flesh time, so you acquiesce and the uncomfortable hug is underway. As a child, I was becoming calloused to fear, and the line between the dark dreams and the light of day for me was becoming blurred.

At the light of day, I would be dashing out the door to scour the surrounding neighborhoods to experience anything other than what would be awaiting me when I came home, which, in my mind, meant sleep. I so loved the outside, never wanting to come home. The flickering of the streetlights warming up for the night was the signal starting my personal tug of war of not wanting to go home. The illumination also meant dinner was almost ready, and the insistence of my single, divorced mother of six that all her children eat together as a family at our indoor picnic table was non-negotiable.

My sisters, Theri and Maria, would have the undesirable task of rounding me up from the neighborhood and the ensuing battle each and every night to find me and then convince me to come home for dinner. They both share the same experience of me kicking them with my high-top shoes all the way home, not knowing all along my real desire was not wanting to eat, but rather what would come after eating.

With no end in sight of this daily battle, I eventually devised a solution to this dinner dilemma. If somehow I could eliminate dinner at home, then I could delay the start of those feelings that had me kicking my sisters into submission—a sure relief to their battered shins.

In the subtlety of not wanting to eat at home for fear of having to sleep, I would have to craft a series of skins to assure a seat at the varying households on our street, eliminating, or should I say delaying, the start of a dream life that in my mind could only be solved by not sleeping. In order to get what I wanted, subduing my dream life, I was willing to go to any lengths to delay the arrival at home, and to me, this was a victory over the fear welling inside me.

Our home sat at the very end of the cul-de-sac, providing a landscape of potential voyeurs to my left and to my right. There is nothing more satisfying to an actor than having a diverse audience to perform to, and let me tell you, our street was full of interesting participants in the building of my circus. I intuitively knew early on that if I could be the one who shape-shifted to the environment around me, the higher the probability would be that I would get what I wanted, and that was not to go home at dinnertime to eat.

The array of venues to perform to was dizzying. To my household's immediate right was the Stone family. Arnold and Kathy were from a part of Texas that never was quite fully divulged, and the source of this secrecy would play out in the lives of their twin boys, Robert and David. Arnold was in the construction business and was a stern fellow who rode a Harley Davidson Police-edition motorcycle with full saddlebags, old-style. I remember the times when he would show us how to butcher the rabbits they raised in the backyard and when he would uncoil the belt from his pants, signaling it was time for some discipline for wrongdoing. I never witnessed the beatings, as I quickly dashed over the wall to the sounds of the ass-whopping Robert and David were subject to on a regular basis. There was no room for error in a house full of errors. Simple words and love were rarely used.

Kathy was awesome and a second mom for me, as she always made it fun around her house. She liked to sew and make all kinds of stuff that were artistic in nature, but a little on the homely side, if you know what I mean. She would teach us how to play canasta, dominos, chess, and other games involving thought and team play. It was fun, but I was always drawn to the abnormal things surrounding me, and Kathy was on my radar.

It was Kathy's walk, or in the summertime when she would wear shorts that the end result of a childhood accident would be in full view. She was run over, and a portion of her leg was chopped away, resembling a bite from a shark extending from her lower hamstring to her upper calf muscle. I never once heard her complain about it, but there were times when she would have to use her hands to maneuver the leg around when she had exhausted it limits. She loved driving her gold Cadillac with the handicap hang tag available when the distance from the car to the entrance of where she was going was too far.

Robert was a beefy athletic type who I loved dueling with, which typically had us always trying to outdo the other, whether it was in table tennis, walking on top of walls, jumping bikes across ditches, water polo, and marathon Frisbee tossing. It didn't matter what it was. We loved to compete. We also liked to fight, and we had our share of close combat, but it was the rock fights I relished in, as I could laser a rock from thirty yards and always put him down.

David, on the other hand, was a frail kid whom we tagged the "Zipper" due to the foot-long scars down the middle of his chest, the result of open-heart surgery as an infant. He was kind and gentle and slow in activity at times, but large in his spirit. He would cry and laugh in the same moment, relying on the crutch of his heart condition at times, instilling in me a desire to protect him from potential challenges, and this included his own family.

The family secret played out as the boys celebrated their birthday on the Fourth of July every year, culminating on their momentous eighteenth birthday celebration, signifying in the American culture a rite of passage into adulthood. Timing was horrible, as Arnold and Kathy sat them down and told them not only were they not twins but they were not biological brothers, either. The pain and confusion this revelation caused splintered an already-broken family, not to mention the Fourth of July was never the same for me anymore, and I'm sure that would go without saying for Robert and David as well.

Now, the culinary delights being served at the Stones' house was amazing, as it would unearth a craving for anything fried, Kathy's specialty. Kathy would whip up some fried foods that would never be allowed at my home, and as a side benefit of not having to go home to eat dinner, I was doing a culinary dance with the varying cultures and foodstuffs on my street.

Fried fish, okra, black-eyed peas, chicken fried steak, chicken fried chicken, gravies galore, and this pan cake to die for. The whole southern culture was right next door, and an added bonus to the daily menu was a huge garden in their backyard, from which Kathy sourced for our meals, including delicious yellow seedless watermelons. Now, I had Tennessee hollers in my blood, but this backwoods oasis was a quick hop over the wall perfectly suiting my desire of not wanting to go home to sleep.

In addition to the food, which nourished my belly, they had an array of toys that would never be allowed at my home. A Recreational Vehicle, BB and pellet guns, wrist rockets, and a round horse trough that, when filled to the brim, subdued the blistering sun on those long hot New Mexico summer days. We built forts in their backyard, looked at dirty magazines, smoked pot and peyote out of a four-foot rainbow-colored bong, and hammered countless nails into living trees because we could. I loved hanging out at the Stone household, but there was one logistical problem, as they were right next door and I could easily be found or summoned home.

To the immediate left resided the Esquire Reggie, with a delicious harem of young ladies rotating in and out of his domicile. They paraded around the front yard in scantily clad outfits, raising the internal temperature of all the men and boys in the neighborhood. They were teasing us for sure while Reggie basked in his rarified air of soft skin and risqué tan lines. He was of high reason and had a devilish sense of humor. Now, Reggie wasn't a source of nourishment for me in the filling my belly kind of way, but his crafted space was nourishing my budding circus in subtler ways. The lessons were vital.

In the summer, I would peek over the six-foot high wall separating our yards to see the young women tanning, tossing over the wall a ball to retrieve so I could talk to and get a closer look at the tanners du jour. Just being a voyeur for me didn't satisfy my insatiable imagination, as early on, I took a desire and then maneuvered my way into situations that would locate me right in the thick of the desire. All my senses needed to be nourished.

My thought was to get closer to the tanning nubile, so I devised the ball scenario that, on face value, would be a common occurrence for a six-year-old when playing—but for this burgeoning wearer of the top hat, it was actually a well-thought-out plan to get what I wanted. I was honing my report with the other sex at an early age, always going for the girl that was unattainable—but for me the process was only a series of actions prefaced by my initial thought. I was learning to connect with a desire, not a human being. A solution ideal for my circus of one—but not-so-ideal for my soul—longing for connection with living beings, not the ones that danced in my dream life and imagination.

Two houses up the street from Reggie's brothel were the Ambroses. Howard, Lorraine, and their children—Rick, Janice, Diane, and Robby—made up this household. Howard's collection of World War II German and American war memorabilia was a fantasy come true for a little boy who wanted to play war. Playing war was not allowed at my house, so I made do by exercising this thought out at Robby's house. Digging holes and trenches to act out war scenes and the occasional firing of a pellet gun to kill birds was filling space in my mind that needed to be quenched for the simple reason it was painted as taboo at my home. I needed to touch the untouchable.

My appetite also found a home here for the varied fruit trees of plums, peaches, apples and nectarines, gorging my little belly throughout the day so I wouldn't be hungry at dinnertime. I loved going over there because it was dangerous and weird and we killed, touching the imagery from my dream life and causing me to lean into the dark thoughts and actions that most kids would run away from. Robby was my muse.

One distinct memory that stood out was the time we wanted to see how long a puppy could stay alive if we buried him, and the initial intrigue for me was death wasn't all that bad, hammered home by my dream life.

This comfort with death had me milling around until it became too real, prompting me as I ran home crying uncontrollably. Gladly, the puppy was never in harm's way.

Now, this experience would have most recoiling from a hot flame. But for me, this fear of the dark that was now an uncomfortable friend in my sleep would have me fearless in my waking hours, moving me ever closer to the scorching flame. It was never hot enough. Never!

Farther down the street were the Shannons—Bob and Judy and their daughter Jodi—a quiet family that went about their daily lives without much fanfare. Bob was a physically imposing man and a Vietnam veteran. The only visible memory of his stint in Southeast Asia was the green fatigue jacket he wore every day and the mechanized hook arm that was covered by the jacket. But it was his wonderful demeanor—a gentle giant, one might say—which masked his intimidating presence, as he always made time to talk to the kids in the neighborhood.

I connected with Bob, finding myself always aware when he was out in his yard doing chores, instigating a desire in me to stop whatever I was doing to watch him exercise his mechanical arm while mowing the lawn or cutting his bushes. His dexterity and precision were amazing, and if you were lucky, he would disassemble the arm to readjust it and, in a moment's notice, click it all back together and resume the clipping, cutting, and sweeping. I don't remember ever breaking bread with Bob or his family, and even though I'm sure he knew about my fascination with his hook arm, the topic never seemed to arise. And why should it? We were friends.

The fascination with his arm would wane, but the lesson was served and the comfort I developed with the physically or mentally challenged portion of our society that become disenfranchised solely for their particular condition would be a soft spot for me in life going forward. And even though I didn't have an outward physical condition, I found myself feeling more comfortable in their environs than with those that didn't.

My dream life had me moving in directions that for most would be uncomfortable, but for me, I wanted to be around people that were visibly different on the outside. The attraction was abnormally strong, as I knew I shared their brokenness, but in my mind's eye, the ailment I possessed wasn't any different, other than it wasn't visible by the human eye. I was lucky because no one could see my pain, but deep down underneath all these growing cast of performers, I secretly wished it wasn't so secret.

Crossing the street and up a few houses were the Roses: Bill, Jeanette, and their children—Billy, Paula, Mark, Patricia, and Glenn. Both parents worked six days a week, so until it was time for them to come home from work, this residence was a playground for me on a constant basis. Now, I spent an enormous amount of time at the Roses' for some devious reasons, but it was the gastronomical delight of forbidden foods that initially drew me to their household. If I positioned myself perfectly in this household, I would be able to assure myself a seat at their dinner table—or should I say a TV tray in front of the television set, which was sacrilege at my home when having dinner, but a common occurrence at the Roses'.

Let's lay out a sampling of some of the foods available to me when visiting this deli of forbidden fruits: Pop-Tarts, chips in a can, ice cream in gallon containers, frozen pizza, Kool-Aid, and Hungry-Man TV dinners, with my favorite one being anything with peach cobbler as the dessert. Sweets like Oreos, praline sandies, and snack cakes up the kazoo. My all-time favorite meal was fried hot dogs sandwiched between two slabs of Wonder bread, accompanied by a hunk of Velveeta cheese caressing either side of the savory meat sticks to ease this delight down one's throat. I would stuff myself throughout my stay, as we would mix in firing bottle rockets or lighting firecrackers to the detriment of various bugs, frogs, and pigeons, all while making sure not to be bitten by the gaggle of ducks and the two geese that lived in the backyard.

My interaction with Mark, who lived in the enclosed garage part of the house, was centered on his bohemian nature, with his turntable and albums of Fleetwood Mac, Tower of Power, Santana, Lynyrd Skynard, and my lifelong devotion to the minister of love, Mr. Al Green. I ended up smoking weed for the very first time with Mark in my garage at the age of twelve. I was infatuated with Patricia, as she became my first crush. She was tall, skinny, pretty, and older than I. Wanting to woo her was my desire, and being near would have to suffice for now as I returned relentlessly for whatever she was serving. She would tease me and I would gladly respond with whatever attention would come my way, with an occasional kiss I was too embarrassed to share with anyone. And Glenn, he was my buddy, my friend, my confidant, and my partner in crime. When we were together, anything was possible and nothing was taboo.

But it was the environment fostered at their household that drew me close and connected with my growing sense of being comfortable with the uncomfortable. It was a free-flowing, no-supervision, anything-was-possible atmosphere resonating clearly with my friendliness with controlled chaos. All the things I couldn't do at home, I could do elsewhere, and when I eventually went home, no one would be the wiser. I could do whatever I wanted, and no consequences seemed to be the result, so why not keep pushing the barriers, I told myself. Hell, I didn't even know what a barrier or boundary was, as I just couldn't wait to leave home to see what I could do next, all under the auspices of not wanting to sleep.

At the very end of our street was the neighborhood gem, the Luceros. Grampo and Grams headed this household that reeked of love, brokenness, acceptance, and let's not forget some kick-ass grind. They were simple and real shedding all masks, smoke, and mirrors.

Grampo Lucero, who worked at the sawmill across and down the boulevard, had suffered a tragic accident, relieving him of his right eye. Most of the time, he would wear an eye patch to cover the hole in his head, and on a rare occasion, he would insert a glass eye in the now-unused eye socket, luring me back for the real show. With glass eye in socket, he had my full attention, so I would hang out while he was tinkering around with the odd car engines dangling from the front yard cottonwood tree. I was transfixed on his every move, waiting with anticipation to watch him pop his glass eye out and spit shine that sucker up and slap it right back in his socket with a nonchalance, like when one picks their nose in public with not a care. The glass eye never floated around. It sat there in his eye socket, frozen, and I have a funny feeling he knew I was watching his eye, so he would tease me by cleaning an eye that didn't move. Funny guy! He was a man of very few words, with a work ethic that showed on his face and well-toiled hands.

Grams was affectionately known as Godzilla for her strong hand in keeping together a family of her own and their offspring in the form of the grandchildren she would raise as well. The majority of her biological children had left the roost, with the remainder being Leo and David, but it was Gino and Duane, the result of her children's broken marriages, who found refuge at her home when it became apparent that living with either of their biological parents would not be possible or maybe even wanted.

Uncle Leo was this swashbuckling type of feller always tinkering with his 1972 Charger, with racing tires, glass packs and a souped-up engine. The rumbling of his car was an early childhood memory, as he always cruised down the street to the cul-de-sac and back toward his home when returning from his latest racing adventure. It was almost like he was taking a victory lap, but no one was really watching — except for me, of course. Aunt David was openly gay and paraded around the house and neighborhood wearing his daisy dukes and a cropped T-shirt with not an iota of fear of being who he really was. I was always comfortable in his presence, as he was completely normal aside from his sparse wardrobe and the moniker of being called aunt rather than uncle.

He had a great sense of humor he directed at himself and his feminine tendencies most of the time, and occasionally, he would deliver a zinger your way and it was cool. Gino was much younger, and our interaction was limited, as Grams kept a short leash on his comings and goings. But it was Duane who would become a partner in crime along with Glenn and me as we would spend time hanging out together and pushing the limits of no limits. We were all hooked in a dark way together as we found ourselves always searching for something we could not find at home, and in time, this would play out in the shadow areas of our lives.

But remember, I was on a culinary dance here, and I was doing pirouettes in the Lucero kitchen, guided by the stern ladle of Godzilla. She was stoic and strong, not because she wanted to, but because she seemed to have no other choice. All the kids on the block were afraid of her presence except me, as I skillfully nudged my way into her apron, and lo and behold, a smorgasbord of gargantuan-sized servings was at my disposal. There was no need to have a second helping of food when she was orchestrating a meal, as it all seemed so bountiful and fresh.

Huge helpings of pinto beans cooked in a broth overwhelmed with the perfect saltiness provided by the ham hocks that broke apart through the long hours of simmering, fried potatoes, red and green Chile, and freshly made flour tortillas. Triple Decker sandwiches with an assortment of cheeses and freshly cooked meats accompanied by tomatoes, onions, lettuce, and pickles, and always a slab of the crispy pig to crown this gastronomical jewel. The macaroni casseroles, spaghetti, meatballs, and lasagna that masked her Mexican heritage and had her standing shoulder to shoulder with her Italian brethren was to die for. But it was the Godzilla burger with the hand-cut French fries she perfected while working as the cook for the Albuquerque Country Club that would be her signature dish. This burger was enormous and delicious, and the perfectly crisp hand-cut fries were heaven-sent.

Nothing was going to get in my way of having an open seat at this household, and a stern old lady with a mean streak not of her own making would be putty in my hands of getting what I wanted, and that was to not go home to sleep.

It was inevitable, I reasoned, with so many days in the week and with those weeks leading into months and months that led into years, that I would have to expand my potential victims—or should I say voyeurs, as the close confines of our street and its limited households would not ensure the overriding fear of having to go home to eat and eventually sleep, so I naturally took my circus on the road. A traveling salesman doling out snake oil and magic soap to the surrounding neighborhoods that were teeming with new challenges and opportunities as my dexterity and imagination would be tested in how I would develop new skins from which to operate from.

The cast of voyeurs were deep and broad as my traveling show traversed a boatload of fences, an *Acequia Madre* (mother ditch to the smaller ones that actually irrigated the orchards, farms, and fields), *Bosque* (a stand of trees composed of giant Cottonwoods and the foreign species of Russian Olive), the Rio Grande River, and the sand dunes that lay at the base of the cliffs created by the meandering Rio Grande cutting its way through the New Mexican high desert millions of years before. The saviors of and victims to my dilemma were one and the same, stretching my young mind and my old soul as I built my burgeoning cast of performers which were unique, diverse, and challenging.

The Zamora family was several fences and a small ditch away, headed by Felix Sr. and Maggie. Mr. Zamora was the Fire Chief for the City of Albuquerque and was highly respected throughout the community. Felix Jr., Chris, and Dodi were all highly talented junior track and field athletes, with a regime of excellence and discipline a common theme in their lives.

The family's other, or should I say main business was horse racing, and their backyard or series of backyards were always full of spunky, unbridled race horses that seemed to not have enough room to exercise their breeding. It was always a challenge getting to see Chris because I would have to jump various fences and an irrigation ditch, eventually positioning me nose to nose in the arena with one of these caged animals. This navigating would result in a game of Russian roulette, with the horse du jour being the bullet and my body the possible victim. Eventually, I would make it to safety and then play—or the dreaded chore of having to feed and water those damn horses. I wasn't humored.

In time, I would have to return home to start the adrenaline rush of having to navigate my way back through the horse stalls and over the fences to a perceived safety of home when, in fact, sleep was on its way. Something in me relished the game of horse roulette, as the potential tragedy delivered by the hoof of one of these eight-hundred pound animals was more appealing than what was being delivered by my dreams at night. Interesting, but there was more than one route to Chris's house, and all the other routes would guide me away from the certain death by hoof, but not me, not I, as I wanted to be as close to the possibility of death and come out on the other side. In my dream life, I never, ever made it out alive.

Traversing a few fences and Reggie's backyard was the home of Boolettuce. He was a gargantuan young man, weighing in at over three hundred-fifty pounds and standing a mere five feet four inches, who rarely left his domicile unless the crawdad fishing was great or if the baseball game was taking place in his backyard. We loved to crawdad fish, as all it took was some string and a slab or two of uncooked bacon to lure out the mudbugs from the brown murky water filling the ditch behind Boolettuce's house. On a good day, we could fill up a five-gallon bucket and the feast was on. Gathering up my mother's prized cookware, we would build a fire in the outdoor fire pit and boil up these delights, garnishing them with ketchup and hot sauce.

Now, Boolettuce loved professional wrestling before it became popular, with Abdullah the Butcher and his nemesis, André the Giant, being his favorites. He would mimic the wrestling moves in the solitude of his room until the opportunity arose, allowing him to quench his insatiable desire to actually place one of us in the sleeper hold or in the camel clutch if you were within striking distance. His sightings were few and far between, and I'm sure his physical limitation was the cause, but I was in his corner, as I silently willed him out of his four-walled prison to play with us, knowing full well he was fighting the same demon of outside fun and inside terror and eventual death. I knew I was lucky, as nothing kept me from getting what I wanted, and I only wished Boolettuce could do the same.

But it was the Van Horn family, originally from Baltimore, Maryland, who resided one mile away from our street, but less than a quarter mile from the Rio Grande, that provided my siblings and me with matches for each appetite.

If the close quarters in our household seemed tight with six total siblings jockeying for bathroom time in the winter before school started, then how about doubling those metrics and the challenges it posed. I guess we had logistical issues in those special physical moments when growing up—sharing bathwater when time was of the essence—but we had it easy compared to the tidy sum of thirteen kids under their roof. Let's say they did a baker's dozen better than we did a half dozen—at least, it felt that way to me. Bill, an engineer at Sandia National Laboratories, and Jane headed up this brood, with Janie, Joe, Alice, Billy, Sharon, Tommy, Brian, John, Stephen, and David in tow.

The similarities between our families didn't stop at the large number of kids, as they too resided on a street with a cul-de-sac, but with a slightly different arrangement, as their house seemed to take up the whole side of the street, almost wrapping around to the cul-de-sac itself. It was exciting going over to visit, whether to play with the pigs in the backyard or navigating your way through their house to find the sibling you wanted to play with. But for me, it was to go see Tommy and Brian and the eventual trip to secret places they discovered when roaming the ditches and surrounding river playground.

One place in particular stood out amongst the rest. Nestled in the towering trees of Itchy Gooo Park was the Blue Lagoon. It formed for only several weeks in the month of June in a dry creek bed lined with tiny pebbles that welled up with the water produced by run off from the snow in the mountains to the north. The water was crystal clear and shimmered of a light blue when the light peeked its way through the dense foliage provided by the Russian olive trees that shrouded its location, enhancing its mystical nature.

The memories of swimming in this mystical place with Brian and Tommy were a rite of passage for me, as they shared this secret as if I were blood. It was as if adding another one to the brood would make much of a difference, since being one of thirteen had its obvious challenges and benefits, so why not fourteen, fifteen, or sixteen?

But it was the bigger-than-life energy Tommy exuded no matter what was at stake that had me captivated from our first encounter. I marched to my own drummer and never followed anyone or anything, but the magnetism Tommy exuded over all whom he touched had me queuing up as well. He was brilliant when speaking, as his words danced around the room, never seeming to drift off like so many others I was surrounded by. He had a zest for life, with all of its possibilities at his fingertips, exercising the dark areas of life openly like he exercised the light areas. No distinction in his eyes.

He was a teacher in the mystical sense, gathering up his life experiences and directing it to help others with his God standing by his side. He would become a wildcatter for oil in Texas and Oklahoma by day and a disciple of his faith with a cause at night. His young life was taken at an early age in a tragic plane crash while searching for something that brought material wealth, but at the same time sharing his experiences with a clarity of language and openness that would change your life if you stopped to listen. I miss Tommy and I wish I could have conversation with him in the physical sense, but I am certain he was one of my angels in the spiritual sense as I drifted in and out of the light and dark of my life.

With all of these beautiful, diverse, loving and, let's not forget, broken characters in my landscape to feed from, I discovered the reasoning behind all this meandering and shape-shifting with the intention of delaying my arrival at home had a serious flaw in its premise. Its flaw was in the delay, because in time, I would have to go home eventually to sleep through pure exhaustion. The constant shedding and dawning of skins throughout the day taxed a well-nourished, physically unlimited, well-reasoned wearer of the top hat, as eventually I would have to lay this weary vessel down. Overwhelmed.

My dream life was only getting more vivid and gruesome, paralleling my desire to outlast these images that terrified me in my sleep and then in my waking hours by living on the edges of life that were available to an eight-year-old. The hidden benefit to all this shape-shifting was the development of a diverse array of performers by simply hopping a wall or a skipping to a yard.

The ability to adapt myself to any environment, like when a cuttlefish changes its coloring based on the background surrounding its present location. In fact, the cuttlefish can process color, texture, shapes, spots, and lines within its mimicking repertoire. Not only will the cuttlefish adapt a coloration and texture of the background to protect it from its predators, but this cloaking mechanism also allows it to lure its prey within striking distance for its own nourishment.

It's not like I was playing with multiple personalities here; I was in this game for survival, my reason concluded. It was one body, one mind, and one desire to rid myself of what terrified me at night, resulting in the learned ability to get what I wanted or keep what I had. Sometimes, my little plan to get my desired result would have an interesting evolution, bringing in more characters, which I willfully controlled without their knowledge.

One experience in particular that comes to mind is when I found myself bored out of my noggin in second grade, feeling the dreaded repetition of spelling words phonically as instructed by my teacher, Ms. Sugar. I guess I was hooked on phonics way before its time. I didn't want to play this game that had me bored, so I decided to mix it up a little and add some spice to keep my interest, or altogether do something else to exercise my true desire to create another performer for my circus.

It became fun for me to figure out how to push the button producing compliance, not furor, from my voyeurs. One does not rise with this gift of being able to decipher which button to push, but it needs to be nurtured and honed with experience after experience. On the one hand, it takes little effort and reason to push the button that pisses someone off because you're not getting what you want or keeping what you have. I reasoned that pissing people off wasn't a sure-fire way to get my desires, but if I could manipulate compliance out of my voyeurs, the odds of success were heightened.

If somehow, I could get the attention of the teacher, allowing me to do something, anything else, I would be satisfied. So I willfully started to spell the words incorrectly, but this tactic would only garner more repetition by the teacher to get it right, and in an instant it came to me. I would spell the words correctly with a subtle twist by reversing the letters, or when I really wanted to throw a chink in the phonics armor, I would spell the word backward. Not only did this sour Ms. Sugar's exercise, but also excelled her hunch I may in fact have some type of learning disorder, instigated by other willful acts propelled by boredom or a lack of challenge to my highly devious intellect.

Soon, I found myself in a pickle, as my mother was scheduling and whisking me off to an ophthalmologist and other health professionals to unravel my misdiagnosed learning disorder of dyslexia. I deftly operated my way through the doctor appointments and passed the eye tests, comforting and assuring my mother I had consumed extra helpings of carrots over the previous few days, allowing me to overcome my misdiagnosed problem.

My simple plan of not wanting to spell words phonically would unravel, and the scale of those who would be brought into my circus for me to dissect and conquer would be a foretelling of how I would operate in the future. My first thought was in fact just that, and what would occur after was the unknown, eventually conquering the unknown by my ability to maneuver my growing cast of performers in and out of the situations to get the desired result.

In time, things would work in my favor. I had no idea what a tremendous toll it would take on the unsuspecting patrons of my circus to be the recipient of this extreme single-mindedness. This formula of navigating through life was taxing. Was another option unknowingly available to me to quiet the dark dreamlife that was wreaking havoc on my waking life? I could only hope.

I turned eight. The clock was ticking.

8

THE MAGIC CURE

My maternal grandmother, Maria Dolores Griego de Chavez—or Nana, as we adoringly called her—was a fountain of strength to my mother during the time when my mother was single while raising six children. Nana lived in a large, Victorian, concrete-pseudo-stone house sitting on a major thoroughfare in downtown Albuquerque; it had a big yard enveloped by crabapple and apricot trees. The house was composed of four bedrooms, a large kitchen, a great room with bay windows for visiting, a dining room where meals were served on the best china at every meal, an attic, an enclosed front porch, and the best asset of the house—a rare find in that part of the country—a basement.

I remember walking in the back door that fed directly into the kitchen where several pots were always simmering and there was always the smell of freshly baked bread waiting to be eaten. The bread was both sweet and savory, and when lathered up with butter, honey, assorted homemade jellies and jams, peanut butter, or my personal favorite apple butter, sent your taste buds directly to nirvana.

Nana's home was nourishing at the subsistence level, but more importantly, the spiritual meal served would unknowingly last a lifetime.

I love those memories in life when you rest your eyes and drift back in time and see a memory from the past, the way the sights, smells, textures, and colors instantly reappear.

As I close my eyes some thirty-eight years later, I can see in vivid detail my Nana making tortillas as she would caress the perfectly portioned balls of handmade dough in her hands, passing it back and forth, from hand to hand, with a slapping motion, eventually forming a perfectly round circle. Next she would toss flour on the counter and reveal a rolling pin — out of nowhere, like a magician retrieving a coin from behind your ear — and with a few flips of the dough and a push with the rolling pin, a tortilla would be formed magically to be nestled on the *comal* for its final preparation. It was mesmerizing, watching her make tortillas, as she kneaded, tossed, rolled, cooked, and held court, all the while attending to my siblings, cousins, and me.

My Nana possessed magic powers, I reasoned, and at the very least some octopus-like appendages to perform this and many other tasks while she cared for us. I was convinced that more than one person should be necessary to make all this happen with ease. Her incredible ability was tested to its limits — and irrefutably substantiated — when it was time to put the younger kids down for a nap. She would settle us in her room and gently scratch our backs, lulling the three to four bodies draped around her into dreamland. Whether you wanted to or not — and in a whisper of a moment — sleep was underway.

Nana's house was a safe place for me. I felt as if a shedding occurred when I entered her home; the skins I deliberately donned for survival during my waking hours were left at the stairwell leading up to the backdoor for safekeeping until it was time to leave. It was safe here, and I knew this deep within my soul. Thoughts of orchestrating my next move to delay my eventual sleep would fade in the comfort of her spirit. Relieved, my focus would shift to playing, eating, and trying to find the key to the cupboard where the homemade cookies and treats were stored for our enjoyment and for the many visitors seeking counsel from my Nana.

But something more powerful had been going on there; I hadn't been able to get my mind around its significance, nor understand why it was there, and not at home, that sleep was peaceful. It was here, at my Nana's home, and the only memorable time in my early childhood that I hadn't feared the nightmares my eight-year-old self always expected. When I slept under her care, the dark dream life I was now expecting would not materialize. I remember falling asleep with her scratching my back and awakening to her still scratching my back. Her healing touch, her healing presence, and her healing words all soothed the brokenness surrounding her, and for the moment, the nightmares I experienced relentlessly were ceased.

What was it about my Nana that allowed her, through the power of touch, to heal me and, for at least that moment, protect me from what terrified me while I slept?

My Nana was a stately woman with a burning desire to lift herself and her family to a status beyond her humble, hard-working heritage. My grandfather, Federico Baca Griego, worked in the roundhouse, servicing the trains that came to his stop on the routes between the Midwest to the West Coast. He eventually settled in as a civil servant, doling out mail for his remaining years. He died at an early age, and I never met him face-to-face.

My mother's ancestral roots, handed down from both parents, went back for hundreds of years in New Mexico. Her earliest known ancestors came from the Spanish excursions into the New World, specifically those that moved north, out of what we now call Mexico, as part of their search for the mystical Seven Cities of Gold. Their path scarred its way up the Rio Grande valley, past El Paso, through Las Cruces and Albuquerque, and eventually led to the outpost of Santa Fe—the crowned seat of government for this newly conquered territory. The Santa Fe Trail kept these explorers close to the living water produced by the Rio Grande, leaving small pockets of families along the way to build communities and change the landscape from high desert to lush fields that would sustain them and those who would follow.

Settling into a territory in which they were outnumbered, the Spanish explorers had no choice but to marry the indigenous Pueblo Indians, producing offspring of mixed heritage. This blending of cultures created a sense of family and longevity, even when the marriages were made for survival purposes only, the spouses perhaps detesting each other. My maternal genealogy emerged from these escapades hundreds of years ago in the isolated outposts dotting the high, desert landscape of New Mexico.

The tiny hamlet of La Joya, New Mexico, south of Belen, was where my ancestral family settled. It was a very ritualistic Catholic community—with hints of the unspoken, but widely practiced, Jewish traditions—and wine production was crucial. The art of cultivating vineyards was transported into this new land, along with old world techniques and foodstuffs. Medicinal remedies and healing ointments derived from the native plants shared by the Pueblo Indians also became a part of our healing culture.

The mixing of religious traditions—Catholicism and Judaism—influenced by the mystical/spiritual nature of the Pueblo Indians practices, produced a hybrid of traditional religious fervor with an equal dose of mysticism. The melding of these three cultures may seem strange, but in reality it broadened the community's line of connection to God, a relationship that had been suffocated by man's insistence on exclusive hierarchy and access to God through only one religion.

Medicine men, shamans, and other indigenous spiritual healers were the forbearers of the *Cuandera*—a term used to describe a woman who practiced natural remedies of healing everyday ailments and who communicated with God through intuition or dream life. My Nana was such a woman, clinging to the traditions passed on from one generation to the next and at the same time pulled by the materialism of the modern world, driving her to be more than those she was most like.

This spiritual duality was evident in the way she never missed mass on Sunday, rosary beads always in hand, while also lighting a candle every Friday night to honor the significance of the Sabbath. A melding of two distinct, and at times warring, religious traditions that, for her, were not strangled by the desires of man to be the one that was right in the eyes of God. She honed and exercised her mystical muscle by learning healing traditions like using natural herbs to make a tea to give to her newborn grandchildren to calm us through the night, to the laying of thinly sliced potatoes soaked in vinegar on ones temple's to cure the strongest of headaches, to the curative method of alleviating our fevers by lathering us in lard and salt and wrapping us tightly before sleep.

But it was her faith and superstition—or better-coined *intuition*—that guided her through the heartache of having all of her seven sons serve in the military to defend our country. Federico Jr. buried in Luxembourg WWII; Robert Eloy—Navy WWII; Raymond Aloysius—Korean War; William Gilbert—Army; Orlando Enrique—Vietnam and Desert Storm; Solomon Rudolph "Uncle Rude Dog"—Army National Guard; and Federico III—Vietnam. She also had two daughters: Agraphia, who passed at the age of six months and my mother, Frances Judith.

Her faith was both complex and simple, as she was moved by a space that spoke to her from within, be it through her dreams of other unspoken communication. She was a healer in the grandest sense, all while locked into a world that was constantly changing. Finding herself stuck between the safety, comfort, and tradition of family and the ever-growing pull to be better than where she came from, pushing the limits of this comfort propelled by modernity and its rebellion against time-honored ways of living life. She practiced natural healing techniques and trusted her mystical gift and at the same time moved her family to the area of town comprised mostly of Anglos, cutting away from the roots that gave her life. She was stoic in nature, but if you ever crossed her, her memory was long and her ability to forgive short.

The matriarch of our family was in a death-defying dance with her faith and mystical practice, which had been passed down for centuries, and the ease of living provided by materialism our modern world promised. I loved her and the comfort she provided. Could it be that the healing source of her touch that allowed me to sleep undisturbed when in her presence was because she intuitively knew what was going on inside of me without me verbalizing it? Maybe, just maybe, if I could share with her what I was experiencing, she could help me even though I reasoned I was helpless.

The terror, fear, and physical exhaustion caused by my dream life had to come to an end. I didn't know if it would be the healing light and touch provided by my Nana who could walk me through this darkness she had comfort with, or if would it be something else subduing the dreams that had me developing a cast of performers in which to live my life through.

My life up to this point didn't seem very complicated, aside from the dream stuff, and if there was chaos at my house derived from being the product of a divorce, I was oblivious to it. It was normal as far as I knew. I pretty much did what I wanted to during the day, whether it was school or playing around the neighborhood.

I'm not sure why my parents decided to divorce, and to this day the truth is really known only somewhere in between my mother's and my father's recollections of why it played out this way. The interesting thing about divorce is it affects each person individually, and I'm positive every one of my siblings had their own unique experience with this topic and in turn, was affected uniquely as well. But for me it was unnecessary to delve into the whys and how comes of the dissolution of our formal family structure, since at the moment I had more important self-survival issues at hand, and if there was any one thing I carried forth from my family unit it is that survival was truly an individual sport.

Maria was the eldest and head cheerleader in the pom-pom kind of way as well as in her desire to always be a leader in the community and in anything she does and does well. Second in line was my brother Juno of high intellect, dry humor, and a serious nature; he loved sports and equally a good book. Third oldest was Theri, who shared mystical gifts from my Nana, had a quiet demeanor, intuitive nature, funny, and was nurturing. Next in line was my brother Mark who I nicknamed "Sparky," not because he liked electricity but because of his industrious nature of wanting everything to be a certain way, like raking rocks or mowing the lawn to leave a certain pattern like one sees on television when watching professional golf. Last was my brother Ralph-David, named that way because my parents couldn't decide on a single name, so they compromised—if you want to call it that—and hyphenated his name, both getting their way. Ralph-David was driven by a competitive nature for anything, be it playing cards or playing horse in our backyard basketball court; the drive pushed him to excel no matter what the cost, because winning was the goal and in his eyes, vital to his survival.

In one form or another we were in the game of life to survive, and our tactics of survival were unique to our own experience, and the methods of navigation would equally be unique. The point was that we needed each other, but couldn't rely on each other in a way that would allow the individual to discard the protective shield hoisted for self-preservation.

There was love, safety, and comfort in our home, but this Darwinian mindset of survival was buttressed by the fact that physically all these siblings and neighborhood kids surrounded you, but in spirit you were on your own and this unfortunately waned heavy on the love, safety and comfort ideal. No one person or persons could be responsible for its germination. What I find quite interesting is that all of us moving forward in life were trying to push away the Darwinian mindset that drove us like the oxen tethered to the yoke and move closer to the love, safety, and comfort that became the collateral damage of lives directed by survival at any cost.

Now how in the hell does this have anything to do with my desire to quell my exhausting dream life that was wreaking havoc on my peace and at the same time was moving me to closer to the ways of the cuttlefish? In short it had everything and nothing to do with it but was, indeed, the onset of the paradox of the foundation of my life constructed by me and me alone. My family life mirrored my physical, emotional, and spiritual shell of being whole and unified when in reality I was lonely and shattered, the whole time trying desperately to unravel my dream dilemma to make it to the next day.

Now my mother, Judy, was hot and hip and there seemed to always be a cadre of potential suitors around the house. One cat that stood out in my memory was Murray, and I'm not sure why but he was cool, but when he talked to me I listened and it didn't hurt he had the greatest Irish setter ever. But what I've learned through life is that no one has the luxury to choose the partner anyone decides to be with—nor should they—and my mother had her reasons why she would sieve through the multitudes and choose Bob as her boyfriend and eventual stepfather to us kids, formalized only after I graduated from high school.

As an aside, both of my biological parents remarried for the first time eighteen years after divorcing, exactly one month apart. Was this pre-arranged? Or was it another miscalculated smoke and mirror debacle centered on changing perception for outside consumption or a willful decision on my mother's part to rule the formal family structure single-handedly without interference? Who knew and who cares? She was doing the best she could with what she knew. She was amazing. She sacrificed much.

My mother was thirty-two with six children when she met Bob, who was all of nineteen at the time. Bob hailed from Pennsylvania and was living in the rectory of San Felipe de Neri, our local church, and was tied into some community work program to serve the less fortunate when they first met. The other suitors would drift away with Bob's presence in our household being a constant when growing up. He never lived with us and never slept over our house unless the festivities of the preceding night took its toll.

The weekend festivities were frequent when growing up with my mother's classmates from college along with my Uncle Freddie Bear and his friends in tow. My father's youngest sister, Kathy, would become a fixture at our house as well when growing up and especially when her boyfriend and soon-to-be husband Al would come live with us after he was kicked out of the dorms while on a college baseball scholarship. Uncle Al was funny, with his thick South Bronx accent and loving nature, and it was always fun when he was around.

While all this stuff was going on at home, I was struggling with the exhaustion of trying to keep my dream life at bay while mixing in surviving my waking hours of character building to adapt to the varied environs surrounding me. Little did I know my terror filled nights were on their last breath at the age of eight when attending Bob's birthday party at his house on Vicic Road.

It was the weekend before his actual birthday of April fourteenth when my mom, Brother Ralph-David, Uncle Al, and I revved up our ten-passenger, orange van and joined up in the celebration. The iconic orange and white van that hauled us off to school, sporting events, movies, and the dreaded mall to shop became our family calling card. With all on board we headed down Rio Grande Boulevard for the short ride that turned out to be a turning point in my life.

I clearly remember the shotgun house Bob lived in, with its main entrance opening up to the kitchen and the bathroom separating a large room to the end of the house that doubled as bedroom and living space. The music was loud, and the adults were doing what they do when having a party, but something was stirring inside of me, changing my physical perception of things that night.

The light seemed different inside the house, with an almost splitting of light into two different colors, like when you open your eyes under water and look up to the surface and you can distinctly see the demarcation point where water and air meet. It was exactly like that, but different. When I was walking around the room or dashing from outside to inside, wherever I moved and looked around, the light at my height and below was darker than normal and everything above my height was a glowing amber color, resembling the light that a lone flickering candle gives off in a dark room. At first it struck me as eerie, but by now I was drawn to fear like flies to honey, and in that moment I saw a lone bottle of tequila resting on the counter above me. It was a beacon. My beacon. It glowed.

The decision to imbibe in any experience was short while enacting the first thought into reality. Taking a quick glance around the room, I quickly put the bottle to my lips and gulped my first drink. Sipping was not in my nature, as I was driven by the fear my sleep life would somehow play out in my waking life and this physical existence would soon end, engaging me to over-experience in everything as much as possible. It was pure magic as this nectar spilled past my teeth over my tongue around my molars and down the back of my throat, settling in my belly. It was mother's milk to me as I instantly recognized its ability to change the growing anxiety I was comfortably uncomfortable with, knowing consciously sleep was only hours away.

My mind was spinning and my performers were at full attention, waiting for the opportunity to be on stage, and then something funny happened I was not accustomed to in this life that had me controlling each and every moment. I didn't have the time to think my next thought as I found myself moving closer to the counter with one eye honed in on the bottle and the other eye scanning the room to make sure the coast was clear, and before I knew it that first gulp turned to a swill. I'm not sure how much time elapsed between each drink, but what I do know is I had no control over this healing nectar that quieted the screeching anxiety in my soul. In no time I emptied the beacon of its light. A lone lightless empty bottle remained. I never liked how the light made me feel, but rather I liked how it made me not feel.

I was drawn to the alcohol flame, and it couldn't get hot enough for me, and I knew this instantly. Before I knew it, Uncle Al was comforting me, as I was now in the van, spinning and throwing up all that had been ingested only hours before. I, and I alone, was the chosen one of my siblings to carry forward the physical disease of alcoholism, as we all were subject to the possibility of catching the disease in the physical sense. It was on this day at this moment I had my first drink—not necessarily my first experience with extreme selfishness that characterize those who indwell in the disease.

It was all about me, more and now, propelled by my dream life to my eventual reality, death. The clock was ticking.

I awakened the next morning in my mother's bed with a throbbing head and a queasy stomach and interestingly enough, dry sheets. Did I not have dreams last night, or did I and couldn't remember them? It didn't matter either way. It was a relief, and even though it felt like a bomb exploded inside me (the trivial), I was feeling overwhelmed and equally perplexed with joy for the first time in my life. It was the first time, except when in my Nana's care, that I awakened with no memory of my dream life that tortured me incessantly night and day since birth (the heart of the matter). It was a miracle!

A miracle I would not be able to share with anyone was the only drawback, reasoning no one knew of its existence so why bother with the whole story. What I couldn't understand was the significance of my miracle cure, casting me to retreat deeper into self-sufficiency rather than a life possibly navigated another way. The peeing in the bed didn't go away as quickly, but since that morning my dark dream life vanished. The only problem now was it was an outside source healing my anxiety, but I didn't see it that way.

Up to this point in life, I had carefully controlled my waking hours to get what I wanted and keep what I had, but in the end, my dream life ruled my life. My reason convinced me I had figured this dilemma out on my own and most importantly and tragically it didn't come in the form of the human touch but rather at the bottom of a bottle, which at first drink gripped tightly around my soul leaving me powerless by its spirit. I was in complete control of life now, without the fear of sleeping and then dreaming, I reasoned, but oddly enough with the assistance of an outside source I could not control. But the real tragedy here was that I had a chance, a real chance, of ridding myself of this dream life without the drink if I only trusted what my Nana was serving me under her care.

My Nana passed away on April fourteenth, only four short days after my first drink. But it was impossible for her nurtured mystical gift to help me unless I was willing to open up this torture chamber, and unfortunately I had learned not to trust anyone with my secrets, and more importantly, to only trust myself when walking through my waking hours. I am sure she knew what was going on inside of me when sleeping and I am sure she was the source of intervention allowing me to rest with comfort when in her care, but that moment in time was gone and what was in front of me was a life incapable of trusting another, since now I was assured I could survive this life and death stuff all alone.

With reflection, I think others intuitively recognized this, "I'm perfect all alone," mentality in me, but it never really struck home until my beautiful friend in Austin, Lyndie, who I have an amazing connection with, shared with me one day after I had shunned her invitation to spend Christmas day with her family and other friends. We were discussing our feelings about each other when she opened her heart and shared what scared her about me: "You do alone too well."

It was the first time in my life someone was being honest with me about my self-sufficiency paradigm for life, and even though her honesty struck deep within my soul, I was not ready to surrender the veil covering who I really was inside. I knew this and relied upon it, I didn't want anybody else to know it as well. I was connected to Lyndie, and this connection was weighing heavy on my desire to pursue her and unfortunately an equal desire to hold on to the veil that shielded who I really was. I wanted desperately to share with her what was really going on inside of me, but in all reality I didn't know how.

Relying on others was too risky and filled with potential difficulties when getting what you want and keeping what you have is paramount, and unfortunately my miracle cure set me on a collision course causing pain and destruction to people, places and things with the real tragedy of keeping me from trusting another.

The ability, and now desire, to have intimate relationships with other human beings was dealt a tragic blow that day on Vicic Road. I was only eight. Nothing could impede the circus now! Nothing!

9
DIZZY-LAND

Day after day, I gathered up the courage to make my way to the library to see what was going to be revealed to me as I honestly mulled over the questions Joseph had posed. Some days I would write for the full hour, and some days I would last about ten minutes before the pain became too much to bear. When I drifted back in time, I felt like a little kid inside a grown man's body; the feelings and emotions willfully pushed down decades ago, dark and deep, were starting to surface, and my resolve was challenged once again.

It's not an uncommon topic in the rooms for those of us that have been consumed by the drink at an early age to stop growing emotionally upon our first swill, and it was becoming apparent to me I was still an eight-year-old little kid creating fantasy into reality so I could be somebody, but not me. The stakes were higher; the finances were larger sums, the people more complex and smarter than I.

Sadly, I was a grown man sitting in a kid-sized director's chair, directing my circus of one with the emotions of an eight-year-old trying, desperately to develop intimate adult relationships. Impossible!

Several weeks into the process of writing my fourth step, it was approaching the end of daylight savings time, evoking a special time of the year for those who gather at the beach to watch the incredible sunsets being painted in the western sky at Windansea. Multiple hues of purple, pink, blue, and gold, illuminated by the orange sun, painted the sky beautifully. The stormy northern swells this time of the year were the highlight to my mending soul. The rising hope one might catch a glimpse of a rare green flash as the sun dipped below the distant horizon had the multitudes gathering on the cliff's edge each evening.

I love the stormy sea and the beauty and strength it displays. The Windansea coastline would be transformed this time of the year, as what was once a tranquil beach only months before was now a landscape of massive stones and boulders, carved by the power of the water and revealed only as the mountains of pristine sand were scooped up and deposited for safekeeping in the ocean until it was time again to return to its former self. I was feeling like the sand, as I too was being hauled off to a special place to be cleansed, only hoping to return anew like the sand that served the human soul at Windansea.

My daily routine of waking, *Sunrise*, community center, sitting with Eddy, Tony's saloon, and now the high wire act being performed daily at the library needed this daily dose of God before I scuttled up the alley to my cottage for the remainder of the evening. With a meal of mashed potato tacos prepared at the best taco shop ever, Don Carlos, by my newfound friends Araceli, Laura, and Diego, I would eventually arrive home with a warm belly. I wanted to rest my eyes, to sleep. This momentary resting of the eyes would soon turn to the exhausting ritual of tossing and turning while my brain flipped through thousands of scenarios that may or may not come true until I was able to sleep for a few hours.

My total being had been able to withstand this exhaustion produced by the lack of sleep for as long as I can remember. If I did rest, it was with unease. I clearly remember closing my eyes that evening and drifting slowly into my thoughts, when soon enough it would turn into the never-ending mind churning, haunting me since my magic cure. It always did. Suddenly, I awoke to the sounds of the early rising Crowned Oriel nesting in the bushes outside my window, chirping his good morning to the sun before the break of dawn. I was groggy, confused, and unsure of what had transpired.

Was it possible I had awoken from unbroken sleep for the first time in my life without the healing touch provided by my Nana? Was I a recipient of another miracle not of my own making or prescribed by Western medicine or the years of melatonin and better yet, my self-prescribed drinking until passing out? Were my sleepless nights now in the past, supplanted by actual natural sleep?

I was the recipient of ten hours of glorious uninterrupted sleep. My body, I'm sure, was desperate for rest with the real miracle being the solitude my mind experienced, as the pounding of thoughts was replaced by quiet through the night. The curse of the night tortured me with a dark dream life as a child and then the unrelenting spinning of my mind to keep what I had and get what I wanted as an adult would now be an experience of the past. It would be the end of my sleepless battle, and I'm sure it had something to do with moving closer to who I really was than who I had become, and as Eddy assured me only months earlier, everything needed to change. Slowly.

He was right! I never expected I would be able to sleep through the night, and as quickly as sleeplessness became a cornerstone of my life, it was now a welcomed memory.

When in Chicago visiting Theri and her family for Christmas, it became a ritual to share with her children, Emilio and Raquel, stories of my childhood and of my family when growing up in New Mexico. With the kids listening intently and interjecting for more details, I would paint up story after story full of intrigue and hilarity, leaving out various details to keep it palatable for the six- and nine-year-olds with the intent that one day the complete unedited versions would be revealed. The kids would be on the edge of their seats, chanting for more details and more stories and I would oblige as best as I could with a wink and a nod from Theri when it was time to edit the current story and eventually when it was time to end this session of story-telling.

One day the story was of how two of their uncles spent an afternoon in Mickey Mouse jail while on summer vacation. In fact, all of my other nephew and nieces: Nina, Francisco, Mia, Isabella, Elizabeth, and Rosalina hade all heard about the alleged incident that occurred at the great theme park where Mickey, Donald, and Goofy roam the streets.

It was a summer ritual in my childhood to visit my Uncle Rudy (a.k.a Uncle Rude Dog) in Los Angeles for several weeks, as he would share his exuberance for life with us all, keeping us on the move, doing one fabulous thing after another. Uncle Rude Dog played a special role in my life and in the lives of my brothers and sisters, as no matter the occasion from baptisms to graduations, he always made the time to drop what he was doing and travel back to New Mexico to share in the celebration. He was special to me in that he was my godfather in the Catholic ritual way, but more importantly a connection for the thrill of life and all its possibilities with an embedded desire to find home away from home.

He tells the story of having to flee New Mexico after a failed attempt to rob a bank at the age of eighteen when he and his co-conspirators realized the teller who would be the recipient of their felony was a friend of his older brother Raymond and had recognized them from the neighborhood. A quick dash out of the bank before any crime was committed and an equally quick dash with a friend in a broken down car on old Route 66 to Los Angeles was the remedy for his soul that wanted to find home.

He built a life one moment at a time, having to use his street smarts and keen sense of humor and gift of the gab to create his claim in his new home the golden state. He would dance from one opportunity to the next, which included creating Circus Royal and the first all-black trapeze artists, "The Flying Souls." He would eventually yet ironically build a successful international business helping others from around the world immigrate to the United States, so that they too could build a home for themselves away for home. But it wasn't the work driving uncle Rudy.

The drive to success was a constant, but with a larger measure of enjoying the success with others and alone if necessary an equal. Nothing in life was an obstacle for him but rather an opportunity to have another experience that would not only be fun for him but for those surrounding him for sure. The experiences I had with uncle Rudy continue to this day and I wouldn't have it any other way.

But this particular trip at the age of twelve would be the first time we were old enough to experience the infamous theme park on our own. The plan was to drop us off at the crack of dawn and to pick us up at five o'clock after a full day of standing in long lines to have some fun. I never really liked theme parks and maybe it was because the suspension of reality one experiences when in this environment was old hat for me and who cares about a made up cartoon character when you can manipulate real people to act in the same way. I'm not sure whose idea it was to bring the contraband in the form of some cannabis and I'm positive it was not one of my cousins. It was the property of one of the neighborhood kids along for the ride.

It seemed to me it would be more edgy to get high while in these environs, since for me it was simply cartoon stuff, not the real stuff I had been dealing with since as far back as I could remember. A trend was emerging for me: the need to enhance any experience that on face value would be amazing for anyone but for me would be mediocre unless I was able to add some level of danger like when the trapeze artist removes the net when performing their midair exchanges.

Upon entering the park, we all roamed together in a pack, trying to find a safe place to puff on the pinner joint rolled for our consumption. It was reasoned we could get caught imbibing inside the park, so we exited the park to puff on a little Thai Stick in the parking lot and then re-enter with a state of mind enhancing its cartoonish nature.

This is where our great plan met its demise, since parking lots at such theme parks have surveillance for car theft and we happened to be a gaggle of kids squatting between parked vehicles and trying to light a joint on a windy day. Within seconds several police vehicles screeched to a stop and surrounded our position and we were busted trying to light a joint—not that we actually got it lit. It didn't take long for the Dizzy-land police to haul us all off to Mickey Mouse jail and there ensued eight terror-filled hours until it was time for Uncle Rudy to pick us up.

After all the other kids were dropped off, my cousins and I all settled in at my uncle's house to see what in fact our punishment would be. Uncle Rudy summoned us all to the bathroom, where he lectured us about the troublesome nature of drugs and what could have happened if we were busted by the real coppers. While this lecture went on, he dug into a paper bag he was holding and started to fill the toilet bowl with what looked like high-grade cannabis. It seemed as though he put his hand in the bag ten times and pulled out one handful after another with a cringe glimmering only in his eye as he was the most serious I had ever seen him in my life.

The seriousness vanished when he attempted to flush the toilet bowl that had exceeded the capacity recommended by Kohler. It didn't want to go down, and I'm sure Uncle Rude Dog didn't want it to either, but he made us all stand there until the entire bag had been consumed. There is no formal police record of the events that transpired while visiting the park that day with my brother Ralph-David, cousins Rudolph and Jeff, and an assortment of other kids that roamed their neighborhood. So the alleged crime can never be proved. But a larger lesson was being served.

This turn of events was disturbing to my circus since I didn't like going along with a plan that, first and foremost, was not *my* plan, and secondly, was not executed well enough to get the desired result. But the heart of the matter for me was we were caught and I didn't like the feeling that simmered in my soul while sitting in Mickey's jail. I didn't like seeing the pain in my uncle's face of having to be something he was not…serious and disappointed. Sacred grounds were being trod upon, jostling a feeling I loved so much, which I coveted and protected at all costs. The feeling of being able to do whatever I wanted and when coming home no one was the wiser of what transpired in my day.

Organically, I was becoming very protective of my circus and the costumes being stored for their eventual display in a moment's notice. I realized I would have to work a little harder at my craft, devising new strategies that allowed for others to take the lead while all along I would be pulling the strings of the fantasy being played out. I was learning to chart the moves one would typically plot out when playing a game of chess. A beginner chess player thinks several moves ahead and a good chess player might think ten moves ahead. But a chess master not only charts out the potential moves they can make, but also the corresponding moves of their opponent would have available and the varied options that would then be opened up to them in order to get what they want — in the game of chess, the goal is to force the opponent into a checkmate, and in doing so, to take their king. My reason was sovereign.

I was intrigued and energized because now I had to massage about twenty or thirty options, all needing to be worked and reworked to make sure I got what I wanted and kept what I had. All while making sure that no one, and I meant no one, knew what was really going on in the confines of the big tent. Don't forget, this was my show and only one person could wear the top hat at a time, and I surely was not going to take part in fantasy again unless I had complete control. If things were going to fall apart, *I* wanted to be responsible. And with hours of mind scrambling under my belt, rest assured I had devised a plan to get out of the problem if it in fact it went awry. No wonder I couldn't sleep!

I found elementary and middle school boring. The real learning environment for me was going on outside the walls of structured schooling, as I was addicted to creating new performers and this could only be accomplished if I was creating new opportunities for metamorphosis. The idea of being a part of something or joining a group had no interest for me, reasoning it would hamper the flexibility to create, which at that point was the only action holding my interest.

This can be tricky business when trying to create anything involving massaging the human ego, because if others don't recognize the feat, then why all the trouble? The goal was to lead without leading, and the ego needed to be sliced down to a tiny portion to make this happen. The skill of the vascular surgeon had its genesis. I recognized I needed other people to participate in my follies willingly, since it was more fun that way, even though I didn't really want to be a part of what they were serving. It was always a matter of mindset. Pragmatic perhaps–or maybe better stated as manipulation.

My brothers Juno and Mark were masterful at teasing and torturing the neighborhood kids with all types of antics. The warm summer nights in New Mexico were ideal for their fracases, especially when they devised the "let's put up the twelve-person tent in our backyard and invite the neighborhood kids over for a sleepover." They would chant scary stories like *La llorna,* the ghost of a woman that traveled the banks of the ditch behind our house, searching for her lost child, a tortured soul who threw balls of fire in your direction if you crossed her path. To the more sinister "truth or dare" games, having us all lean toward the dare because the questions they would ask were designed to make you choose the dare, which was their intention all along. That was fun!

The dares ranged from climbing walls to reap the fruits from the prized apples trees at the Garcia's house, to shitting in a paper bag and placing it at the Apodaca's doorstep and lighting it on fire while ringing the doorbell as we all watched from a safe vantage point for the door to open. Eventually, the dares would venture into streaking naked up and down our street.

My brothers had no intention of watching over us throughout the night, which was part of the negotiation with my mother in erecting the tent. As the dares became more sinister, the crying would ensue, and before you knew it the tent would be empty and all would be nestled in the comfort of their own bed. Juno and Mark loved this "truth or dare" game so much that it dovetailed into the formation of a gang called the "Black Mafia" with the initiation into the gang being its only premise and purpose. Little did they know how much this helped me soothe the desire to try new experiences as well as the learned experience of not wanting to belong to a group for fear inclusion might lead to the cessation of the new experiences. How so you may ask?

I don't remember the exact number of members that were christened into the "Black Mafia" without having to be initiated, but I'm sure the older kids in the neighborhood were grandfathered in as long as they participated in coming up with new initiation rites that needed to be performed by the younger kids who wanted to join. Make no mistake, this was a game, not a gang. I was game.

I was licking my chops because this was perfect for my plan of experiencing new things and not having consequences as I reasoned that my brothers were sanctioning these antics, so getting into trouble was not in the cards for *me*. The deal was, if you performed several dares you would become a member and would then be allowed to come up with the dare to be performed by the next pledge. Let's say I was more interested in performing the dare than coming up with one, propelling me to be one hell of a willing participant and in time, the only willing participant.

As a non-member. If I got a whiff of an upcoming initiation ritual, I would insist on participating, and the attraction for me was knowing that there was no actual risk that I'd be asked to join after performing whatever dares they had concocted: I would rifle a snowball at the mailman, Leo, pummeling the fedora from his large, round, shiny black bald head, causing a welt above his brow; I would place sixteen penny nails under all four of Mr. Ambrose's truck's tires with camper attached as he drove off with his eventual return and the ensuing deflation of all four tires that he had to repair in the rain; I would dash into the cavernous warehouse of the sawmill, where Grampo worked, to scale the three-story high sawdust pile, disfiguring its perfect cone shape as I tumbled down its height before dashing back out to avoid getting caught by security; I would go *au naturale* and gallop through the hotel lobby and curiosity shop of the Sheraton hotel across the street; I would light a smoke bomb and toss it into Rowlands Plant Nursery retail area during regular hours, watching as the patrons and smoke billowed from the building.

These antics and many more went on for years…an unspoken agreement between the members of the "Black Mafia" and me. It was accepted fact that I would never be allowed into the gang. In their mind, the initiation only counted if the pledge was performing the dare against his will; I was *willing* to do whatever they dared, without the hint of unwillingness. But as much as I loved the spotlight — knowing all along that I would be getting what I wanted, new experiences, and keeping what I had…a circus of one — they equally enjoyed watching me carry out each dare.

I was fearless and without limits now, and these experiences just added to my quiver. I learned it was better to make others *feel* like you wanted to be like them than it was to actually be like them, especially if you wanted them to willingly participate while you were getting what you wanted. Calculated deceit.

In high school, I was interested in sports, basketball in particular, and girls always kept my interest, but school and the learning it provided was of no interest to me until I had the pleasure of being taught by Ms. Lovato. I think most people have the experience of finding a mentor outside the home, someone who unearths in them a previously unidentified interest or desire, someone who is the catalyst that leads them to their ultimate direction in life. Ms. Lovato, with her long flowing dark hair and dark rimmed glasses, was my first muse, and as it turned out, the only one to garner my attention in the confines of a structured learning environment.

Every semester of every year that I attended Albuquerque High School, I took a class she taught. They were mainly history and civics and other humanities related subjects, which did arouse my intellectual interest, but more importantly it was the way in which she taught the classes that had me hooked. She would talk not just about facts and dates but about how people in history made decisions and how the decisions they made affected not only those surrounding them but the course of history as well.

Ahhh, finally someone was talking my game and I couldn't get enough! The game of shaping time and the future for a desired result was right in my sweet spot. It was the only time I can remember that I was actually *present* in the classroom, not wanting to be somewhere else. It was under her tutelage that I realized the importance of studying people, history, and how one can move thousands. I wanted to be one of those people who moved the masses, who made a difference, who changed lives, who cared for those who could not care for themselves.

The humanness she painted on these historical characters was amazing and I was inspired, yet it was not her teaching style that most enamored me, rather it was the feelings she instilled in us all that we too could change the course of history. She challenged us to look beyond our perceived limits and envision the capacity to be a catalyst for change in the places we live in—"but don't stop there, make change that makes history."

I knew what I wanted to do in life, and I guess I never had those childhood fantasies of being a policeman, forest ranger, or engineer when I grew up, because for me, making it through the day and the night was all the fantasy I could handle. Now, with my dark dream life in my past and the remnants of that time transforming into the control of each and every event in my life, I was now ready to do what everyone else seemed to be doing and that was to chart out the rest of my life. The thought of calculating each outcome in life provided the comfort I always sought.

The career I would pursue, the family I would create, my retirement at a pre-determined date up to death all mapped out like the precise table my Nana would set up for every meal. I wanted to be in government, since I reasoned they had the most control and the biggest impact. But local and national government was not big enough for my ego, so I decided that being in the foreign service would be the stage that could hold all that I wanted to accomplish in life. The intrigue of being in foreign lands, always on the move, taking part in shaping history on a global scale was rummaging through my consciousness at the age of fifteen. My circus demanded more. Unknowingly, my ego was my foe.

At this point, the ways of navigation for me were set in stone, and with an ever-growing circus to draw from and add to, my destiny was predictable. Or was it? With a constant tweaking of each and every moment, all I needed was to somehow move through higher education and make this happen.

Deep within my being, I knew I would make a difference someday and that it wouldn't be of the material kind but rather of the compassionate kind to aid my fellow broken human beings. My survival tactics summoned by my dark dream life had me leaning into the brokenness surrounding me and my resolve to make a difference was single-minded.

The subconscious connection to something dwelling within me, moving me, which could not be spoken nor understood through logic, had me grasping for the light in my life—I knew it, but I was incapable of harnessing its power at that moment. Life's roadblocks would be looming for sure as I hoisted my luggage of not uncommon but unique experiences on my back, hoping they would further, not hamper, this single-mindedness. I wanted to help. Did I have the courage to be who I really was? Would I be sidetracked by modernity?

I thought that if I could only dig a little deeper before the landfill of my modern life consumed me, I might be able to tap this source calling out to me, calling me to be who I really was all along. But what I didn't and couldn't foresee was the inability to make a plan and see it through—or more to the point, the continual aborting of the missions in life: spiritual growth, school, people, relationships, family, places, and profession. They were all well thought out missions but unfortunately yoked with a habit of always cutting the life out of my experiences before their natural endings.

I was being hamstrung by the first thought entering my mind, which ironically gave me life. It was my umbilical cord for survival and I needed it intact to breathe, while at the very same time it was choking the calling I had deep within my soul. The idea being if the calling was not exercised it would be the death of me in every sense. The death of the soul preceding the physical death is by far the most excruciating feeling one can experience in the human frame and I was hoping this would not be my destiny. The rabbit was thumping away at my soul. I was the culprit.

Where do I start? Do I throw up on these pages? Story after story highlighting my ability to control and manipulate one scenario after another! The countless drinking and occasional drugging bouts were extraordinary and amazing involving others, but those people were not necessary in my circus of one. I didn't really need people to make things happen, they just made it more fun. Who am I kidding? It was about me having fun and my voyeurs would have fun if they could hold onto what came next. It was all about me. Always was.

My innate ability to capture other human beings for my own enjoyment and at a whim cut them out of my life because they didn't fit into my next plan was a special talent. Tragically, I was able to trump that precious life skill by being able to ice-out people, places, and things, including God, as if they never existed, while moving through life's scenes with not an iota of remorse or regret. I would become the only nourishment the circus needed for sustenance while sucking the life out of those surrounding me. This would not be the normal icing-out when you eliminate the people, places, and things, but rather I would keep them around to serve the circus without their knowledge when in fact I had severed the connection eons ago. They had no idea. When I cut without cutting, I never looked back.

I reflected on my time at *Sunrise* and recognized that the gory stories were common and now boring but what was really interesting was how people walked through life while at the same time exposing the continual broken nature of our nature and the passage through this brokenness to the next and never-ending challenges of life.

What was eating at my soul was this abortion of every single experience in my life for fear of not being able to control the outcome. When I didn't foresee the desired outcome, or when something seemed less attainable, I would start up the engine of thoughts and instantaneously I would chart a different course that would be filled with half measure, ensuing success and in a moment's notice eventual termination. I even cut short the experiences that were going perfectly well, since waiting to see what would happen next could not be controlled, by my reason. The beauty of life by learning from experiences was being short-sheeted by my own will. Simply, I was scared of what I could not see.

Where do I start, I ask myself? My teenage years were filled with common themes, but this heart of the matter stuff like all of life's jumping off points is christened after our high school years when we become responsible for our own decisions...or do we?

10

SCARED TO FAIL

Now the court system in California was jockeying for my conviction and financial resources. I was very well aware of the consequences before me. In the past, with a highly functioning circus at my side, I experienced success a majority of the time in my previous battles with the law. Blessed with great counsel and some amazing luck, I avoided the potentially damaging consequence on the freedom front that comes with multiple convictions and the escalation of the charges to a felony. A felon was not a performer in the circus, but I'm sure if I had no other choice, I could carve up a few to concoct a player that would not only succeed, but also prosper in prison.

The desire to have no consequences was delusional. Consequences are inevitable when making a decision. Any decision. My current situation testified to this fact, but my survival instincts ignited full measure, propelling the top hat to spin back in time to see how I escaped some of those charges in the past. More importantly, was it possible that this current charge in California, lucky number seven, could possibly have the same welcomed outcome?

Three no convictions—or should I say, the charges were dropped with prejudice—and one mysterious night on a military installation where the charges were never filed, which in retrospect would have been a federal charge, not this state stuff that I became immune to. Now Jaybird, my counselor, always made the process seem surreal as he handled my chronic yoke with a bedside manner of a professional waiter—which, by the way, there is nothing better than having a wonderful meal served by someone who touches your space at the right time coupled with the right amount of clever banter to make a meal taste that much better.

His tableside manner was precise, cutting through the legalese to get to the heart of the matter to see how we could absolve the situation or, at the very least, minimize the repercussions. Cleverly serving me the exact amount of hope to ease my anxiety, while bantering me up to provide the space I needed to let him harbor the weight of my situation so I could continue directing my circus of one. I don't remember the exact cases and what number in sequence they were, but I do remember how we, or should I say how Jaybird made it happen with an equally gargantuan dose of grace from above.

One case was thrown out because the cop mysteriously couldn't make it to the hearing and the statute of a speedy trial had exhausted its limits. Not sure why he could not make the court date and the reason was never mentioned, as I was instructed to leave the courthouse and never look back, and I never did look back, reasoning some things are better left unknown. Kind of find that funny because of my insatiable desire to know why things work, but for some reason, I didn't want my circus to be impeded, and this advice seemed to provide comfort.

Another case had the same fate, but when I was arrested, there were two cops present upon arrest, complicating my freedom. The district attorney's office only needed one of the cops in court when presenting the case before the judge, decreasing our odds of pushing out the case to the last moment so the cop would have a scheduling conflict. Our tactic of massaging the system, hoping both cops would not be able to show up, was not in our favor, so we decided to negotiate a deal with the D.A. That's when Lady Luck reared her ugly head again, giving an adrenaline shot to the circus on the last possible day before the statute exhausted its limits to a speedy trial. I was not sure what was happening, but the odds of both cops having conflicts in their schedule, thinking the other would be able to make the court date and not communicating to the other, was plain lucky. I'm a Sagittarius—what can I say?

Now, my political view is not swayed in one direction or another, and the thought of joining a political party and being labeled with a particular lens grated at my desire to have flexibility, wanting the freedom to be able to learn and grow and not be saddled with having to toe the line when it came to my political views was a must. I have been registered as an Independent since the age of eighteen, and even though local and national politics bore me, my voracious reading habit had me viewing all angles and participating in our democracy voting every time the opportunity arose.

You may be asking yourself why I'm sharing this and what it has to do with getting out of another DUI. Go ahead and ask yourself that question, and then sit back and settle in for the connection between these two phenomena. I have voted for Republicans, Democrats, and Independents, and if my memory serves me right, I have even pulled the lever for the Green party on occasion when the other options were ghastly.

It was the 2000 election for the presidency of the United States that had me muddling over the choices presented by our two party systems and the non-player Green party. I remember I wasn't too sure of any of the candidates, but I liked the bravado of the little Texas governor and his desire to provide some order to the disorder the office of the presidency in my eyes had suffered over the last four years. Of all the reasons one had to vote for a candidate in the election, I was voting not so much for the candidate, but rather for the preservation of the position our presidency should rise to, and I didn't see the same old thing, just better in what the incumbent party was offering in the form of change. I voted for Bush.

Numero cinco was already in the books, as we were now playing the delay dance with the D.A.'s office on scheduling a court date, when lo and behold, our precious number forty-three announced he would come a-visiting to the land of enchantment. I believe Bush carried New Mexico by less than four hundred votes, and my vote on a weighted scale was pretty valuable in retrospect. Now, I'm not a political rally kind of cat, and for the life of me, I didn't acknowledge his intended arrival and number five's court date being the same day, but what would come to light was absolutely brilliant. The cop never showed up to the hearing, and the judge had no choice but to throw the charges out...again.

It wasn't until several months later when the connection between my court date and the arrival of forty-three for some political rally came to light. Now, my family was aware of number five, since this charge instigated the lame intervention I quickly danced around, but what currently raised my mother's feathers was, while watching the local news one evening, she thought I had received an additional DUI.

An investigative reporter from the local ABC affiliate was doing a report on how the court system was failing in regard to convicting DUI offenders, and during the course of this piece, my picture was flashed on the screen as an example of how a simple case of DUI slipped through the cracks without a conviction. The piece went on to detail how my non-conviction was the result of the police officer being scheduled at the last moment to escort number forty-three.

Now, I am sure my mother was aghast at seeing my face plastered on the television and the equally yet unspoken thought of what others may think of her "perfect" children, as I reassured her it was not another DUI but the same old one without revealing it had been number five. It doesn't really matter, because in the circus, who's really counting anyway? Certainly not me, and remember I never cared what people thought of me or my actions or inactions in life.

Bottom line is, I had escaped number five because George W. Bush was our forty-third president, and maybe, just maybe, I had a little to do with a historic election that played out perfectly in getting what I wanted and keeping what I had. The show must go on!

My desire to beat the system, any system, was still strong, especially since I had doled out the dead presidents to make sure I wasn't fired from my job. Even though my current counsel was lackluster compared to Jaybird, we had an angle and were successful at the DMV hearing, so why not pursue a trial by jury and see what happened next? If we could prove I was in my house and not on the back porch, a huge hole would be exposed in the D.A.'s case. Freedom from the consequences was a distinct possibility. I would be able to turn in my keys and my commitment at *Sunrise* and set my sights on South America.

The desire to act on a lot of old habits had diminished over the past several months, with the big ones being drinking and self-edited honesty. I no longer had the desire to drink, and I no longer had the desire to edit the truth. The connection between the spiritual experiences and the new way of navigating my way around Windansea at first was disconcerting, but now was a welcomed friend. Nevertheless, the fantasy of walking away unscathed from lucky number seven was tantalizing every part of my being. If successful, I would be off and running, this chapter in my life would be over, and I would be able to restart the circus with, at least in the short-term, sobriety.

At the same time, I recognized I was still on shaky ground, with one wrong move rattling the growth growing inside of me. My saving grace was the fear of losing what I had gained. With my court date only days away, a funny feeling was stirring in me again, embracing that once-unwelcomed feeling hoping I could learn to trust it. But this time, the genesis of the feeling wasn't in the form of another human being. It was different. It was a feeling from within, a spiritual experience for sure, and I knew I couldn't bend the truth again to keep what I had or get what I wanted.

It was the melding of my subconscious and conscious thoughts for the very first time in my life, and this time, I didn't need the assistance of another to do the right thing. I shared with Joseph my decision, and he concurred, leading me to plead guilty to number seven and let the consequences play out. It was a critical moment in self-honesty for me, as I had finally relinquished delusion and fantasy in the form of a verb.

I would still have the thoughts of self-deceit, as we all do in the human experience, but now, I would not act without at least having a second thought. I could no longer orchestrate the circus of one in its present form, and a new muscle would need to be formed and nurtured as I navigated my way around Windansea on my bike one moment to the next.

Really! Why? In my gut, I acknowledged if successful at maneuvering past number seven, I would abort my current excavating projects. It was a significant moment in my life, narrowly escaping my formula of half measures and not completing something from start to finish. It was a close call. I battled myself to the last possible moment, but that moment had passed, and for now, the will to continue with this fourth step stuff and see what happened next was all I had.

But what I didn't realize at the time was the hidden blessing of pleading guilty to lucky number seven. It was the consequence of nine months of court-mandated DUI classes that created a void in my planning paradigm. It allowed the time to take a deep breath and exhale with the added luxury of not having to make life decisions in the short term.

In all reality, the fight of my life was directly in my path, a collision of my will and the circus it created versus the uncovering of my life to my roots. What I would need now was all the courage, strength, and grace I could take hold of to carry me through. Simply, I needed another miracle.

My adolescent life was a blur with magic cure in hand, and now, I needed to decide what to do next after high school. It only seemed logical that I would go to college, since all of my older siblings had done so. I rarely studied in high school and never developed study skills and somehow was able to pull off the grades and test scores to apply and gain entrance into Creighton University, a Jesuit school in Omaha, Nebraska. The circus was nimble and deceptive. But did the circus have the resources to fool everybody in higher education, including myself? The high possibility of failure would be my savior.

Fearful of failing and conscious of my secret of not having the skills and study habits to be successful in a highly charged Jesuit environment, I decided — or maybe it was decided for me — to go to junior college and play college basketball, while at the same time learning discipline and study habits for the first time in my life. I knew the circus had exhausted its academic magical powers by skating through elementary, middle, and now high school, but that was not going to be possible in college. With "scared to fail" as the active ingredient, drastic measures were needed if I was going to change lives like Ms. Lovato encouraged.

No normal junior college would do, as this was a military school. I needed more than study habits to get me through college, and this institution was ideal in providing the ego-bending assistance to the areas of my life desperately requiring attention. My brother Ralph-David was held back a year in middle school, and we graduated high school together, furthering the myth that we were twins; we were not. I guess we both needed the forced discipline offered at New Mexico Military Institute, and if playing basketball was the salve making this decision more palatable, then that worked for me.

The summer after graduation went quickly, and before I knew it, we were off to an experience that, for me, would change my life forever in so many amazing ways, which had very little to do with study habits, spit shining shoes, eating at attention, playing basketball, drilling with a rifle, topography map reading, and setting up claymore mines—all of which I perfected. What was unexpected for this wearer of the top hat was the oasis this environment provided to experience new people, places, and things. Every experience up to this point in life had prepared me for this exact experience perfectly, and I was salivating for the possibility of me, more and now!

Now, all new cadets must arrive one week early to endure what is called "Rat Week." A week comprised of learning how to do the basics, like standing at attention, saluting properly, shining belt buckles, shining brass, spit shining shoes, making a bed with military corners, marching in formation, what uniforms to wear for what, and a lot of physical training. It was what one would call boot camp in the regular armed forces, but compressed into one week in the tiny hamlet of Roswell, New Mexico, widely known for its extraterrestrial sightings. A time to assimilate all of the newly inducted into this new culture, as well as to level the playing field and get everyone to be the same when we are all completely different on the outside and inside formed by our previous environments.

With every shape, size, race, and socio-economic class represented, how does an institution at least on the outside make everybody feel the same on the inside? One method deployed was the psychological badgering to break the spirit of an individual down to the level of a "rat," with the intent of building everyone back in the same methodical way, creating a bond with those sharing the same molding experience, and in turn, crafting a sense of responsibility for each other. This psychological molding of our oneness continued for the remainder of the first six months of my freshmen year.

The second tactic employed in the early hours of "rat" week was simple and a highly effective self-leveler of our uniqueness on the outside, creating that same feeling of oneness. A haircut — or more accurately, labeled a buzz cut!

In the first hour of my first day, I was marched away with a bunch of other knuckleheads to the post barbershop to have our uniqueness erased from our beings one by one. It was painfully obvious most were having a difficult time with this process, evidenced by the shocked blank stares plastered on these nameless faces. The air in the room was thick with discomfort as you were forced to watch the next person get in the chair and instantly see them change drastically into a new form they were aghast at as well. With the long line of uniformity filtering into the room and the constant chatter of the drill sergeant chuckling at your misfortune, a growing pile of locks carpeted this torture chamber disguised as a four-chair barbershop, representing the only sign of who we used to be.

My timing was impeccable and my luck dazzling. When it came time for my turn in the chair of uniformity, presiding over the room was my troop leader, who recognized my name. While the hair clippers arched over my cranium, causing clumps of hair to fall to the hair-cluttered floor below, he barked out an order that on first thought seemed odd, but at the same time had me leaning into the dark of me.

He roared, "You've got pretty hair, Rat Raby, and I want you to remember this day forever, so grab some of you hair and carry it around until I tell you to throw it away."

As I bent down to pick up what represented my uniqueness, it dawned on me that the shaving of the domes of my fellow "rats" served its purpose of creating uniformity, and now suddenly, I would be the only one carrying around my locks and, in a strange way, preserving the circus of me. I carried the fistful of hair around in my hand for the next two days, and I loved every minute of it. The circus was excited at developing new ways of adapting to this environment, while all along making them think I was one of them with the entrenched desire to never join the club. The Black Mafia experience served me well.

With the buzzing of hair clippers and the chirping of the drill sergeant filling the room, it was my nature to scan the environment to pick up on the humanity surrounding me. I was eager to add to my circus, and this was all new stuff for me, and for all intents and purposes, I had a lot of roles to fill if I was going to make my stay here successful. But it was the look on the faces gathered together in the room of uniformity that would be etched in my mind forever, as if a landscape of their lives were painted on their faces for all to see. I could see and feel what others were hiding, a gift resulting from hiding from myself for all these years. We were scared. How could we not be?

New Mexico Military Institute was a unique incubator comprised of a junior college preparing kids who wanted to go into the military as officers and a high school for the well-to-do in our society who could afford to send their kid to this expensive boarding school, with discipline being the guiding force. Some kids didn't belong in this environment but found themselves saluting *ad nauseum* as a result of being challenged socially and or academically. But the kids that really stood out were the ones thirsting for love from their parents, who in their own right were suffering from the effects of materialism brought on by wealth coupled with the pressure of being socially relevant.

The end result left little time for a child whose only remedy was to exercise the dark areas of life in place of what was missing and desperately needed at home: love. It was the pain masked on these nameless faces that exacerbated the emptiness and all-alone feeling I had been uncomfortably comfortable with since my first memory. I knew what they were feeling without words being exchanged, and I wanted to let them know I too shared their pain, with the only thing being different my own experience. So many kids were sent here for the wrong reasons, and it only drove them deeper and darker into the shadows of their lives, since now you had to be even more creative to activate the ingredient that made the pain go away.

It wasn't all gloom and doom at the institute since the manicured environment was ideal for those who may need a dose of discipline, confidence building, and some good study habits. The academics and athletic facilities were second to none, and the food was plentiful and hearty, with three squares served daily. Having three meals a day was a shock to most of the kids, regardless of what economic stream you filtered from to get here, but it would be the ritual of eating at attention that stamped the extremes of this environment forever in your mind.

After all the personal hygiene, decorum, room inspection, and daily roll call completed, the entire corps would march in formation, singing and stepping in cadence to the drill sergeant's bellowing song of choice. It was fun marching, singing and rising early followed by all-day activities of school, managing your shining duties, keeping your room spotless, athletic training, and basketball practice, all topped off by mandatory study hall. With the crescendo of hunger peaking at dusk, we finally entered the mess hall, where the food would be brought out to the table family-style. Our rumbling bellies ached for some sustenance and were greeted with heaping plates of meats, starches, and vegetables. This was where the mind training came into play, and if you were still labeled a "rat," you had to eat your meal at attention.

Now, I challenge you try this at home while floating yourself back in time to when you were in your late teens and full of salt and vinegar and, at the very least, a bushel full of self-reliance with the definitive answer to everything. First, you have to sit up straight in your chair, with both feet planted firmly on the ground in front of you and a fist space between the back of your chair and your back, and this was the easy part. Arms must be rested in your lap, and you must stare straight ahead during the entire meal. In order to start the process of putting food on your plate, you would have to formally request permission to eat, and only when it was granted could you start putting food on your plate to methodically consume.

It would go something like this: "Staff Sergeant, cadet Raby, A.F., request permission to use my utensils to consume my meal."

Throughout the meal, if you wanted anything, including the twins—salt and pepper—another helping, or some more juice or water, a formal request must be asked and permission given before acting.

This was just the beginning of the eating process, because when granted permission to eat or drink, you had to get the food from your plate to your mouth, and this could only be done in a forty-five-degree angle. After every bite, the utensil must be returned to rest at the top edge of your plate, with your arm returning to your lap while you chew your food. The size of the bite on your utensil must be measured as well, and if your squad leader thinks you're shoveling too much food in your mouth, he can request for you to respond to him, meaning you had two chews and a swallow before you had to speak up.

Everything was squared off in this environment: the corners of your bed, the changing of direction when walking, and now when eating, one eats a square meal. If the squad leader was in a good mood during the last five minutes of a meal, he would grant permission to eat at ease, and this was where the real eating took place at every meal, as the shoveling of food was underway to keep from going hungry.

I loved every part of these games, since I was only here to get a little discipline and some desperately needed study habits. This was old hat for me, with an ever-growing tent of performers, mastering the game of making people think I wanted to conform by actually doing what they wanted me to do, and excelling in it, while all along, my insistence to keep the circus independent was being nourished the whole time.

I would never be one of them because that was too easy, but what I didn't know at the time, the real challenge in life was to be who I was, not all these other things that allowed me to get what I wanted and keep what I had. Make no mistake, I was in complete control with the façade of being controlled by others. The dark was looming.

The underbelly of this environment whose surface reeked of discipline, honor, decorum, shiny shoes, snapping salutes, and the aforementioned squared everything was not unlike any other institution that's composed of human beings toiling with their humanity. A lot of kids matriculated here for all the right reasons, and an equal amount for all the wrong reasons. Loneliness, home sickness, feeling different than, and not feeling loved are all representatives of the intense pain experienced in the human condition, as these traits and many more were all present and accounted for at the institute.

Most institutions' sustainability is centered on successfully manipulating and cloaking human feelings and emotions under the guise that if you make them all do the same stuff over and over with insane repetition, it will compensate for those feelings, allowing them to rise above the individual pain to find union with others. The union is the emphasis molding the individual to become a part of something larger, with the side effect being the loss of uniqueness and individuality.

Under this formula for group building, a "we're in this together" attitude arises, allowing for a space to be created within oneself of trusting another, even if it was not desired. The light and dark is present in every institution, and at N.M.M.I., it was oozing from every stoop, parade field, daily room inspection, and cadet walking these storied grounds.

If one wanted to exercise the dark area in their life currently being researched, it had to be pushed deeper and darker, since this environment itself demanded new ways of navigating if you wanted to act on those feelings, but at the same time didn't want to get caught, which would result in two distinct consequences. Getting kicked out of the institution was the last measure and rarely used, but the first, more debilitating, and often repeated was the demerit program in place to curb the desire to act out.

If one exceeded the ten free demerits given weekly, since we all know perfection is a delusion recognized even in this squared environment, one was forced to give up the only free time you had on the weekends to work off excess demerits. For every hour of picking up trash, cleaning the communal bathrooms, or the dreaded task of gearing up in fatigues and boots and shouldering a drilling rifle to march in a defined pattern would earn you one hour of credit for every demerit over the allowable limit. Some kids had hundreds of demerits and would spend every weekend for the whole year trying to make amends N.M.M.I.-style, and believe me when I say this: there was a lot of exercising outside the lines that never ended up with marching to the beat of your own will on the weekend. Regardless, there was a lot of marching on weekends!

Alcohol and drugs were prevalent in my neighborhood when growing up, and I had seen about everything before I attended N.M.M.I. But what I was surprised by was the accessibility and the quality of drugs that were available at this institution.

Most kids were not from these parts, and in fact, we had kids from other countries, especially from Mexico, Central America, and South America. The rumor was that they were sons of high-ranking military officers, who were sent to learn English and get a head start on the military life that seemed to be in their future, whether they desired it or not.

We had kids from extremely wealthy families. We had kids whose fathers were politicians, both in state and national politics. We had kids from the barrios, from the urban ghettos, from the rural areas, from the east, west, north, and south. Every imaginable walk of life was on full display, and in this confined and controlled setting, some of the best urban spices available.

Now, I didn't partake in the pills, cocaine, or other delicacies readily available, but on occasion, I would puff on an apple caressing some very kind pakalolo. I was too scared to partake in the forbidden fruit of drugs, as the fear of being caught and the possibility of revealing my secret was a chance I was not willing to take. What was the most prevalent, and on face value, the hardest to hide, was readily available to all: alcohol.

With the hope I could exercise this shadow portion of my life with safety, I set out to dabble in the healing spirit while in this environment that desperately needed some bedside manner. The seed of exercising the spirit—which, on first glimpse, seemed impossible to make happen here—was planted during "rat" week, as we were cautioned on the severe punishment for drinking, and in the case your roommate had been drinking, making sure he didn't sleep on his back because cadets have drowned in their own vomit while passed out. If this happens, roll your roommate on their side and call for help. It was all the room I needed to start the planning and plotting, since its tacit approval in my eyes was granted by sharing this information.

I wasn't afraid of death, and I wasn't afraid of drinking and its consequences, knowing it would only be a matter of time before I could corral up the perfect person to purchase some booze. Every month or so, I was able to get a janitor or the barber or a newly formed acquaintance from town to purchase a case of beer to be consumed in one sitting over an hour because we didn't have a lot of free time. The planning and control of each session took weeks to devise, making sure getting caught was minimized. My unsuspecting friends were a recipient of a well-crafted plan sourced from my circus, but in their eyes, it was a freak opportunity to get drunk. My Dizzy-land experience was coming in handy. I was in control without being in control. What was not in my control was whom I lived with.

My roommate situation was a little more precarious, with two roommates in the first sixty days after my arrival. My first roommate was Tad from Northern California, a product of a naval family pressuring him to follow in those footsteps. He had been granted a provisional entrance into the Naval Academy, as long as he did well in his year stay. There were probably a dozen kids in the Corps on a similar program with the other military academies, and to this day, I'm not sure why Tad had to spend a year at N.M.M.I. before entry, but something never smelled right with him. I'm not talking figuratively, but literally!

He was a good white kid from a good family, taking accelerated classes, and was meticulously sharp, making it a little nerve wracking trying to get my shoes and brass as shiny as he seemed to. Now, I'd played war in Robby's backyard, but this uniform and inspection stuff was unfamiliar to my circus, and I was grateful to have such a serious student of this game to help me along the way. He taught me tricks, and I watched his every move to get my brass and shoes up to snuff, knowing if I could emulate half of his deportment, it would allow me to succeed and, most importantly, keep the circus of Me intact.

We got along well, and I really liked him, but within the first couple of days, a lingering odor seemed to fill the room, and I couldn't put my finger—or should I say my nose—on it. It smelled of warm milk, with a slight sour note at the end. I'm sure if you poured a glass of milk into a Riddell Cabernet wine glass, let it sit out for a few days, and then lifted said glass to one's smeller, a hint of what our room smelled like would be represented.

Meanwhile, there was so much stuff to learn and keep up with in those first few weeks that a strange, slightly unpleasant odor could easily be ignored, and for the most part it was. It was equally plausible that I was starting to get used to the smell since I lived with it, and don't forget, I had in my circus the learned skill of being able to get comfortable with the uncomfortable. Pissing in my own bed for one. The odor would intensify, going unnoticed until it slapped you in the face when walking within a twenty-foot radius of our front door. The mixing of the fresh air and the funk exposed his secret.

Now, Tad's shadow masking abilities were elementary in relation to my own, as he knew the source of the funk and was now determined to resolve the situation on his own. The putrid sour milk smell wafting through our room was now mixed with an alcohol-based blend of bad cologne. An ill-fated attempt by my roommate to hide or dilute the toxic smell, but a common experience when we try to cover up our flaws with the intent to smoke-and-mirror the issue so no one will notice and no one will be affected. Tad had the foot funk, and Dr. Scholls, baby powder, musk oil, gasoline, and even Agent Orange for that matter would not suffice to knock down what he had stored up in his dogs. His desire to cloak the smell only compounded the problem, as this highly toxic mixture would instantaneously generate a sweating of your taste buds, propelling one to gag and throw up whatever was in your stomach, and if nothing else, a pleasant dry heave.

I had compassion for my friend, and I was comfortable with being uncomfortable with his odor problem, as I too had experienced my odor issues, going to all lengths to mask my problem that, in reality, was the trivial of what was really going on inside of me. No one wants to be found out with something that could possibly alter the perception others have of us, revealing what may be going on in their lives, so we generate ways to cover it up, with the real tragedy being something greater is at stake here. The heart of the matter never gets addressed, and we learn to adapt to the next environment, to the next masking opportunity, until we find ourselves being a shadow of who we really are. I'm not sure what his reasoning was, and it really didn't matter. I never requested to be transferred to another room, but within several weeks, my troop leader, which happened to be the same cat that had me carry my hair around in my hand for two days, sourced some compassion and informed me I was being transferred to another room in the next several days.

I was sad for Tad, knowing he would be rooming by himself for the duration of the year, and in some small way, happy for him as well. I understood his dilemma, knowing the relief you experience when you are exposed, the trivial, but the show still keeps rolling because the heart of the matter is never addressed, and that in and of itself is to be celebrated.

You see, it's never the things we direct all our energy at to try to divert attention or change perception that thrusts us deeper into delusion or fantasy, but rather, it is the same self-directed smoke-and-mirror jostling providing the temporary breathing room to move to the next opportunity to do it again. The duality of acting and reacting at the same time to alter perception is truly unsustainable, since we never get to the heart of the matter, where the possibility of change is plausible. Short-term relief followed with long-term pain assured this inevitable outcome.

Now, basketball was the medicine to temper the blow to the ego of having to go to military school, and in all reality, my skills were decent but not worthy of the talent recruited to play on our team. After "rat" week, we were allowed two hours daily to play pick-up games amongst each other, and it was very apparent we had some extremely talented players.

Darius was a wiry point guard with mad handles from Washington D.C. and was as quick going forward as he was sideways and backward. Brown, who was in my troop, was a man amongst boys, standing six foot six and a solid two hundred thirty pounds, with skills defying gravity. He had handles like a point guard, a post-up game he often finished with a dunk or sweet spin off the glass, and a silky jumper from any range. We had Patrick, a long skinny post from South Carolina who was strong around the basket with a solid midrange jumper, who needed a year of academic growth prior to being admitted to the Citadel on a basketball scholarship. There were a few other cats with powerful court résumés that never made it past the first three weeks of school, as the military regime of being told what to do and how to eat was too much for their ego to absorb.

The gem of all this coalesced talent was a svelte six foot three, two guard out of Pojoaque, New Mexico, named Billy, whom I had never heard of before, and we lived in the same state. He was the class 3A player of the year, with skills allowing him to play anywhere on the court. He could play the point, the two or three guard, and if necessary, either post position. He was the smoothest, most fluid player I've ever witnessed in person, while massaging a basketball with a thousand intuitive moves so graceful, they must have been choreographed. He moved at one speed while everyone else moved at another, and when the competition adjusted, so did he, recognizing the greater asymmetry between his tempo and the opposition was necessary for him to create space to dominate the hardwood. I connected to Billy immediately. With a sharp mind and funny bone to match, he seemed to be more like me than the others. We shared meals together, studied together, listened to music together, trained together, drank beer together, and made sure no one knew what was going on inside our beings.

It was very evident to me I would be hard pressed to find playing time on this team, and for me, that wasn't a big deal anyway, as I could use this oasis, the gym, from the tightness surrounding these storied grounds. The intent all along was to develop some skills that could further my academic goals, getting me closer to the Foreign Service. I would do anything to make it happen, as long as the circus was in total control. No gray area allowed. I would gladly ride the pine.

Initially, our team was purposely compiled to compete with anyone in our league, the formidable Western Junior College Athletic Conference, considered the toughest junior college conference in the nation. In fact, the reigning junior college national champions, Midland Junior College, were ranked pre-season number one in the country, with three other teams from our conference in the top twenty.

Within a few weeks, our towering team was dwindling by the day, as the two kids from Florida could not make the transition and were sent home on the bus to a future unknown. Some of the other players were racking up demerits as the tidal wave of forced change was starting to take its toll with some our best players. Some were bending and some were breaking, finding it interesting when, void of the option for elective change, our first reaction demands a defensive position to preserve and protect the ego and pride. The pride and ego are sensitive creatures and will use extreme measures when their sovereignty is at stake or when it's not our idea or will to change.

I despised being forced to do anything, and I had compassion for my fellow cadets who were battling change not of their own will, but for me, this was another venue for my circus as I quickly adjusted, forming new performers in order to draw from this fountain of potential experiences what I needed. I needed academic discipline and the strength to overcome my fear of failing at this higher education stuff that my four older siblings had conquered, knowing if I tempered my ego and pride and allowed the institution to think I had conformed, I would be able to get what I wanted and keep my circus moving forward.

The intent of the conformers was equally strong, with the only difference being the final destination. My will trumped and outlasted many strong-willed foes and institutions. Deeper lessons were soon to be served. I wish I had known. We all do.

Now, Brown was a gentle man-child from Louisiana who was weathering the storm as best he could, and it was apparent he knew this was his last opportunity to make a run at the basketball dream he was destined to realize if he could only get past a few hurdles. Brown was a twenty-year-old freshman in junior college, with two kids at home and a new girlfriend — Tree — from town. Tree was about six foot one and happened to be about seven months pregnant, but that didn't stop Brown from having relations with her. He would make us laugh, saying he was going to put a "baby on top of a baby." None of his background or life circumstances were going to keep him from reaching his dream of playing professional basketball, and I believed he had the talent to do as such. He was a tower of strength, but there was one obstacle that might get in the way, and a memory I will take with me to my last breath.

Brown's room was several doors down from my new room that I shared with Mark, a cool cat from Conroe, Texas. It was customary during our Sunday through Thursday three-hour mandatory study time to take a small break to grab something to drink or go to the communal bathroom. During these breaks, I would see Brown intently hovering over his books and would always extend a strong greeting to inquire if he needed anything from the snack machines. This ritual of taking a break and our shared greeting was in its third week when Brown asked me if I could help him with one of his assignments. I gladly offered my services.

In fact, I would do anything to see this cat on the court against our upcoming competition, knowing the attrition rate of our basketball team was extremely high over the past several weeks for various reasons, and if I could help in some small way, I would. It was a strong possibility my impact on the hardwood would play out without ever actually lacing up a sneaker—by helping Brown with his studies.

Overall, Brown was jovial, lighthearted, funny, and quick-witted, but on this occasion, an air of meekness settled over the room. It was as if when I entered the room, this imposing human physical specimen, who only hours before was showcasing his skills on the hardwood with spins, fakes, hesitations, and dunks, was now a scared little boy sitting in his chair, surrounded by the sterility of our environment. I would never forget the look in his eyes when he asked me to help him read and comprehend the story for his English class. It was a look I knew too well, even though I never saw myself in the mirror when having those feelings of being vulnerable with a hope I wouldn't be judged for what I was about to reveal. The difference was I never had the stones to be as vulnerable as Brown exhibited that evening. My ego wouldn't let me go there.

As I gazed down at the table where he was sitting with the same book he had been hovering over for the past several weeks, it was now evident what he'd been battling the whole time. I looked him straight in the eyes while simultaneously pulling a chair up to his table, and we started from the beginning, phonetically sounding out the words to Dr. Seuss's *Cat in the Hat*.

My phonics training back in first and second grade had finally been put to use, spending an hour every night with Brown, as I was the only one he trusted with his secret. We would sit in his room and work on all his assignments, only speaking when it pertained to the work at hand, and only after we had risen from the table would we resume the lighthearted banter customary when exchanging with Brown. We were locked in this military dance together, albeit for different reasons, but with a goal in mind of making it through so that we could get what we wanted and keep what we had: our secrets.

Brown would only last a few more weeks, as he had conquered his pride and ego in one instance and had shared it with another—myself—but the ego and pride is a selfish lover, always wanting to be nurtured in every situation in our waking hours. He would have one too many encounters with an overzealous cadet who wanted to make him do push-ups for the silliest of reasons, prompting Brown to threaten an ass-kicking with a one-handed throat choke up against a wall that had the young white kid lifted several feet off the ground. He would survive the choking incident but would be yoked with over a hundred demerits, and now faced with the thoughts that his only free time would have him marching on weekends was too much to bear.

When you're dismissed or choose to leave, no formal notification is announced to the rest of the corps. When it came time for study hall, I passed by his room, hoping to see his face, only to be greeted by a dark, empty, sterile room. I was wishing for another reason to explain his darkened room, and like many times in life when we know what has transpired, we sidestep the truth.

I went to sleep with the thought that I would see Brown in the morning when we assembled into formation for our daily ritual of chanting, marching, and singing our way to breakfast. I loved sitting with Brown. I loved him teaching me to be vulnerable, and I loved seeing honesty by another human being as he showed me by example to be honest with my deepest secrets, even though I could not.

The man-child was gone, and I would never see his face or hear his wonderful laugh again, but his subtle and brief influence on my life had been monumental, although I was unable to take action as he had done. Our team was mortally wounded. I moved on. I had no other choice but to rely on me.

The basketball team, with its dwindled ranks, had us overmatched in about every game we played, as our competition took full advantage of our overall lack of size and athleticism. Our mascot name was the Broncos, and even though we were underdogs in every game, we were never outplayed in regard to hustle and desire, having no choice but to play up to the level of our competition. In each game, we would run out of ammunition, exposing our lack of talent with an assortment of turnovers and foul trouble, and with Billy and Patrick out of the game, our ability to stay close would eventually morph into a blowout.

This static nature of our games' outcomes would weigh heavily on our team members, who in general experienced winning at the high school level. The overall demeanor, despite our continuous ending up on the short side of the stick, was quite jovial, which I believe was a direct result of the sitting, eating, and standing at attention ritual. It was a relief to be free to win or lose without a defined roadmap or demerits involved.

Colonel Richard Toliver, one of my earliest spiritual mentors, would always say, "We were not baptized in lemon juice," meaning we had to have fun in life, no matter how difficult its path. Even though it would be years before I would meet and study under Col. Toliver, it would be this state of lightheartedness our team embraced that had our team fine-tuning our nickname to the Bron-choke-os.

My role was limited, spending a lot of time riding the pine and hoping my hard work in practice and some opportunistic foul trouble by my teammates would get me a little playing time when the current contest's outcome had been settled. I was a six foot two decent post in high school and a slow point guard with limited handles in junior college. Extremely overmatched against every opponent I had to guard or when bringing the ball up the court to run the offense. But little did I know I would have five excruciating minutes of fame on the basketball court play out in a West Texas town recently made famous by president number forty-three. His hometown.

It was early January, and the Bron-choke-os had traveled to Midland, Texas, to play the reigning junior college national champions, the Midland Junior College Chaparrals. They were a powerful team, with their starting five already committed to play at the Division I major college level after their junior college days were exhausted. They had not lost a game all season and were still ranked number one in the country when we came a rolling into town in our red and white short bus affectionately called the Broncomobile.

The Broncomobile had a strange sense of direction, or maybe it was a lack of funds, but after each game, our trusty wheels would guide us to our post-game meal, knowing beforehand its destination. Kind of like when placing horses in a new environment, you place them with others horses that are familiar with the area, allowing them time to bond, as the experienced horses will show the new horses where the water and feed is. This Broncomobile's rubber had worn tracks in these pastures in West Texas for years, as it somehow knew the direction to every McBronco's—McDonald's—in West Texas.

We were aware what was going to happen before each game and where we would be eating after the game, but the in-between and the final score was the unknown excitement that had us lacing up our shoes and diving for loose balls until the final buzzer sounded.

The arena was packed, buzzing with energy to witness a sacrifice on the hardwood, which ironically pushed our team to do our best. It was one player in particular from their starting five I had heard about from our returning players upon my arrival. He was the reigning national player of the year and bigger than life in reputation, but when I set my eyes upon him for the very first time during warm-ups, I thought he was in junior high school. Standing at a generously listed five foot six, with a frail frame and an interesting patch of discolored hair on the side of his head, was none other than the iconic Spud Webb.

Now, Spud would eventually go on to sign with North Carolina State, who had recently been crowned national champions on a now-famous last second shot game in the "Pit" in Albuquerque against Akeem "The Dream" Olajowon and Clyde "The Glide" Drexler. He would spend the next decade in the NBA, showcasing his high-wire act with the top players in the world alongside and against the likes of Magic, Michael, Bird, Barkley, Kareem, Malone, Ewing, Dominique, and many others that arguably defined the greatest generation in basketball. He would become famous for winning the NBA dunking contest against men almost twice his size. He wasn't any of those things yet; he was just an extremely quick point guard with an incredible vertical leap and a shooting range from deep, with a very humble and meek presence.

He never uttered a word or showed any emotion. He was singled-minded in his method and detached from every moment, as if all this stuff he was orchestrating on the hardwood was an out-of-body experience. I've never seen anyone move so quickly and change directions and not lose speed or balance while commanding total vision of the court and each player within its boundaries. I envied his ability to command the room while not allowing anyone in the building to really connect with who he really was. I instantly knew this supremely talented human being on the outside was equally complex and in control of every move he was making on the inside. We were connected without ever speaking a word to each other and never have to this day.

I was soaking up every moment, loving the caliber of my competition, but I was playing my own game within the game being displayed on the court only several feet in front of me while commanding the last seat on the bench. A game of not really wanting to be doing what I was doing—playing basketball—with a desire to move on to the next thing, while only giving half measure to what I was doing at the moment. I was alone again in a packed arena, isolated in my own thoughts of tomorrow.

The idea being it will be the next thing providing the comfort to the emptiness I was currently feeling inside, with a result of tragically missing out on every experience including the one right in front of me. The common human experience of peeking around the corner to see what one can make happen next, rather than experiencing what was currently being experienced at the moment. I was altering my own experience, robbing myself of the lessons intended for me all along as I willfully became more isolated with single-mindedness by developing that first thought, long ago, into reality. But today was the day when an equally well-reasoned, single-minded character who happened to be wearing sneakers squeaking his way around the hardwood would alter my paradigm of reaching for tomorrow to soothe the present.

I was elated and resolved to the fact that I would be getting very little playing time in any of our games, and especially against the caliber of competition we would be facing tonight in this oil mecca of West Texas. I was a voyeur sucking the energy out of the arena, ready to watch the show and eager to see how this experience could possibly add to my circus, and the only thing lacking at my side was some type of festival snack food like a corn dog or turkey leg and a soda pop to sip on while I witnessed this inevitable massacre. It didn't matter if I was sitting in the cheap seats or positioned with front row action in life, as inevitably, I always seemed to be thrust on stage, no matter the circumstance, and this would be another example of my luck.

Several minutes into the game, our starting point guard picked up two quick fouls trying to check the elusive Spud, and while the thoughts of this experience were spinning in my head, I heard a voice call my name but was unsure of its origin. The only thing connecting me to my team was the uniform I was wearing and my position at the end of the bench, with several open seats between my teammates and me.

I was alone again in this experience and couldn't stop the racing of my mind as it plotted the course of my life while I sat in the cavernous arena with an iconic sports figure only several feet away. I heard my name again, and in a fraction of a second, I realized I was going to have to check back into the moment and check into the game playing out in front of me. Not only was I going to have to guard Spud, but I was going to have to run the offense while he guarded me with my limited skills. What happened next was pure magic.

As I stepped over the line to enter the court in an instant, my body was transformed to a place where time and space slowed down and everything seemed to take forever, as the room became eerily quiet, when in fact, that was not what was happening. I was probably on the court for five total minutes, but it felt like an hour. Every bounce of the ball, every squeak of a shoe making a cut of direction, every grunt of the bodies clashing for a rebound echoed in my mind as I felt myself moving to the flow happening around me with one distinct thought. That this was where I should be at this moment and nowhere else; and for me up to that point in time, this thought would be a first. I was actually engaged with what was happening, as if each moment was being catalogued for some other purpose I could not understand.

Now remember, I was slow to begin with, and currently matched up against this zenith donning sneakers, found myself exerting maximum effort, but to no avail. I made sure to stay between him and their basket, and that was even true when we had the basketball on our side of the court. I was playing defense when we were on offense, and that wasn't enough to stop Spud from sprinting past me with ball in hand while I watched him rise to the rim, gazing up to look at the bottom of his sneakers as he finished off the play with a thunderous dunk of the basketball. The bottom of his feet were at my eye level as I witnessed firsthand Spud dunking the ball on me at least three times in the brief five minutes that seemed like hours. I was happy to be in the moment experiencing what I was experiencing and equally happy to be pulled out of the game to take my seat at the end of the bench where I belonged all along…alone.

The suspension of delusion and fantasy, if only for a brief moment, transpired on the hardwood in a sleepy West Texas town, and my tutor was a basketball wizard named Spud Webb. I never quite grasped the significance of the moment and how it could have possibly changed my paradigm of controlling each outcome by letting happen what was going to happen next.

The opportunity was lost as I brushed it aside to continue weighing the significance of what was going to occur in the future as the only vital ingredient I could control, providing the only safety and comfort I would desire. I did not like the five minutes on the court, and in all reality, it was perfect because I was finally engaged in the moment.

Unfortunately, my reasoning convinced me otherwise. I was perfectly in control as long as everything played out my way. I didn't realize it at the moment, but I was becoming encased in the cocoon of my own active ingredient…my way…with the emerging inability to navigate away from me, more and now.

The N.M.M.I. experience was amazing. I excelled at all levels and quickly moved up in rank in the last half of the year to staff sergeant. I would be approached by the administration on what my plans were for the next school year, as they wanted to promote me to an officer and give me my own troop to command. The offer boosted the ego, giving me the confidence to succeed at the next academic level. Was it time to jump ship again?

The inability to let what might happen next, happen next was peeking its ugly head around the corner as I opened the possibility of accepting the offer to attend Creighton that had been deferred for a year. I was ambivalent to the military lifestyle, other than the childhood fantasy of playing war, but soon found myself thriving in this environment drenched in decorum, tradition, discipline, and honor, with a growing respect for our men and women in uniform. Maybe this was the avenue destined for me to achieve those lofty global goals?

The desire to stick it out and see what was going to happen next was present. But my umbilical cord of survival of acting on the first thought that came to mind was the guiding force behind all my decisions, having me play this military game so I could move on to the next thing, since moving on to the next thing was the thing, if you know what I mean. It was a great experience.

But I was unbendable. I was going to abandon what would come next, reasoning my path could only be directed by me if I wanted everything to go my way. What I didn't realize was that my way was neither good nor bad; it was simply my way.

It was the predictability of the environment and a deep-seated idea that joining something would detract from the opportunity to have an unlimited supply of experiences, propelling me to pull the rip cord on what was going to happen next toward the unknown in Omaha, Nebraska.

11
OPPORTUNITY LOST IS AN OPPORTUNITY GAINED

It was becoming very apparent to me the defibrillator of my life was the perfect storm surrounding me at Windansea, with the eye of the storm being *Sunrise*.

A new character would enter the room in the month of May, and his influence on my fellow *Sunrisers* and me would encourage us to dig a little deeper to move beyond the topical skin and flesh of our experiences and related feelings. It would not be enough now to examine the flesh of our experiences, as now we were being led by a man who not only went to the bone of his experiences, but went even further, tapping the marrow that gave his physical structure life. There were a lot of bright, articulate, passionate people in the room who worked daily at exposing their frailties and how they were working toward a solution that would benefit not only themselves, but also those who surrounded them, and our new friend Sung would command us to go deeper by his example.

I was now thirsting for the magic happening in the room when human beings gather and metaphorically strip away clothing to stand naked amongst one another with the intent of building anew. If I wanted a new foundation to build my life upon, I had to get naked in front of others. I thought I was seasoned to do, as such with my experience as a child instigated by my brother's escapades that had the neighbor kids running for the comfort of their own beds and had me stripping off my clothes and running into occupied hotels.

Even though I had done a lot of work and could have easily been satisfied with what I had uncovered to this point, coupled with the monumental changes already achieved, it was very apparent to me that I had only used half measures in the naked arena. Stripping off my clothes in front of total strangers was self-serving. Stripping in front of another human being to reveal what I was feeling inside was fraught with anxiety fueled by the possibility you might find out who I really was, rather than who I wanted you to see me as. But as I learned by showing up at *Sunrise*, what I needed, what we all needed was a heavy dose of our new *Sunriser* Sung, and to a bunch of human beings addicted to the self, we eagerly listened when it was his time to share what was really going on in his life.

In the human experience, it is a common theme to start placing people in their respective categories before they utter one word, categorizing a person before they open their mouth for the very first time. It is often at first glance that we start sharpening the Ginzu knife, preparing for the ensuing slicing and dicing up of people with the sole intent of making us feel more comfortable in relation to who we think we are. I'm not talking about ethnicity, but rather how style and fashion today are a driving force on what status you will be given topically.

Sung rolled in to the meeting wearing an Adidas sweat suit with a chain hanging from his neck and a pair of highly priced basketball shoes loosely laced up. He was a baller, a rapper, a kid from the inner city with a cool swagger who, for whatever reason, pulled up a chair and sat down, listening to the sharing going on in the room that day.

It's customary after the reading of the daily reflection to pass the book around the room so everyone had a chance to read it for him or herself before it was time for their share. The book was passed to Sung, and he rummaged over the page and gently placed the book in his lap, waiting for his time to reveal who he really was.

Now, I don't exactly remember the topic, but it was the month of May, meaning we were studying the fifth step. This was the step where you share your fourth step with another. The step where one learns to open up and get naked with another human being, tossing away all ideas of being judged by another and truly trusting another human being with your deepest and darkest vulnerabilities and secrets. The shares were especially powerful that day:

The freedom and willingness to share and expose our feelings is joy. When we are confused we have to be willing to share this joy...Ricky.

Codependence can be changed into loving and caring, when we take care of ourselves first...Rod.

Better to be a live dog, than a dead lion...Mark the scientist.

Not clinging to a certain answer for something, but rather being open to what comes at you...Deborah.

The challenge is to change the real fears in life, not the fears of our mind...Larry.

Seeing the qualities in another and seeing those imbedded in you, freeing one to exercise that muscle inside me, deep inside me, to have those qualities for myself...Jimmy.

Life truly is a journey of change...Larry.

I keep what I share, not what I have...Ricky.

The learning can never end; and if it does, we slip into the old ways of working with the material of life. Through listening we have an opportunity to change... Joe — Oklahoma.

How quickly can I let go of what doesn't work...Larry.

Don't hold back anything in life...Not succumbing to the easier, softer way...Deborah.

The inability to engage with another human being in a manner where I can share my feelings and emotions have stunted my growth...Molly.

Running toward the things that are harming me are comforting, managing the symptoms versus the root of the problem. When we address the problem, the options to navigate at our disposal are now unlimited...Deborah.

Do you know why God is not working in your life? Because youre not giving him any room...Jimmy.

When it was time for Sung to share, it was if he looked directly into each one of our souls and spoke a language we all understood. Sung's heritage was Korean, and when he opened his mouth to speak to us, it was now very apparent his outward costume was in fact a shell, not who he was. I was relieved. His English was limited and his understanding of the reading was sketchy at best, but therein lay the blessing and lesson he would share with us all.

With tears rolling down his face, he shared his story of how he ended up in this room, hoping his worst fear of being judged by his culture and family for being an alcoholic would not be his reality. A cultural black-balling would ensue if he showed any signs of not partaking in drinking weighed heavy on his soul. He had never stepped foot in a meeting before and had never heard the sobriety razzle-dazzle, but that did not stop him from getting to the heart of the matter. He was naked and exposed on his first day and would continue to share in his limited English with us over the next several months.

Initially, we collectively thought if he could only understand the reading, he would be better served at understanding his own troubles, so we would take a collection and Deborah would go online and purchase him a Daily Reflection book in his own language so he could follow along in the meeting. We were blinded by reason. We were blinded by the desire to help. Most times, helping is not helping.

The amazing thing is he didn't need that damn book; we needed him to share his life with us without the filters language can provide. His shares were raw and not thought out. Using the perfect words to hopefully mold the perceptions of his audience was not possible. When you don't have all the fancy words to cloak your true feelings and emotions with the intent of not letting people know what's really going on, then you find yourself saying what you feel. Not unlike a child when the innocence of life is still their reality and what comes out of their mouths is what they feel and most often is the truth, whether we like it or not.

In the human condition, the will to put all the right words together with intention can sour one's ability to be honest, damaging the ability to share what is really happening inside us. I was masterful at crafting the right words to get what I wanted, and now with the example unknowingly served by Sung, I was hoping to move through life with fewer words and more feelings.

Omaha, Nebraska?

Now, my old man dropped off Ralph-David and me at military school, and that was cool, but it would just be the two of us as we hopped on a plane for the Midwest in late August. I'd never visited Omaha before, and for all intents and purposes, my travels outside of New Mexico were limited. The jolt of the landing gear on the tarmac was the signal we had arrived, and I couldn't wait to get off that plane and start moving toward my plan of making positive change in the world, as now I was confident and prepared to succeed academically with the structured study habits learned at N.M.M.I.

What I remember most about that moment in life, when I left the climate-controlled temperature of the plane's cabin and stepped on the jetway connecting the plane to the terminal, is the blast of heat and humidity, sucking the very joy out of the thoughts dancing around in my head only seconds before. I'd never experienced heat like that before, and it was nine o'clock at night; in retrospect, I believe was the first sign my well-designed plan of quickly whipping through this undergraduate school would be just that…a plan.

Over the next day, we stumbled around Omaha, picking up the needed essentials, like toiletries and the now-vital fan to blow hot air on me so sleep would be a possibility. It would be the first time I could remember my old man and me hanging out and doing stuff together, and it was cool. I'm not sure if I was expecting some type of encouragement or words that would ease me into this change of venue, sharing his life experience with me when setting out on a new adventure with the high probability fear and doubt would occur along the way. Not a chance.

What did happen was a hug in the parking lot as he left to go back to New Mexico. It was the first time in my life I felt connected to this man, who in all reality was a stranger. I didn't know him and he surely didn't know me, but I was hoping maybe this would be the start of a connection that went unquenched so long ago. I was ready for the academic challenge and not so ready for what was to happen next. Next in the sense that it was not a part of my well-thought-out plan; a detour, a roadblock, a bump in the road that would jostle my circus.

My roommate Chris Dracup was an ordinary fellow who was born and bred in Omaha, with no real peculiarities as far as I could tell. He was small in stature, with a wispy bowl haircut and a pair of wire-rimmed glasses, necessary only when he was reading, which meant studying. He was pre-med or pre-dentistry or pre-something that had to do with a plan on getting out of school on an accelerated basis, like a lot of the kids on my dormitory floor. These kids had a plan and were executing it with a passion and desire that had them pushing the limits of competitiveness.

Creighton had programs in three different disciplines—Law, Dentistry, and Medical School—allowing the brightest and best-prepared to accelerate through undergraduate school and move into the discipline of choice. Only a few would be eligible for such a program, and if the will was strong enough to outmaneuver the competition—fellow students—one could be that much farther ahead in the game of life and what was expected of them through family, societal, or plain, old self-imposed expectations.

Now, I was accustomed to competition on the athletic front and, to be quite frank, was not motivated by its pressure to outperform my teammates to get more playing time. The early-on survival tactics learned around the family picnic table had me insulated in my own will, resulting in not really giving a damn about what anybody else was doing and why. But isn't worrying only about myself a sense of competitiveness in and of itself? Up to this point in my life, I had not been faced with an environment where reason alone was used as the anvil to crush the will of those who wanted what you wanted. I was intrigued, and at the same time, something didn't feel right about dismantling someone else's dream so I could achieve mine first. This was not about learning. It was about setting the bell curve and winning.

The majority of the kids were from middle- to high-income families, educated at private denominational schools from the Midwestern part of the country. An overwhelming majority of students were from the Catholic denomination. It was a Jesuit university, whose tenets were not unfamiliar to me. I had been brought up in the faith and even done a two-year stint in middle school at San Felipe de Neri, our local church's learning center. I was comfortable with the idea of being surrounded by people who believed in the same things, but what I was uncomfortable with was the mean-spiritedness when defending the faith by the student population. The "us versus them" mentality was absent from my upbringing in New Mexico, where distinct cultures and traditions were prospering side by side. Unfortunately, divisiveness was the staple being served in almost every spiritual conversation in this environment.

I had no real spiritual depth to offer in the discussion, when chopping away at another tradition was the basis of building up the belief system one was defending. But what I did know was the feeling inside of me when confronted with this "us versus them" mentality didn't feel right. Maybe I was connecting back to my Nana that honored and practiced with ease warring religious traditions to find a higher understanding of God? I was wrestling with this spiritual dilemma, but at the moment, it was trivial in my stint at Creighton, as the heart of the matter, or at least what I thought was the heart of the matter, was to conquer the academics in this highly competitive environment, where winning meant you had to assure someone else was losing.

With a wide array of interesting actors on my floor that kept my interest high on the humanity level, it was a welcomed sip of nourishment to my thirsty circus, unknowingly becoming the balancing stick to the cutthroat "me first" mentality that flowed on campus. It was almost as if the admissions department made a concerted effort to put the misfits and those that didn't quite fit with the others on the same dormitory floor.

There was Masa the Japanese exchange student, who didn't speak a word of English except for his current English tutor, a cassette tape plugged into his Walkman. He would sing every song by the English band The Police, unable to understand the words he belted out from his belly. He nodded and smiled a lot when he couldn't understand what was going on, and that pretty much meant all of the time. He was frozen in his own language, and he too, like Brown, would be reading the prose from Dr. Seuss, as the gateway to this environment would be locked if he could not open the door with understanding.

Across the hall and several doors down was Milton, the exchange student from Gonzaga University who was from Thailand. He had transferred for a semester for no apparent reason other than to experience another part of the country before he finished school and headed back home to work in his family's textile business. He was a cool cat and a Bruce Lee fanatic, with life-size posters plastering every available space in his room. He was a seventh degree black belt in several fighting disciplines and had an array of weapons I'm sure were illegal, but he didn't care. Sharpened throwing stars, knives, nunchucks, batons, and swords all adorned his room. He would wear his fighting regalia and perform exact routines from Bruce Lee films with the aforementioned weapons. He was nutty and funny and was always finding time to make everyone feel at ease, a strange demeanor since at any moment, he could take your life and you couldn't do a damn thing about it.

Several doors down the hall were Tom and Gabriel, an odd couple at the very least, with brawn and strength being their common denominator. Tom and Gabriel were both Pre-Dentistry, and they had been unknowingly pitted against each other for the few slots available to accelerate them through undergraduate school to whisk up a doctorate in dentistry.

Tom was a big white kid from Kansas City with a gentle demeanor.

Gabriel was from Hawaii and a mixture of several Asian cultures, with Filipino/ Chinese being the dominant strains flowing in his veins. He was stocky, strong, and the kindest heart that welcomed me without condition. I would spend two summers living in Hawaii visiting Gabriel and his extended family, comprised of his childhood friends. It was an experience that deeply moved my circus, shedding a light on a dark corner of my life, since I had not experienced people who sustained friendships since childhood. I loved that they knew so many things about each other, an experience that escaped this wearer of the top hat solely focused on me, more and now.

My circus wouldn't allow for intimate relationships to occur. Nevertheless, I was profoundly nourished by this experience. But it was his striking smile with dimples I can still see to this day when I close my eyes and reflect on his character. It would be the friendship sticking with me forever, even though our connection would be broken by my own selfish action, never to be filled by another human being. I missed our friendship, and its loss drove me deeper into never allowing a connection to move me in that way again. I would never be the same, and even though I tried to reconcile years later, the damage was done, and I would never see his smile again. Heartbroken. Still.

My performers were adapting to my new friends in this highly competitive, religious tradition-charged environment that pushed the individual to the forefront, where I truly was most comfortable. It had always been about me, more and now, centering me in an environment that fostered and encouraged that desire, propelling me exactly where I wanted to be… in charge.

In retrospect, everything was ideal academically and I had made some really great friendships, but something inside of me was stirring up unease. The environment was not to my liking. I could put up with the religious tradition bantering and the cutthroat competitive nature, but it was the Midwest small view of the world that had me questioning the overall learning environment. I guess I had global visions, but the vision and small-mindedness apparent in my current environment could not be overlooked. I needed more stimuli, other than cramming my face into a book to get the desired grade to propel me forward while at the same time setting someone else back. The thought made me nauseous.

I would learn how to study for a test to make a certain grade, but what I did not learn was how to apply what I was learning to my own experience. I wanted more and I needed more, and everything in me said to stick it out, that eventually it would get better. Unfortunately, this feeling would not go away, haunting me every waking moment.

The circus was being choked in this amazing learning institution, leaving me no choice but to abandon it to seek out an environment suiting my vision of being nourished academically and environmentally. I could not and would not let anything get in the way of hindering the growth and prosperity of the circus, and a small setback and blow to the ego centered on failing to stick it out would not get in my way of moving forward. The show must go on!

While attending Creighton, I met a kid who had returned from a semester abroad in England, sharing with me his life-changing experience. The school was great and tough, but it was the culture and the enormity of the experiences available that he insisted was the heart of the matter. I wanted what he had, and with that thought in mind, the one semester stint at the University of New Mexico necessary to be eligible for the study abroad program was quickly devoured. I soon found myself on the train from Gatwick Airport to meet my new roommates for a semester that truly changed my life forever.

Upon my arrival and after all of the formalities of checking into school, I was quickly whisked away to my flat, where I would be staying for the next four months and, if I had anything to do with it, an opportunity to extend my stay.

The flat I would share with five other students from the States was situated on the border demarking the neighborhoods of South Kensington and Knightsbridge, positioning us directly across from the Victoria and Albert Museum and several blocks down from Harrods department store.

As it turned out, two of my roommates were from New Mexico of all places, and the other three were from a small liberal arts school in Nebraska. Quite ironic, I left Creighton because of the perceived small-mindedness of the environment and couldn't wait to leave New Mexico because it was too small for my lofty ideas, and now here I was, where I'd always dreamed of being on the international stage, finding myself surrounded by what I'd desperately tried to escape.

At first glance, not funny but perfect for me personally and a common human expectation that never comes to fruition when we make geographical changes to improve our lot, with an eventual understanding that wherever we go, there we are. Frustrating realities for quick-fix artists. I was hoping I could hang on to the bigger picture in front of me, rather than get bogged down with what surrounded me at first glance, potentially derailing future experiences if I allowed it.

The cat I shared a room with was a strange fellow named Goose, who was short in stature, with an extremely long torso, short bowed legs, a red mane of hair, and an admitted condition of eczema that had him shedding skin everywhere. A smattering of skin wafting in the air as he moved about paled in comparison to the foot funk I had endured at the Institute. This arrangement would be a piece of cake—with German chocolate being my favorite.

He loved eating Cheerios and Sugar Pops. He would bore us to death by constantly beating his patriotic drum, comparing everything here to home, missing out altogether on the experience at hand. In his mind, no matter what he was comparing, it was a gazillion times better back home than here. All I could think of was how insane his thoughts were, finding myself now in London with a very recent personal experience of living in Nebraska. No comparison. Light years. Goose was the typical ugly American knucklehead, who continued to shower us with his single-mindedness for the duration of our stay, which coincidentally was the same mentality that was choking my perceived lack of personal growth at Creighton.

Unknowingly, Goose was my savior, as he taught me to leave home at home and to embrace the culture at hand with an honest intent. Goose was teaching without teaching, as his formula for meandering around his new environment would be all I needed to do the exact opposite, and interestingly in unison with my own skin-building paradigm for life.

If I approached the locals with sincerity about wanting to experience their culture, they would oblige by opening their hearts and home, that soon enough would have me off the beaten path of tourism, smack dab in the middle of a culture or experience not possible otherwise. I would hone this idea birthed during my meanderings as a child, carrying it forth no matter where I landed in life, opening a plethora of experiences and people eager to share their home and heart with another, precipitated by the fact I was willing to leave home at home—and for me, that wasn't hard to do. In an odd way, I was always trying to find home.

Now, my other roommates, Mark and Brad, seemed to be okay fellows, but we didn't click past the formalities of living together. But it was my instant connection with Gregg and particularly Kevin that had me leaning into the darker, mischievous, no limits to all the possible opportunities that were available to a nineteen-year-old in one of the greatest cities in the world. It reminded me of the feelings I had when I was a kid hanging out with Glenn and Duane as we pushed the limits of no limits, knowing in my gut I could do business with these two cats. The connection was strong, as we all loved music, reading, wit, women, alcohol, and anything to do with the extraordinary. None of us wanted what we had already experienced in life up to this point, fueling the desire to cling to each other in a foreign land while soaking up as many experiences as humanly possible.

Our initial bonding occurred when ascending the ladder giving access to the roof from the interior building stairwell which, by the way, was on the list of things not to do while living in the flat, with expulsion from the living quarters the consequence. We would hoist Gregg's yellow boom box up to the roof with an assortment of local beers to catch a glimpse of the sun and, if possible, the surrounding spires, domes, towers, and clocks signaling the landmarks that make London's history.

I was intensely listening to the storytelling being tossed around on our rooftop playground, with a personal desire of finding out how deep and dark these cats could go if I in fact decided to work that side if the aisle while in London. Personally, I had made the decision before departing for London to tether the dark of my life in the basement of my being, knowing full well the consequences as a guest in a foreign land would be severe if I found myself on the wrong side of the law. But with a constant spinning of the mind and an unquenched desire to overindulge in any experience, it was necessary to know, if needed, who among my new friends could dance with me in the forbidden fruits of life. The bantering and chest pounding continued for hours on the rooftop, only briefly pausing when one needed to take a jobbie or a piss or when the beer ran out, necessitating a run to the midnight store that lingered in the basement of our building.

It was here on this roof I had my first introduction to the spice curry, indicative of the East Indian culture that was a vital part of this city's landscape, as were all the conquered cultures in this modern megapolis by the long reach of this empire years ago. Eclectic and cultured made the stew of modern London extremely tasty.

On the first floor of our building was an Indian restaurant constantly churning out engorged, pasty-skinned Londoners. The exhaust system from the kitchen scaled the building and deposited its fumes amongst our rooftop tanning, drinking, and music salon. We would spend hours up there singing, laughing, and drinking, and when we scaled the ladder down to rest for the evening, along came the smell of curry that had chiseled its way into every pore of our being. It took me a while to get past this initial experience with curry, and now it is one of my most loved spices in all its forms and ethnic culinary uses. I love food!

It was a surge of growth on so many different levels for me personally, especially with regard to other cultures. I had grown up in a land that embraced the Anglo, Mexican, and Native American cultures, but this was elementary compared to living in an international capital for people from all over the world. The circus master was happy with his new arrangement, excited to shed new costumes so I could add new performers to my wardrobe for life. Scholastically, I would take classes on British History and Culture, International Politics, Economics in the Emerging Third World, European Prehistory, and let's not forget the best class ever—Shakespeare.

All this British and European ballyhoo I was learning about was nice and someday hopefully useful, but to be able to study Shakespeare and then to go Stratford-Upon-Avon to see Ben Kingsley perform *Macbeth* was nothing short of brilliant. The class met once a week, and we would gather in the park next to the British History Museum, where our professor Mary Bess held court. The class requirements: come prepared to talk about the play we were studying and with one beer for yourself and one beer for the teacher. Our class would also meet once a month at night to see a play, with most of them being experimental renditions of the material we were reading during the week, which was always prefaced by a mandatory pub crawl to set the mood.

One performance in particular touched me deeply, when we gathered to see *Othello* at an East End location whose set decor was composed of a pitch-black theatre with the only illumination being candles lighting the stage.

It awoke what I tried to damper when crossing the Atlantic, the struggle with the light and dark in my life. The use of a lone conga drum to direct the cadence of the play was the audible effect that mimicked the ebb and flow of emotion in the human condition being displayed on stage. An amazing interpretation of a play written hundreds of years ago, with a modern twist using light and sound, magnifying for me that not much has changed in how we humans act or, better yet, react when faced with the light and dark of life. I pushed these thoughts aside with new experiences. Anything new made the battle palatable.

I was absorbing culture like never before, recognizing I had been lucky to have an early childhood experience with culture and heritage. My culture went back a mere three or four hundred years or so, and here in my current neighborhood, there were houses older than that, domesticated by the same family one generation to the next. It was so eye-opening. I would never be the same.

In no time, I was off scouring the city, experiencing its delights and embracing its energy: the symphony, museums harnessing the goods when one happens to be on the right side of imperialism, museums showcasing the artifacts that propelled our world into industrialism, experimental performance art in the Thames warehouse district where audience participation was a must thrusting Kevin and I into the crowd hoisting a sledge hammer and beating a car to the pulsing rhythms of a punk band, and Jack the Ripper walking tours. I was game for any new experience I could get my teeth around. I couldn't get enough and London was up to the task. I was in new experience heaven and my circus was on fire!

The unique sociological cauldron stewing in London and its immediate countryside was molding my thoughts: hanging out at Speaker's Corner in Hyde Park watching and learning how people with varying thoughts and ideas struggled to voice their concerns, long afternoons wandering the Tate gallery, Trafalgar Square, England versus Ireland World Cup qualifying football match on the pitch at old Wembley, Piccadilly Circus, Covent Garden and the British History Museum with its amazing collection of Egyptian mummies, artifacts, treasures and let's not forget, the Rosetta Stone. Weekend trips to Canterbury Cathedral, St. James Palace, Stonehenge, Dover Cliffs, Cambridge, and the Welsh countryside were proving to be voluminous to my tent, as some rearranging and cataloging was now necessary. I was graced enough to see the Royal Shakespeare theatre company perform several times, which included the first running of *Les Miserables*.

All this culture and life was amazing and more than enough to fill a waiting tent dripping with desire to be nourished, but something was missing. My old friend needed some attention. Needed some love. I found myself reaching out, calling out to the dark in me to make the amazing time I was having even better. No net needed now, and with our rooftop dance complete, Gregg and Kevin were ideal. Music would unlock the chains.

The music scene was amazing as Gregg, Kevin, and I rummaged daily through various rags, looking for the next show to see, hoping to quench a desire to absorb music not replicated elsewhere. We used the Tube as our primary mode of transportation to get us to the venue du jour, which meant late night shows throughout the city.

A favorite venue would be the 100 Club in Covent Garden to catch punk bands, with a memorable headliner being Peter and the Test Tube Babies. It was my first live punk performance in this cavernous underground club, consisting of creepy little rooms spindling off from the main room, with a bar in each corner lighted enough to barely make out the person right next to you. A sighting of Mick sipping a pint was customary.

The highlight of the evening was being frisked to get into the club and the encore song sung by the babies titled, "Rocky's Got Aids," for the newly outed Mr. Hudson. The chorus and the hook were one and the same, as the band repeated over and over, "Rocky's got AIDS, AIDS, AIDS, Rocky's got AIDS." With the crowd thrusting its momentum toward the stage while simultaneously thrashing into one another with elbows and fists roaring with approval. I found myself getting wrapped up in the frenzy, with an elbow here and a push there, noticing something strange starting to occur that I had not seen before.

As the zealous fans were spilling the blood as a sign of their own expression, I noticed one, then two, and before I knew it, a hundred people spitting in the direction of the band as they screeched their instruments to their limit with passion. The band was not turning from the spitting, but rather leaning into the crowd, until I could see human bile dripping from their faces. Apparently, spitting was a high form of flattery in the London punk scene in the early eighties, and it was smashing. I love spitting!

With a night full of new experiences, it would be our journey back to our flat that massaged our fondness with the unknown, since by now, our musical adventures had lasted into the early morning hours. It was our dependence upon the Tube that navigated us beneath London's topography during the day that was now closed for the evening, when it shuttered at midnight, positioning the three of us trying to find our balance and direction on a single high wire masked as concrete, cobblestones, and blacktop beneath our feet. The now-unfamiliar cityscape was our new playground as we stumbled around in the dark for hours, trying to notice a familiar street name or building to guide us home.

Three teenage Americans rummaging around the streets, mesmerized at the life-sized posters posted around the city announcing a band's new album or the most recent Hollywood release. We were in no hurry to get home and could have easily accessed the bus system if needed, but we relished in being lost and finding new ways to navigate our way home, while at the same time scraping off the sides of buildings posters for our intended archives. Gregg would find a gem as I hoisted him on my shoulders for what seemed like an eternity as he methodically removed, inch by inch, a full poster of the album cover of the Clash's *London Calling*. We would repeat these shenanigans several times a week; as the music and booze flowed, so did our ability to not care if and when we got to our flat. We found home with each other on those long nights wandering around London. Our time was magical, even when sequestered in our flat.

The flat consisted of four bedrooms, one extremely long hallway linking all the rooms with a bathroom at one end and a shared living room at another, with a tiny shotgun kitchen bisecting the length of the flat. The living room was a gathering spot, as we stored the empty cans of the varied beers consumed above the ledge of the bay windows that faced The Victoria and Albert. The room had a table, chairs, small sofa, and a faux fireplace with a heating element attached that we could ignite to provide some heat when needed. In this space, for the rest of the building's occupants, we would perform a play about the first Thanksgiving, written by Kevin, with a part for each one of our roommates. I played the Turkey nibbling at Kevin's ankles.

We had fun living together, without too much drama, when a unifying cry of a boob alert had all the roommates scurrying to any window to sneak a peek at our neighbor across the way, who loved undressing in front of her window. The slow, methodical striptease taking place several times a day was a bit too much to handle for a bunch of undersexed teenagers. With a high-pitched scream announcing the show had begun, a stampede to get to the lone pair of theatre binoculars for a close-up view of our vixen was a prize worth risking leg and limb. It would take several months before Kevin and I, unbeknownst to our other roommates, consumed enough liquid courage one evening to make our way over to her flat to make an introduction. Virginia was her name, and Australian was her accent as she invited the two of us up to her room to chat.

It would be one of those lessons in life not realized until you literally place yourself in someone else's shoes, and since we were so intent on our own view across the street, we were missing the bigger picture. This one-way mirror lens skews the bigger landscape, narrowing the possibilities that can be experienced. We saw what we wanted to see, but the beauty of the other side of the coin wasn't revealed until we were able to see from her vantage point.

It so happened that when we gazed across the street to see what Virginia had been looking at the whole time, it was a very different view with identical intent. Virginia's flat was positioned directly in front of our loo, and she had a bird's eye view of our shower and what went on in that scrubbing environment when one tried to relieve the built up sexual tension through self-pollinating. All along, the voyeur was being watched, with neither party privy until now. A beautiful lesson when we allow all the angles of a situation to be viewed before deciding on the final analysis, providing twenty-twenty vision to the heart of the matter. Refreshing.

With the semester halfway over, Gregg, Kevin, Goose, and I decided to travel as a pack across the channel to take in the sights and varied cultures the continent had to offer. We would take the all-night train from Calais to Basel, with our first destination being Zurich. The trip was christened the Pastry Tour, with a photo op on Lake Geneva to freeze the moment in time. We would make our way to Milan, followed by a harrowing two in the morning cab ride to a hostel from the train station. Up early the next morning on a train south, and then east to Pisa, with a final destination of Florence for several nights. We would find refuge in a monastery at night, and in the day, we would soak up what this wonderful city had to offer.

The food, David, The Duomo, gelato, the countryside, and some of the most amazing street artists who would use colored chalk to replicate some of art's most famous scenes in great detail on the sidewalks. *The Last Supper, Mona Lisa,* and Dante's *Inferno* would rise from the gray pigment of concrete to a three dimensional masterpiece that would be washed away by the next morning. A wild night with some crazy Canadians in the monastery that had a curfew and nighttime noise restrictions would shorten our stay.

Back on the train for a quick ride up the coast, with stops in Naples, Nice, and Cannes, with an overnight in Monte Carlo, followed by a day of rest, long overdue to sun-starved white kids looking for some beach time. An unwelcoming cold Mediterranean framed by rock beaches had us rising early the next morning in search of sandy beaches farther west, with Spain the intended destination.

A standing-room-only train quickly doused our thoughts of sand and warm water as it rumbled along the coast of France through the night, testing our will to go any farther. Our ride eventually came to a halt in the town of Port Bou, straddling the French/Spanish border, allowing some weary legs to get a little stability under them with a little food in our famished bodies. A short dance on the tracks to Barcelona, where some amazing tapas and let's not forget the national dish and my favorite breakfast food, pig, filled our bellies as we washed it all down with delicious red wine. With the nourishment of our bodies and bellies handled, we were now off to see some Gaudi filling our imagination and souls. Back on the train again, through central France, with a day of sightseeing in Paris, and then back to London to resume school.

It was an amazing week of travel, hastily done with way too much train time to fully grasp the essence of any one particular place. A lesson carried forward in life: only with time and a slower pace could one truly develop an understanding of a culture and destination.

Oh, I guess I should explain the Pastry Tour. Kevin was coming up with all types of goofy pranks and skits for us to perform throughout our four-month stay, and he suggested we make our fall break a memory for a lifetime by partaking in pastries in every country and town that we found ourselves passing through.

We dabbled in amazing chocolate éclairs in Switzerland, canolis and fruit-filled tarts in Italy, custard and whipped crème-filled flaky buttery croissants in France, and powdered cookies in Spain. No matter where we were, Kevin was white boy rapping, as I break danced on every railway station floor, finding time to do a little pastry shopping before we moved on to the next destination.

We were butter in Kevin's hands, as his imagination was broad and odd, only needing some willing participants to carry out the first thought that came to his mind, and I was always willing for anything new to experience. A match made in heaven, or could be a place a little darker with no limits or barriers. I was only hoping.

The experience of traveling as a pack gratefully was in the past, as Kevin and I quickly set our compass on a fairly well-known playground for adults across the channel and north of Belgium. Gregg was beating to his own drum at the moment and opted to spend a long weekend in Russia, with a chance of exercising his own shadow material by himself. With a short school week that began on Monday and ended early Thursday, we could plan out an early afternoon train ride to Dover, a connecting hydrofoil boat ride across the channel to Oostende, with a final destination by train to Amsterdam.

Physically, our outward appearance was interestingly similar as far as our hairstyle went, and for me personally, a constant back and forth from long hair to short hair. Kevin had thick blond hair pulled back in a ponytail, and by this time, my Indian heritage was serving me well, with long locks past my shoulders. I was never the ponytail type of cat, rather allowing it to fall in my face with a tuck behind the ears to allow for peripheral vision.

We would set out on this four-day excursion with the clothes on our back and black trench coats to keep us warm from the elements. With high anticipation welling in our souls of being able to stretch our limits in this oasis where nothing was taboo, the train's wheels screeching to a muted halt when we arrived in this city's gargantuan train station.

With multiple pints of Stella Artois in our bellies while en route, we set out to find a place to roost for the evening, intending to spend as little time as possible sleeping, while enacting one thought to the next with rest assured when we returned to London. We canvassed the hostels in the city centre, and they were full for the weekend. We were not lugging around backpacks, so we didn't necessarily look like students, just a couple of sketchy long-haired cats looking for some new experiences.

Somehow, we lost interest in finding cover for the evening as hunger, frosty Heinekens, and a coffee bar with mind-altering smoke that happened to be our first thought before we left London some six hours ago was being exercised liberally. We would walk miles up and down the canals to various bars and coffee shops, smoking and swilling to our heart's content, and when not lounging in an establishment, we would peruse the red-light district, gawking at the items for sale. Sex was the intent. It consumed my entire being. It always had. This was fun!

Every imaginable size, shape, race, and nationality was represented behind the red shimmering light that silhouetted the windows on this now cold and wet night. We should have been cold and probably were wet, but we did not feel a thing as our desires had us ducking in and out of tiny streets and over bridges to indulge in as much as possible. Large women, ones with whips and chains, oriental persuasion, African beauties, and one who was so skinny, it was grotesque. At the moment, I didn't understand the significance of this display, nor did I understand true beauty is in the eye of the beholder and this sex mecca was an honest interpretation of that fact. If you could dream it up, it was available.

We would roam from one establishment to another, drinking, smoking, resting, and eating, and when en route to another den of indulgence, we would try to pick out the girl we would pay for our evening's dessert. It was our first time purchasing sex, and we were scared and excited at the exact same time, lengthening the time it took to find the right one for this momentous occasion.

With hours of imbibing under our belts by now and the available lighted windows starting to dwindle, we decided upon a tactic that provided safety in our minds and fantasy in our loins, with a stunning blonde and brunette sharing the same red-hued window. We would go in together and give each other moral support, hoping this long-awaited fantasy would be better in reality. They were fun, cute, and easy to talk to and, I presume, sensed our uneasiness and suggested we all hop in the bed together and have some fun. With a quick glance and giggle, Kevin and I commenced to take off our clothes and hop in the sack with these two vixens, with laughter and protection high priority.

The assumption one can make is the quicker the escapade, the higher the profit margin for the ladies, and let's just say a query about how much hashish we smoked before we arrived threw a wrench in their business model. This was serious business and a long-awaited fantasy that took way too long to make into reality.

Inexperienced with very few moves, we were being directed by our hosts on what to do next until the moment when we both glanced up and over at each other and started to laugh uncontrollably. We were naked with huge piles of clothes at the foot of the bed and two beautiful professionals, and all we could do was laugh at each other. I love Kevin and I love to laugh with him, and this love for life and the light that we both brought to the darker edges of life is what would bind us together forever.

To the relief of our hosts and their now-weakened profit margins, our business had been consummated, and all that was left was to sort through the pile of clothes and reassemble our outfits, and with a customary European double kiss to the cheeks, we said *adieu* to our first encounter with the famed ladies of the red-light district in Amsterdam.

Our lovely vixens asked us where we would be sleeping for the evening, since it was way past the check-in time for the hostel, and it dawned on us that we forgot to secure a nest for the evening. They suggested a friend's small hotel down the street that had a peep show and red-lighted windows on the ground floor, with a few rooms for rent by the night above. We had so much laughter together that these two gals went out of their way to call ahead and secure the room for us, as by now, we were running on fumes and needed a place to rest till dawn, when the bars would reopen and the indulgence could resume.

We didn't sleep that night. We rested, took separate baths, and laughed about what had occurred only hours before. But it was not what had happened that connected Kevin and me, but rather, it was what we could be doing next — the next thought that must be delivered into reality.

Over the next three days, a lot of the previous night's navigation would be repeated, with one small minor detail, and that would be the decision to purchase a block of blond Afghani hashish to take back to London to share and sell to our American comrades. With four full days and nights composed of the greatest fun tickets on the planet as far as we were concerned and little, if any, sleep, we started on our journey back to London, retracing our steps with a calculated arrival back to our flat around midnight if we could catch the last train out of Dover to London.

It was our first time carrying illegal contraband across international borders, and for some reason, the benefits heavily outweighed the consequences, if in fact that thought had come to mind. Our timing was precise, as we were able to catch the last hydrofoil across the channel to Dover, with an hour in between our arrival and the departure of the last train to London for the evening. I guess the four days of frivolity caught up with us, as we both fell asleep on the boat ride across the famed channel, with an awakening of the boat docking to eventually pass through customs to declare any goods.

Jointly, we made the decision to go to the bottom of the boat, where the vehicles were stored, and depart the boat from that exit, hoping we could scoot past customs and get to the train station for the hour ride home. Our plan seemed to be proceeding nicely until we departed the boat, and in the distance was a van idling to pick up any passengers on foot to take them back to the customs entry. The only drawback now was we were deposited to the back of the line at customs, possibly closing the gap on our ability to catch the train back to London as we had anticipated. Our rear exit strategy would backfire, making it through customs but missing our connection to London. The next departure time wasn't until six a.m.

A seemingly harmless decision to spend the night catching some shut-eye in the nooks and crannies of the train station could have been a death-blow to our freedom if I had not acted on a funny feeling churning in my gut. I would act not on reason, but pure gut alone, stashing the contraband outside the building while we rested not but fifteen meters away. I could keep an eye on the goods while at the same time resting. While drifting off to a light sleep, I was awakened by Kevin asking if I wanted some tea or a biscuit. I opted for the tea and waited for his return before fully engaging in rest, when out of nowhere, a customs agent approached me and asked to see my passport and wanted to know where my friend went.

Over the next sixty minutes, I was questioned about our travel, where we lived in London, why we were in the train station, and would I consent to a search. I answered all the questions and was searched, with nothing to be found. The customs agents had waited for us to separate and unknowingly had us under surveillance since we'd stepped off the boat, trying to bypass customs. At the same time I was being questioned, Kevin was undergoing a barrage, as they were hoping that a chink in our armor would be revealed if they caught us off guard.

The sun would be rising soon, and before we embarked on the train ride back to London, I quickly dashed outside and retrieved our package, since that initial thought would not be completed into action if I had left it in the bushes. A subtle yet critical moment in the building of my circus, furthering my will to get what it wanted and keep what it had, regardless of the consequences. I was now without fear. Troubling.

Another opportunity missed for personal growth, as somehow reasoning I was the active ingredient in allowing for our freedom to proceed. Altogether forgetting something else was calling out to me, reaching out to me to guide me through and past my own will.

My will was strong, and this weekend experience with Kevin would prove that chaining the dark in me to the basement of my life was not necessary, since no harm was done and no consequences were realized. It was time to move past this life-changing experience and move beyond this stage of formal education so I could make the impact I felt inside of me so long ago.

I was on the edge and it was sharp. Just the way I like it. The last twenty years have been fruitful and at times trying, but I was in full control with a bevy of performers to call upon when needed. I was ready to carve my path in this world, just not sure of the nature of the nutrients I would need to sustain my circus along the way. What I did know was that I needed no one to make life happen one thought to the next.

The wheels were in motion, and even if I tried, I couldn't stop the momentum I had built up to get what I wanted and keep what I had.

I was in trouble. The wheels of my circus caravan were starting to unravel, and I knew it! I was no longer in control, with the illusion of being under its comfort.

12
CHANGE NOT NECESSARY BUT DESIRED

I had nine months of sobriety under my belt, and I was finished with my fourth step—except for one small section that kept creeping up on me at the oddest of times. Joseph was getting ready to move at the end of July and had been asking me if I was ready to do the fifth step. I mentioned my unfinished section. It was my sexual inventory uncovering that had become the thorn in my paw, as I thought I had completed it with full measure when lo and behold I would be riding my bike, eating, or swimming in the ocean when a person and event would instantly reappear out of the chasm of my mind and I would have to add them to the list. The list was moderate in length, but what bothered me was I had forgotten these people I shared intimacy with and they were now being revealed through this new clarity I was experiencing.

This act of self-honesty was slowly allowing me to recognize my role in all my relationships without regard to their length. I discussed this with Joseph, and he suggested I write an entry to those I could not remember at this time, but more importantly to see the repetition in my behavior and how I could actively learn from my past. I wanted to be as thorough as possible and this tactic seemed to get to the heart of the matter, so I quickly dashed home and finished the entry, hoping the next step, *numero cinco*, would be a little easier.

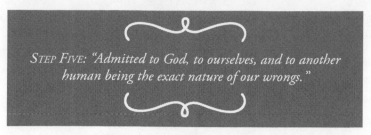

Step Five: "Admitted to God, to ourselves, and to another human being the exact nature of our wrongs."

With the continual chipping away at my ego and pride over the last nine months, I was finally ready to sit in front of Joseph and reveal to him verbatim what I had been mulling over and extracting from my memory, which was now in writing and for the first time in my life an honest rendition of my past. The opportunities to abort this current mission of changing everything in my life over the past nine months had been numerous, and with the tilling of my past via my fourth step now in my rear view mirror, I was ready to share the uncovered truth with another human being.

So many things had changed over the last nine months, but the most striking change had been my ability to share my feelings in a room that at first was composed of total strangers and now had been transformed into a room of friends. It hadn't been easy to share when in front of total strangers, and it had become even more difficult when these people became my friends—now I had developed relationships and truly cared for them. What I feared was my reptilian ability to freeze out feelings when feeling vulnerable with another human being, limiting the ability to have real intimacy and connection—a connection I wanted and needed so desperately if everything was going to change, but in the past I cut out before it became too real.

I was flying solo now, without the circus to fall back on, and this instilled in me a feeling, not a fact, of surely being on shaky ground. It's a common human experience when we are trying to mold the perception of others rather than letting it rip and finally being genuine with what lies within. But at that moment I was blessed and relieved that I would only have to share this stuff with one other human being, and Joseph would be my litmus test to see if this life of honesty could actually be a foundation to build upon or rather another jumping off point to a future directed by my will alone. Another turning point was in my sights. Life is full of them, with most occurring daily, hourly, breath-to-breath.

The setting was quite different and less sterile than when we had met several months ago to start my fourth step. For step five, we met in his backyard, sitting around an outdoor glass table under the brilliant blue sky with the hint of salt from the ocean wafting through the air. It was a quiet morning that first day, as if a memo went out to the entire yard maintenance crews buzzing the neighborhoods that some important business was being conducted outside and serenity and peace was desperately needed. I heard this once at a meeting:

Heaven grows quiet when a person sets out on the path to restore their soul, spiritual condition and dignity...The path leading them toward whom they really are...Larry.

The hope of heaven being a happy place full of conversation, laughter, and exuberance would suddenly come to an abrupt halt, recognizing this sacred event in a human's life demanding quiet and full attention. I needed it. Heaven sounds fun. Living like that in the human flesh, more fun.

Surrounded by grass, bougainvillea, an unusual dwarf palm tree, bird of paradise plants, trumpet lilies, and Joseph's calm demeanor, I was ready to see if this bloodletting would be a source of separation from my past, an understanding of my part in those experiences, and a chance at healing so I could move forward in life like so many before me experienced by doing the steps. I was purely relying on someone else's experience as I walked through the gate to sit with Joseph in early July, hoping all this exhaustive and torturous uncovering when implementing full measure and bone marrow tapping honesty could possibly shed some light on my perceived dark and unknown future that was previously only lit before by manipulation and control.

I was still holding on tightly to my former paradigm for living life, reserving the right to return to my old life if this honesty stuff became too real for my palette. Creating and reserving for me the space to return to fantasy and delusion and my beloved seasoned cast of performers dwelling within my tent, to implement one amazing thought after another was the backbone I needed to press forward. In all reality, I had no faith this step stuff would work—I was doing what I was told to do—and with a gargantuan dose of grace, I was walking through the experience with honesty, hoping sustainable change was at the end of this weary trail. I guess I wanted change, but I was unsure of how much change in fact I wanted, or better yet needed.

We started at the top and slowly worked through the questions Joseph posed only months before, which now felt like forever ago, and the answers I painstakingly mulled over and now put in ink. I hesitated to read what I had scribbled down for fear of being judged or, the worst-case scenario in my mind, of exposing my human flesh that had been protected by the armor of my circus since my first memory.

The circus I created was the insulation from the dream life that tortured me at a young age. This served me well, and over time it morphed into a desire to overindulge in any experience. Unknowingly, this process blossomed into the barrier that hampered any possibility of having any relationship with another human being, including God, into adulthood. Bottom line—I didn't want anybody to know who I really was and I didn't want to know who I really was either. It was too much to deal with, I reasoned, and without the insight of reflection, it worked well enough.

This was virgin territory for me, exposing who I really was out loud to another rather than the ping-pong banter within my own mind when questioning my navigation settings. It was an atrophied muscle never exercised, so you can understand my resistance to relinquish the grip on how I orchestrated my life since birth. It was miracle time, and I was hoping something was going to happen before we got too far along with me self-editing verbally what I had written down, knowing full well it would be impossible for me to push the restart button on this process again. I didn't have it in me.

I was only going to give this step stuff one shot with full measure. I hadn't even started the fifth step and the pull from my old tracks in life were steering me back to me again. I was desperate and needed something to kick me off the tracks of safety and comfort…my way. I was looking for a Hail Mary, a last second shot to win the game, a double-breaking downhill putt from twenty feet, some fireworks—anything to enhance the show, because that is what the circus served when things became uncertain in life.

I truly believed I was the miracle maker and only included the assistance of others—and when absolutely necessary God—when the odds of pulling something off were deemed too far-fetched, and even then I trudged alone. A loner in every sense was an illusion in and of itself. I was surrounded with love the whole time. I chose isolation. It was an illusion of safety. Clinging.

Luckily, before I could start self-editing, Joseph interrupted my stuttering and suggested we pray before we proceeded any further. It was perfect and exactly what we both needed at the time. It was an opportunity to stop, pause, and ask for guidance and direction; This was not our customary mode of operation. To stop and ask for guidance from God, whom I believed in but never really trusted implicitly (especially since I had this well-tuned reason to rely upon), was strange but at the moment oddly comforting. Maybe I could trust? In the past, my reason wouldn't let me. My reason was sovereign. I was God.

We spent the next four days, three hours at a time, going over in detail each answer and my part in the creation of who I had become. I had no one to blame for what became of me since exiting my mother's womb. I was comforted with the realization I alone had created this life of smoke and mirrors, surrendering to the idea of total responsibility for what had occurred, and more importantly, I could actually use these experiences to help myself going forward and when needed, to help others.

All the promises Joseph shared with me several months back, which his sponsor had shared with him, were now looking plausible for me when only months earlier had seemed impossible. The jewel box of my life, a circus of one, which at one time seemed gluttonous, was overflowing with experiences I was grateful for and thoughtful for their potential use in the future when another was in need. The me, more and now didn't seem so important to my survival anymore but oddly would now be my treasure chest going forward in life. Interesting yet equally baffling.

Step five was complete, and Joseph was leaving town for new assignments and in my mind's eye the hard part was over, or was it? Challenges lie in wait.

I was back in New Mexico, finishing up my degrees in Political Science and Sociology with the goal of getting back to London as soon as I possibly could, but something was churning in my soul and I could not deny its presence.

When in my last month of residence in London, I had received a letter from my father, sharing with me his plans on getting remarried. It was full of emotion and honesty, wanting me to understand his desire to spend his life with another human being and more importantly not wanting to be alone anymore. I knew this feeling of being alone, and it gave me comfort, but something inside of me connected to his desire of not wanting to be alone even though I was perfecting this state of being in my own life. When reading his letter, I experienced that same feeling of being connected to this man when he hugged me in the parking lot at Creighton.

Could it be that we were connected in this "all alone" game that was self-inflicted? Maybe we were not strangers as I surmised by his lack of presence. Was it plausible I was seeing myself in a different form through my father as he perfected his alone paradigm for survival? Bottom line — I wanted to connect but didn't know how and was too afraid to ask for help or guidance on this vital life decision. Who could I ask? By my choices I had made sure there was no one to turn to.

The thought of making a choice that went against the grain of me, more and now was on the table. Unfortunately, this decision propelled me toward uncharted territory that would eventually have me leaning into the dark to seek comfort when the light became disappointing. The light experiences in life, whether perceived or real, do not always provide a feeling of happiness. Nothing is simple. Being human is complex.

It was his honesty that I had not experienced from another human being, let alone my father who was a stranger in the details of his life, finding myself drawn to a connection that was unknown to me. I wanted more of this, but how could I get what I wanted and connect with a man whose life was centered on his business? He was there, financially, but all the rest seemed like he was unsure of what to do with all these kids he fathered. I didn't know his story. What was his life like when growing up so I was unsure of his own intent? Had he known what to do? Had he ever had a role model? Did he make other choices that didn't include his children?

I wanted to know more about this man and was drawn to the idea if I could help him out and get to know him better, all these questions would be answered, putting to rest this desire to connect — then I could resume my plan of going back to London and making the impact indwelled in my being since inception. I successfully orchestrated four schools in five years and graduated with two degrees and it wouldn't hurt if I delayed implementing my next thought while I connected to this man and repaid him for what he had done for me. The funny thing is I was unsure what he had done for me and not sure why I felt like I needed to repay him — other than the money thing. It wasn't about the money; it was about connecting in a meaningful way with another human being that happened to be my father and a complete stranger. Do you smell paradox again?

My beeline through higher education had been circumvented with stops and starts and some serious regional, national, and then international navigation. I was able to piece together in my short stays some highly valued and unique performers for my tent that couldn't be possible any other way if I had not aborted one mission after another. I wanted deeply to connect to the friends I had met in each locale, but that desire was trumped by my internal compass of getting what I wanted and keeping what I had, driven by a self-will centered on survival. Each decision was critical to my survival.

My will was strong, and I excelled in this higher education game; with a few more years of graduate work under my belt, the culmination of the thought at the age of fifteen would be at hand. The decision to change course was made without hesitation, delaying additional schooling for the moment to wrestle with this desire to connect with this stranger. I had never before in my life, up to this point, put aside my desires for something I didn't understand and could not control, but the draw to find the essence of this feeling could not be brushed aside, at least not at that moment.

Now the booze and occasional recreational drugs I was partaking in during the past four years were typical for a college student and in line with my desires to complete my degrees and kick forward, not kick back, into the next phase of my life. Kicking forward was a phrase Uncle Rude Dog would use when he was faced with a turning point in life and the initial mindset he created to push him toward his next thought. This short but sweet phrase allowed me the space in my mind to not wrestle with my conscious understanding of the role alcohol played in my life and its unmanageability upon first swill and to simply move forward. Internally, I knew I could not control the elixir, but at the time, my will was strong and my desire not to fail had overcome, for the time being, this dark corner of my being.

I realigned my compass and settled in on the second floor of my father's corporate headquarters, crunching numbers with his bookkeeper, Hank. I was a fish out of water, making it difficult to navigate to safety. I was relying on another to make me feel safe. The darkness was closing in.

How in the hell had my father amassed such material wealth with an admittedly precarious educational background cemented by the fact he was pushed out of high school with diploma in hand rather than graduating from this institution by deeds? Suffering from dyslexia not diagnosed until later in life, he had been driven by an early childhood memory, propelling him to excel at any cost, whether it was his own health at risk or the family he drew from his loins. A childhood memory willfully sequestered in the gallows of his being unshared with anyone was the guiding force behind his single-mindedness, leaving no option to the choices he had to make if survival was possible.

My father, Phillip, moved from Fayetteville, Tennessee, with his younger sister Evelyn. The move was conducted while his youngest sister, Kathy, was still in his mother's womb. Mother Kathleen harbored a stoic nature, but underneath was composed of love and kindness. The icon of this side of my DNA was my grandfather Ralph, who moved his family to New Mexico in the late forties due to a heath emergency. My Papa suffered from tuberculosis, and this relocation was a last ditch effort to save his life, tearing his family from its roots with a final destination to the high dry desert climate of Albuquerque to possibly squeak out a little more quality time on this earth.

Arriving with one half of a half lung, he was quickly admitted to the local hospital with a prognosis confirming his family's worst fears: six months to live. Even though my Papa would live another thirty-three years, a miracle in and of itself, his health would be precarious at best with an oxygen tank in tow wherever he went. Compounding this was a weakened heart working overtime to move his blood around his ailing vessel, straining to pump blood between shallow breaths to extract as much oxygen from his depleted delivery system.

It was no coincidence the same heart that worked so tirelessly to keep him going and on occasion would fail him, would be the organ that changed countless lives directly and indirectly. He knew life was precious, and he consciously lived it one breath to the next, stretching the modern call of living in the moment to the extreme. He had no choice physically, but he did have a vigor and vim for life, choosing not to wallow in his plight but rather commanding fun no matter the situation, perfecting the tightrope walk sans net decades before I was born. I was not alone. We never are.

He loved his grandchildren, horses, cornbread dipped in buttermilk, cold pork-n-beans in a can, catfish, ice cream, butterscotch candy, feeding ducks, cigars, gambling, baseball, Cadillacs, whiskey, and the scent of a beautiful woman. He was vaudevillian in nature without a formal stage, as he moved about his day from one place to another, entertaining family, friends, and the potential clients he came across, allowing him the opportunity to sustain his family and the dark areas of his life.

He would make a lifelong friend in the sanatorium: Esquire William Marchiando, whose mercantile family resided in the northern part of the state with a lineage going back hundreds of years. This dynamic duo was always angling for the next experience, using their skills of language and generosity to maneuver around the state, selling watches and Bibles to get them to the next town where whiskey, women, and a card game proved to be the real moneymakers and the intent all along. He loved people so much, and with his new lease on life, that even though he had the gift of turning fun into material fortune he never, ever forgot about those in need, especially the children, and unfortunately at times at the expense of his own family. Sometimes the light has shadow areas.

One of Papa's partners in crime was a true vaudevillian, or rather should I say, the brains behind the performers orchestrating the shows entertaining the small cities around the southwest. His name was Mike London, the promoter for a traveling show that today would be the low budget equivalent of the WWF. It was championship wrestling and the kind Boolettuce loved so much.

At the time, New Mexico was a large state in acreage with a relatively small population, so it was only a matter of time until Mike and Papa would join forces at the bar and card table for some well-timed banter and revenue sharing. Multiple-day gambling parties at local hotels filled with cash, booze, women, and plenty of trash-talking built a bond between these two men, one only possible if you're telling your story without filters. They moved past the formalities of what they had in common, fun, moving effortlessly to the heart of the matter a shared desire to help children in need.

An unknown shared life experience that molded their own lives was the mortar to a yearly event they practiced without ulterior motives. Papa and Mike would pool together all their funds/winnings, and every Christmas Eve after all the five and dimes had closed, they would be granted special access to buy up all the remaining toys at a discount until their money was exhausted. Hoisting the toys into multiple vehicles, they would spend the rest of the evening delivering gifts to the kids that otherwise would have gone without Christmas if not for all that gambling, boozing, and womanizing.

This blurring of the lines between the perceived dark and light of life was not a conscious decision, and could it be they were in their own battle of navigating the light and dark of life? I find it interesting, the insistence no one knew where the gifts originated from, and more secretive, the true origination of this idea. They were giving because they could, and recognition was not necessary, and maybe—just maybe—that allowed for their own show to go on…the show must go on!

Now Papa and my father dabbled in various business enterprises with an emphasis on door-to-door furniture, appliances, and cotton carpet sales in the early fifties. My grandfather was a marketing genius, and on occasion he would have to stretch his innate abilities when a deal would have to be rerouted to achieve financial success.

With a knack of convincing others an idea was grand, he would garner a truckload of new appliances on credit with a marketing slogan to create demand on slightly damaged appliances. In reality there was no bargain, and there were no damaged appliances, but magically now a demand was at hand. And this is where he had to reroute because customers were sending back the appliances, concerned they would be charged for undamaged goods. Papa solved this dilemma with a ball-peen hammer and a little elbow grease and with a few whacks to the appliance he sent it back out for delivery with another satisfied customer in the fold.

My father trumped Papa's gamble by financing a truck load of carpet he turned into a money making machine, one customer at a time, housed in a former plant nursery, growing the business into a multi-state operation that serviced the movie studios in Los Angeles, to the military bases in El Paso, Texas, and everything in between.

With a large presence physically and energy-wise, Papa filled any space no matter its size, always finding communion with others as he relished in building relationships lasting well past his departure from this earth. Papa was magical with people but at the expense sometimes with those he was closest to in blood evidenced by a deep cavernous rift with my father.

This rift was compounded by a constant inability to communicate in a safe, honest way, culminating in a handwritten letter from my father to Papa, delivered by my brother Juno to Papa's casket, which was incapable of holding his enormous character. A truly tragic moment in my father's life when the words he so desperately wanted to share all along with his father got mixed up in the will of his own first memory. A memory that until recently would not be shared with anyone, becoming the yoke he would be tethered to for the rest of his life.

It was when my father was nine years old and his family newly arrived in Albuquerque with no relatives or friends or community structure to fall back on that would be the backdrops to his first memory. Papa was in grave health in the hospital, and with little or no financial resources to bridge the gap my father hunkered down with his family in a garage across from the hospital to find refuge from the streets and the cold high desert nights.

As my father huddled with his sister and mother on a concrete floor, all sharing one blanket, he vowed to himself in the silence of the shivering cold that he and his family would never, ever be poor. A vow that to this very day has him rising at the break of dawn to hustle to work, even if no one else is around, finding refuge in the thought that if he is making it happen, he will never be poor. A common occurrence in the human condition: strangling the ability to achieve balance in one's life unless drastic measures are embraced.

The inability of these two polar opposites to communicate was centered on a life experience that moved them further apart even though they were blood. Papa sought joy and communion out of everything in life, blossomed by simply having a second chance. It was a yoke he willfully collared, giving what he had to others no matter what. My father would be driven to succeed materially, not for the sake of it, but weighted by his fear of an early childhood memory that kept him single-minded, missing out on the moment-to-moment joys of life based on communion with others his father had mastered. Both wills were strong and equally intent on having their way, even at the expense of those they loved most.

I find it interesting that even though blood is a strong vein in the construction of our character, it's the experiences in life that move us deeply when choosing between blood and the heart of the matter. The individual experience must be honored and uncovered for honest communion with others. If not, the struggle to find common ground is futile. Tragic.

On the treadmill of work in my early twenties, I found myself stuck on the second floor, crunching numbers, tabulating gas taxes, and collecting money. It was not the experience I was expecting when I made the decision to reconnect with my father. He was busy orchestrating a business strewn across four states, and little did I realize at the time, even though he had up to a hundred employees it was a one-man show.

In a way, I guess you can say he was wearing the top hat to his own circus and there was not enough time or the skill sets on either of our parts to communicate in a way that might bridge the gap created so long ago. I was bored and unchallenged, and with graduate school at The London School of Economics at least a year or two away, I had to soothe the uneasiness residing in my own circus. I needed some me time, reasoning I had sacrificed me, more and now for the possibility of understanding what stirred in me and my desire to go at this life alone seemingly perfected by my father.

The work was a dead end for me, and I knew it on my first day, I just wasn't sure what to do next, and more importantly, not ready to give up on the connection I desired but was unable to understand its genesis. My intellect was sound, but it was the heart stuff baffling me every time I dabbled in its domain, and with no real life experience of reaching out for help to understand this dilemma, I retreated to the essence of what I knew best, what worked every time I became uneasy, my first thought. What had been missing over the last four years was the unabashed delving into the areas of my life I suppressed while climbing the higher education ladder, one fear of failure-ridden step after another. It was time to let my hair down and maybe make some friends while I simmered in the uneasiness of my inability to make a connection with my old man.

In my last semester of university, I had met an odd fellow named Mike who happened to be breaking up with his girlfriend and in need of a place to store some personal items while he took a thirty-six-hour bus ride down to the Yucatan peninsula for a month of rest, relations, and relaxation. Mike, collared with the nickname Spike and massaged into the moniker Stick by my brother Sparky, was milking every last cent of his student loans to find what vocation suited him best. With the gift of the gab christened by being the only son of a Midwest General Motors dealer, parlayed with a penchant for creating things with his mind exercised by his hands, he would lean into the artistic side of his being and create wonderful drawings, paintings, gargantuan steel sculptures, wood furniture with inlaid exotic wood species, and anything that had to do with the unusual.

I loved his free flowing "take it as it comes" attitude and the overall air that he breathed no matter how impossible a feat seemed to be, because Spike, Stick, Spear was not repositioned by fear. I was drawn to his creativity and spunk for life, hoping that this kid from Menasha, Wisconsin, would allow me to reach beyond myself to slowly make a genuine connection with another.

Upon his return, we decided to be roommates, sourcing my archives I reached out to my next-door neighbor whose domicile provided nourishment in the form of tanning young nubiles when I was seeking refuge from my dream life as a child. The Esquire Reggie through the years had developed a highly connected law practice with political roots that reached the governor's mansion in Santa Fe, providing him the resources to purchase The Eller Building in downtown Albuquerque.

It was the first two-story apartment building in the downtown area built in the 1920s that had modern amenities. The majority of the suites had been tweaked to accommodate law offices, but their layouts were unmistakably residential except for one untouched two-bedroom suite in the middle of the second floor — available for Spike and I to seek shelter. Wood floors, mosaic tiles, claw footed bathtub, push button light switches, and windows on a pulley system allowing them to fully recess into the sill. It was hip, it was cool, and at night essentially we were the only ones around with full freedom to exercise our desires.

It didn't take long to become efficient at work by day and considerably less time to be exuberant for whatever the night would reveal when work was done, exercising any form to alter the nauseating feeling churning inside my gut. I had made a crucial navigational error by returning to New Mexico, thereby delaying me, more and now. I didn't have any friends to speak of, so I decided to nudge my way into Mike's world and make his friends my own.

Jerry "cousin Gersano," an amazing artist and skilled craftsman from Albuquerque via New York; Steve, a funny quick witted fellow from Los Alamos, New Mexico; Kenny, a sculptor of steel and wood from Chicago; Scott, a printer and lithographer from Philadelphia; Mike, a deep-reasoning fun-loving lad born and raised in all places Albuquerque; and a soccer player from New York by way of Santa Fe named David — this would be the core of people I would surround myself over the next several years as I fully exercised the shadow area of my life. Sex, drugs, alcohol, and music would be the common denominator that moved us from one venue to the next no matter the day of the week. I would roam The Fat Bar, El Madrid, The Monte Vista Fire Station, and the historic El Rey Theatre for its revolving line up of local, regional, and national musical performances that conveniently happened to be only one block from our flat.

I loved the bohemian nature of my friends, Mike's friends, allowing me to tap into an area of my life I loved so much but had not known its existence until my experience in London. They were artists driven by a passion to create something out of nothing, and I loved how free they were from having to be something. It was as if the creation of a single piece was the intent not where it was going to take them and that felt right in my soul. I love music and I love the art world, and it warmed me inside to be on their side of the fence so to speak. I have no artistic skills and cannot carry a tune or play an instrument, but being close to them, almost living through them in a way, made me feel full. Unfortunately, a growing emptiness, not researched but present, in my gut constantly opposed this feeling. I was full and empty at the same time.

I found myself struggling to rekindle a character in my circus, allowing me the ability to commune with these cats. How could I navigate my way into their circus in a genuine, not contrived, meaningful way that enhanced the aura of not being attached to an outcome they seemed to thrive on when creating their pieces? I wanted to be a part of this cadre of free thinkers and as far as navigation was concerned the polar opposite of my single-thought-then-implementation mindset. If I could just connect with them in the meanwhile, until I navigated my way back to London it would make my decision to stick around seem worthwhile.

It was an unusual twist for me in my life, as I was trying for the very first time to create a space for myself in a group. How could I fit or did I fit? The circus loved this new challenge of being in a group with no intent of controlling the outcome, which seemed to be the foundation of the group, verbalized or not. If I wanted to be connected to another or in this instance a group, I had to exercise a new muscle, and my fear of joining had to give way to the possibility of altering my ability to have unlimited experiences. I was game, needing to reposition myself over the next eighteen months, and if I couldn't connect with my old man I wanted to connect to something and these cats were fun and new to my circus.

I was well-seasoned in the shadow areas of life, and with minimal investigation it was apparent this parallel circus, without an identified wearer of the top hat, relished in mind-altering substances to enhance their craft as I did when wanting to enhance the extraordinary. It might be the chink in the armor of their circus, allowing me to nuzzle my way deeper into their world like I did as a kid at the dinner table of my unsuspecting neighborhood patrons. I was trying to find a niche in this new environment, so with a simple checking of the boxes I reasoned with a steady job I had the necessary cash flow to keep the frivolity in session around the clock if needed, since most were stretched financially as most are in college. I could use the disappointment of not connecting to my old man and the monotonous crunching of the numbers by day to enhancing the environment for as many as possible at night.

Never really caring about money and for all intents and purposes not having much to share but more than those who surrounded me, allowed me to be more than willing to keep the fun going because I needed to change the way I was feeling about being in New Mexico and working for my father. As quickly as those feelings of disappointment arose in my consciousness, I summoned the vascular surgeon to cut away the pain by immersing myself in making sure the fun never stopped.

It wasn't like I didn't know how to have fun or that I needed to buy my way into this circle it was simple. My friends and I liked changing the way we were feeling and they had their reasons for imbibing in the edges of life, not just chemically but artistically, and in this we connected in a strange way. The relationships were symbiotic, and let's not lose sight of the undeniable fact that I was in complete control of my circus while performing in theirs.

Now this vigor for sharing the wealth was not a strong vein in my DNA except for my Papa of course, and I didn't see the point in keeping it all when my experience in life back to my childhood dream life had set in stone the concept that life is fleeting, so I might as well enjoy it with as many as possible before the show was over. IRAs, savings accounts, investments, stocks, and simply putting some money away was fruitless for someone with an embedded feeling that living past another single day was a crapshoot.

On several occasions I would be convinced to participate in some type of modern day retirement fund that would provide at the end of forty years of savings a tidy nest egg, but that too would be short sheeted, as I cashed in those attempts as tools for survival, not luxury as positioned by the fancy-pants kids on Wall Street. I was settling in for unabashed fun, hoping at the end of this interlude I would be able to have some relationships rather than constantly filling my own till, finding that type of gardening now boring. How things change, slowly.

Our flat was ideal for all night parties, with our own private parking lot and a front and rear stairwell leading directly to our abode. Ralph-David would move into a one bedroom that shared a common wall, proving to be useful when it was time to keep the fun in play. I would purchase multiple kegs, and we would store the untapped ones in his bathtub until the tapped keg was floated, setting Gersano in to motion as he commandeered a hat to solicit funds for the next keg sitting next door bathing in a tub of ice. Several of us would walk down the back stairwell and up the next stairwell to Ralph-David's flat to hang out for a while, creating the illusion of having to go purchase another keg, eventually wrestling it down the stairwell and back up our stairwell to a thirsty crowd.

Without interruption our cassette geared sound system bumped to the beats of Cameo, Edie Brickell, REM, Terence Trent Darby, Peter Gabriel, Dire Straits, Van Morrison, Elvis Costello, and The Brothers Johnson all while the keg samba played into the wee hours of the morning or someone detonated a pipe bomb in the front stairwell or the bowl full of urban mushrooms were consumed scattering our patrons to less populated confines, a prerequisite when tripping on the organic acid.

It was all good times, good times had by all with a proud circus master spinning his top hat for the next thought to solidify his connection with another. All this was well and good, but the fact remained I was uncomfortable in my own skin. A reprieve was needed.

Finding myself uncomfortable in a town that never felt like home, hoping to connect with my blood, and instead I found myself diving deeper into the shadow areas of my life to find comfort. In no time my circle of friends had quadrupled, navigating without barriers in an underworld I had willfully quashed when in undergraduate school for fear of its strong pull. I had been afraid to let this area of my life roam free, which only fourteen years earlier saved me from my dream life. The dark in my life was becoming my light, saving me once again. So it seemed.

I surely wasn't going to fail at work with the least amount of effort needed to succeed, so I moved the unused energy to what gave me comfort. A very common action when one phase of life is providing safety and comfort and another is the opposite. I'm not sure I was consciously seeing that movement in my decisions, but I don't think humans weigh what make us feel safe and not safe, as we organically move in the direction providing the most comfort. And for some of us, we like leaning into the unsafe areas of our lives when that direction provides the most comfort, nurtured by our experiences.

Safety for me was not building a nest egg for the future financially or the creation of my own family, which is a common theme when that experience eludes us as a child. It was so simple for me and easy to execute as I lived one thought to the next, only separated by the former thought coming to fruition. The troubling spot then was my circus had been exposed to a feeling exposed by my father, a feeling of wanting to connect to another in a meaningful way. With that option at the moment stunted between the two of us, I now found myself mechanically going through the motions professionally, albeit highly functioning by day, and changing tack hoping to connect to another by night. I had a little money and a lot of time, so why not connect before I have to pull up stakes to continue my circus across the pond?

In a way I was living my college life after I graduated from college, since it was the first time in five years I had lived in one place longer than a year, and I was enjoying the expansion of the circus to include friends. The circus now had friends and not just internal performers. I had my own place and an appetite for the extraordinary.

The extraordinary became the ordinary for me, as I unknowingly dragged my friends down the road of what thought was next, implementing the thought into light speed reality when the alcohol and the not-so-occasional drugs fueled my engine. But over time, even this method of new experience generation was starting to get boring, forcing me to mix up something in my current model, knowing full well that London was now only a year away. My nightlife was doable, but I had to change up my day. I had not given up on the potential connection with my father, but at the time it was futile and I needed to be challenged when coincidentally Maria came a-calling.

Maria found herself back in New Mexico, newly married and struggling to find her own groove of what to do next. An MBA was in her sights, since being dissuaded from going to law school, so she reset her compass to the business world with a decision of choosing between UCLA and Stanford to further a new occupation. The decision was tricky, having to choose between staying in New Mexico to work on her new marriage and jetting off to graduate school to fulfill her own dreams. She didn't abort either mission but rather changed course choosing to get a degree locally and helping my father run a new business.

In time my father's taste for this new business would sour, and Maria's interest would develop into a plan of purchasing the business from my father with the rest of my siblings being part owners. Saddled with this new acquisition, Maria was aware of my desire to go back to school and offered me a sales job to increase my fortunes before I set off abroad. She had no idea this offer in the meantime would quell the lack of inspiration and boredom I was experiencing at my current employment.

Up to this point, I had never sold anything in my life — except for the high grade Taos Indica I would finance and Mike would sell to all his friends, keeping the creativity soaring on campus and rent paid for Mike after the profits were divided. Whether it was evident to me or not, somewhere in my vascular system the gift of gripping that ball-peen hammer and whacking away at whatever came my way to create another happy customer was emerging. I loved the creativity it took to help someone meet their needs and at the same time weave in the sell without them knowing.

My mentor in this industry was Gail, a recent graduate of Louisiana State University with a degree in interior design and daughter to Colonel Toliver. I never learned formal sales tactics to garner a sale, but rather I tagged along as she provided solutions for the client by asking a thousand questions, magically transforming them into a vision the client could not see when describing what they wanted. It was a consultative approach effectively taking the edge off being in sales, which eased my current state of mind of not wanting to be that sales guy who makes your skin crawl. But it was the conversations we would have about spiritual matters on those long drives to see customers that provided the soil she would need to plant the seed of hope in me. I was without hope, and somehow she knew of my desperation. Our connection was truly mystical.

My territory would have me driving as far as six hours one way into the tiny hamlets of the Navajo Nation and Hopi lands servicing the clinics, schools, and government offices that provided for its people and to an Air Force base in southern New Mexico that was the home of the world's most powerful fighter jet, the F-118A Stealth fighter. But it was the Native American experience that would prove to have most effect on my growth, as it afforded me the opportunity to connect with an underserved portion of my heritage in an amazing way by genuinely wanting to be helpful. And if I sold something in the process it would be a bonus.

In my eyes and spirit I was amongst family when in the homeland but still treated as an outsider linked undeniably by a connection of being hoodwinked by outsiders for hundreds of years. I worked diligently at providing sound solutions and honest pricing, but no sales were achieved until I had showed up long enough to earn their trust. It wasn't about providing what they needed at the right price; it was about making sure I was committed to being around in their eyes and not another outsider who came to make a promise and never to return again. It was simply about trust, nothing else, and I honored it. The lesson was deep and served, changing my perception not only on my own culture, but the culture of sales in general if integrity was the driving force behind all my actions.

I was learning without being taught, and my experiences were the catalyst for this new growth. Unbeknownst to me my fortunes multiplied without having to use the marketing tactics deployed by my grandfather, but rather taught to me by another strain of my blood…the dynamic duo of Gail with her deep Christian faith and by my native brethren with time honored mystical ways. It was the last place in the world I wanted to be, New Mexico, and the last profession I wanted to be associated with, sales, but at the moment it was an unexpected experience that I relished in while waiting for London to call.

13

MUSICAL DOG

Rapidly approaching year one of sobriety and feeling free from the gluttony of my past, I took a deep breath, one that lasted the whole month of August, resting in the glory of my honesty with a new lens attached to view my past and present one day at a time.

I had mixed emotions about Joseph's departure. I was happy he was gone, because it forced me to see if I could trust another in the same way. But I was pessimistic at best. The possibility of our connection happening again seemed too far-fetched, and I didn't want to take the chance of the next one not being up to snuff. I recognized my personal growth over the past eleven months and the freedom from the drink now in my past, so why all the pressure to get another sponsor to finish the steps? On the other hand, I was quietly sad he was gone and was thankful for his honesty, which allowed me the freedom to evolve in ways that were nothing short of a miracle.

The struggle to provide full measure to anything in my life over the last eleven months had been overcome, I surmised, and in all essence the hard part was over with step four and five scratched off the list. If I never reached out to get another sponsor, no one would really know, since by this time I was opening *Sunrise* every day of the week along with being the treasurer. I was engaged in the program up to my gills, and no one would question my resolve.

Joseph had been heaven-sent in my eyes, touching every part of my life, but what I could not shake from my reason was that no matter how helpful this sponsor relationship was to my current evolution, it still infringed on the autonomy of my circus. I guess the real question was whether I would get another sponsor or tip toe out of the program with less than half the steps finished unable or unwilling to trust another...the heart of my problem all along. In the blink of an eye, half measures were swirling again.

The good news with all this mind maceration underway was that the trust I was developing with Michael when it came to sharing the thoughts I was normally having in self-imposed mental isolation. It was easy to share with Michael. I'm not sure it really played out that way, but rather it was Michael's ability to read my pain and desperation that he too experienced when our minds go crazy with thoughts without the release valve of sharing with someone else possible or even wanted. He reached within me and pulled out what was so apparent on my face without the cast of performers to hide behind.

Michael would query me about a new sponsor, and I would share with him my thoughts of not getting one or better yet wanting one. He would listen and suggest we pick out a few potential sponsors in case I changed my mind and wanted to proceed with the steps. What was interesting was that Michael was moving to San Francisco in the next week or so and my release valve would be gone, and I'm sure his suggestion was more than just that, as he knew the probability of relapse without the full experience of the steps and sponsorship was slim to none. I wrestled with this decision, but with Michael's encouragement I identified two potential candidates, in case one wouldn't accept my invitation to be my sponsor.

Both candidates attended the Saturday men's meeting, *Sons of God*, which I had been attending for the last year or so. I loved seeing men in this meeting getting emotionally naked, peeling away the layers of pride and ego thereby exposing them to share deep intimate parts of their lives.

The healing spirit oozing from the four walls provided a sphere of safety, allowing one to gather the courage to uncoil years of pain with a bunch of strange men. It was a safe place to tear down the walls of life and commune with men in a way women naturally do so well when sharing feelings and thoughts with each other. Grown men, in the physical sense, sharing out loud with the full range of emotions, encompassing laughter and crying in the same sentence at times when the reality and release of what had been stored inside for decades passed from their lips.

It would be the lubrication needed to allow the recipients of this un-covering, if one were really listening, to unlock another layer of one's own troubles and thoughts. This meeting allowed me to reach deeper spiritually than ever before in my life as I witnessed the transformation of men from all walks of life sharing a spiritual experience founded on non-filtered, gut-wrenching honesty. Their exposure allowed me to unveil myself.

Having made the decision to ask Jerry to be my sponsor, I anxiously arrived early to the meetings, trying to catch him to see if he would accept my invitation. I waited several weeks for Jerry walk through the doors. Nothing. My mind was ruminating with whether to stay the course and get a new sponsor or maybe it wasn't meant to be and I needed to readjust my sails back to the course directed solely by me. I was hoping this new feeling of confidence wouldn't germinate old methods of navigating. The all too common human experience of when things start to turn in our favor, propelling one to question the desire to wait patiently for what will happen next by actively trying to make this new feeling even better. The active ingredient can be costly. I was an expert at altering my own experience with one aborted mission after another to fall back on for reference.

With the reins of my life being gripped tightly once again, having emotionally all but changed course, Jerry finally walked into the room. I knew the window of change was closing, and before I lost the courage to follow through with a plan foreign to my solo survival tactics, I quickly greeted him, asking if he had some time this week so I could pull on his ear to see if he would consider being my sponsor.

He looked directly in my eyes and said, "I don't need to sit down with you I will gladly be your sponsor."

I was relieved and grateful I had listened to Michael — and so was that small space inside me that words, reason, or religious training couldn't understand. It was my emerging intuition that had been suffocated since birth by my paradigm of living life unable to move past my first thought. In my past I listened to no one including the voice from within. Ego.

Within a couple of days Jerry met me at my cottage to sit on the magic couch, and I began sharing the essence of my fifth step I had shared with Joseph two months back. I was willing to start the steps over if he thought it was necessary; pausing, he began to clearly lay at my feet his view on my experience, whittling it down to two vital components: I had a spiritual foundation to build upon, and in his eyes had very little resentment. I was amazed with his assessment. How did he know me so well?

Simple, I had ripped open my chest with bone–marrow-tapping honesty, knowing my life was on the line, and in a few short hours he had understood the intimacy of my war only because he had experienced his own similar war. The only thing separating our experiences were the details driving the emotional experience, but shared because one doesn't have to over-explain to understand how it made you feel inside. He suggested we start with steps six and seven and if I did some reading we could meet next week to go over those steps and move on to step eight and the dreaded step nine.

STEP SIX: *"Were entirely ready to have God remove all these defects of character."*

This step separates self-improvement from God-improvement, and based on my track record of trying to do the same thing but only better, time after time in my life, and seeing only short-term improvement, I was ready to surrender. This step took a direct shot at my whole paradigm of living life as the sole wearer of the top hat in my circus. All along I thought I could remove my own defects of character, but if I was really going to have a sustainable transformation I had to do this differently. If I was going to be the conductor of my own spiritual transformation, wasn't that another misguided attempt founded on ego? This was not about religious perfection that I had tried in previous attempts to redirect my circus to the light of life, but rather it would be centered on simply having a spiritual experience so I could be useful to others. Step six gratefully understood.

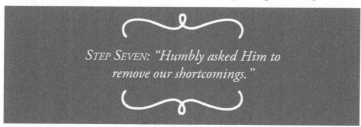

STEP SEVEN: *"Humbly asked Him to remove our shortcomings."*

It's not necessarily the things I have identified in step four as defects or assets, but rather I offer all of me to my higher power, so that what is not useful to others can be removed. A common mistake is that we think we have identified to our higher power what needs to be removed through the fourth step process and that if these things are removed all should be well. A ridiculous spiritual assessment of what was best for me and in turn my fellow man, continuing in a less diluted process but nonetheless diluted the me, more and now paradigm that had me killing myself only a year ago. In short, the self-help process was over and I was going to have to trust my higher power what was best for me and for the lives I would touch going forward. The pure essence of faith was trusting in what cannot be understood, and I was relieved to understand this significance.

Sitting down with Jerry and going over steps six and seven was comforting—I felt as if he had understood my entire life. He would share his own life experiences, and I soon came to realize that we did not share a similar background, which at one time was necessary for me to be able to trust another. I was getting comfortable developing another relationship with another human being that didn't involve my circus, as I experienced safety when sitting with Jerry while working deep spiritual waters.

Jerry mentioned the provenance of his own sponsor experience and that Bill W., one of the founders of the program, had in fact sponsored one of his earliest sponsors. I had a direct link to the foundation of this program. With an unusual comfort resonating in my being, I shared with Jerry a planned trip to New Mexico for a friend's wedding in a couple of days and asked if he thought it would be a good idea to start with some amends, step nine, to those I damaged knowingly and unknowingly over the years.

He quickly pounced on the opening: "Read steps eight and nine and I can meet with you tomorrow." He also suggested I write down a list of people we could discuss to knock off the edges if in fact I decided to meet with them.

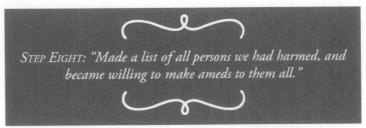

STEP EIGHT: "Made a list of all persons we had harmed, and became willing to make amends to them all."

Jerry's strategy was subtle, having me devise a list before I had time to find a reason not to make a list of the people I had damaged along the way. The fact was I had left a large swath of debris in my wake as my circus quenched its own thirst, not only physically but also emotionally, one thought to the next. This surely was going to open some wounds, and I was grateful to be able to identify those I still had contact with that might need some mending by my own humility. I was conscious of my acts and now willing to identify my reckoning with those who knowingly or unknowingly participated in my circus. My list was now ready and so was I. I hoped. Scared!

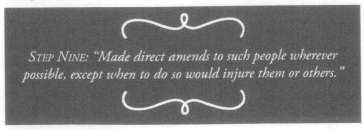

STEP NINE: "Made direct amends to such people wherever possible, except when to do so would injure them or others."

Building long-term, intimate relationships was a non-starter when the goal is having a highly functioning circus. The eligibility requirements for making my amends list had an extremely low threshold. I had lost contact with most and some I knew reconnecting with would only cause more harm than good, so I set out to simply put right what was wrong with those that made my list. Jerry gave sound council in regard to being humble and sincere when making amends, and that no matter how sincere an attempt, sometimes amends cannot make it right. If that is the case, then it should be left alone. If I found myself only making amends to make myself feel better, then nothing had really changed in my character over the last year other than I had stopped drinking. One last suggestion from Jerry was that I pray before making amends, so that my higher power was guiding my intent and words.

In my mind, step nine was posing the most unrest as it exposed two vital areas of my life I had protected at all costs: my circus and the dark in my life. It had taken me all of ten months to get a sponsor and complete with full measure the first five steps of the program and in one short week with a new sponsor, I had traversed steps six through nine. This rapid, yet thorough, pace didn't leave much time to think about the ensuing dismantling of my circus and the revelation of the depths of my dark side to those who had been watching the show all along. They knew more than I thought they did. They always do. My thespian skills were not as good as my ego suggested.

The continual chipping away of my ego and pride allowed me to take Jerry's suggestions instituting humility and sincerity for good measure, and magically, what I feared most in this step process became a glorious blessing. It was the first time for the majority of those I sat down with that weekend where the conversation had some real depth and honesty, at least on my part that is. The need to control each and every outcome had been relinquished as I walked through my amends list one by one, hoping I could parlay these experiences into a day-by-day, or better yet, moment-to-moment paradigm for living my life.

It was a new beginning for me and for those relationships, any relationship, to see what the future may hold, and I was excited to complete the steps as soon as possible to see what was going to happen next.

My departure date for London quietly passed with no one knowing its occasion except for me, as I found myself mourning its loss and at the same time reveling in the uncovered gift of sales along with the creation of some friends to exercise the unknown boundaries of my dark life. I was having fun, outweighing the desire to help those unable to help themselves. I recoiled into me, more and now.

Now in my mid-twenties, I experienced exhaustion from having to escape my terror filled childhood and then the battle to succeed in my early adulthood guided by the fear of failure. The isolation in my circus was deepening, and the inability to connect in a meaningful way to another human being was the only plausible outcome for me, as I willfully mixed another batch of mortar, experiences, to see if I could rise above my choices to see life in another light. I was sinking.

I knew something was wrong. I just couldn't find the right tactic to maneuver my way to peaceful waters. I leaned into what gave me comfort, regardless of the consequences. I knew full well the fun would be short term with the end result being what I experienced in my dream life as a child—certain death, and this I hauntingly embraced.

Despondent, depressed, and feeling worthless, I shrouded these feelings during the daytime with my performers in full bloom at night, caressing each situation with precision so no one would know what was really going on inside the circus of me. I was looking for an outlet that would allow me to rest in the possibility of not having to separate the light and dark of my life in different camps. The effort was taxing my human frame.

The idea that all of what comprised me in and out of my circus could come to the forefront fully exposed, allowing me to be me. Unfortunately, over the years I developed a tragic survival tactic that didn't allow for me to have peace under the roof provided by my tent, as the volume of my performers I maneuvered with throughout my day and night left the completeness of me out in the cold. I was alone when surrounded by my own cast of performers.

I found myself having trouble navigating the day and night in my life once again, hoping another miracle would lead me away from my old tracks. My reason was not able to reconcile that I was composed of the most basic human characteristic: the duality of being a sinner/saint, good/bad, and light/dark at the same exact moment in time. My mind, body, and spirit had not developed enough through experience to understand the complexity of our human nature being composed of both the light and dark. I was looking for a way out, a way to express all of me in a safe respectable way to the voyeurs of my circus and out of nowhere a dog came a-calling.

My brother Mark introduced me to Miguel, as they were sorting out their own circuses while at the same time furthering certificate hoarding doled out after undergraduate school...an MBA.

Miguel was born in Redlands, California, and raised in the tiny hamlet of Vegita, New Mexico, only a short stone's throw away from my ancestral hamlet of La Joya. Over the years we would connect to see live music at the El Rey Theatre and when available, imbibe in the urban spices to enhance the evening. But it was always about the music. A shared pull of the heartstrings binding us together like the connection I found in Gregg and Kevin while in London.

Miguel had spent a semester in London as well while attending undergraduate school at Grinnell College. It was a welcome surprise to find his intellect and sensibilities in common with my own. An instantaneous connection not verbalized, as our shelled exteriors were too hardened with ego and machismo to recognize its significance. We were connected. It was all fun and games at first. Not for long.

In time with our individual circuses churning our contact faded until Miguel reached out with a business proposition. He wanted to open a live music space/ bar and was looking for a third partner. Knowing I was already involved in another business, he was looking specifically for a small investment but more importantly, tapping my social connections built by my circus over the years. In essence it was his idea and venue as he brilliantly crafted its heart and soul while I assisted him in any way I could at developing our clientele while our third partner would handle the back end of the business.

With a heroic business plan in ink we set out on this adventure severely undercapitalized to effectively run a live music space supported only by the liquor we purveyed. It was a risky model when you put the emphasis on the artist rather than the spirits to keep the doors open. I trusted Miguel's intellect, but more importantly, I just trusted. This trusting business was foreign soil for me personally and not essential when orchestrating a circus of one, but we were mystically connected, and at the moment that's all that mattered.

The liquor license was obtained and a space was leased in downtown Albuquerque on Gold Street only several blocks from the Eller Building. An emerald green, marble bar top from a famed nightclub that closed down due to a cocaine situation would be the foundation of the shotgun space with a stage facing the depth of the bar. A combination of used beer coolers and keg dispensers along with the highly prized leased ice machine and dishwasher would be the backbone to the operation. But make no mistake—the space was designed for music and nothing else would steer us from this intent. A space, a liquor license, and an opening date were all in place and the only thing needed was some sweat and hard work to make it all come together, and luckily a surprise was waiting in the wings to push Miguel and our ragtag team of friends to open this long shot dream.

It had been four years since I had arrived back in New Mexico with the intent of building a relationship with a stranger who was more like me than I wanted to acknowledge. The attempt failed not because of desire but rather a lack of the necessary tools to develop a relationship based on safe, honest, respectful communication. I guess we both had the ability to do this when we wanted to keep what we had or get what we wanted, but were unable to when it was for the sake of having a relationship with another human being—in this case between a father and a son. I shared with my father what my new endeavor was, and without hesitation he jumped in with vigor unmatched by any of us who actually had our sacks on the line. As most of the work would be done at night and on the weekends, we had to get this open and running to make sure the house of cards we built this upon would not crumble under the slightest pressure.

With no room for error, we calculated our cash flow at opening would be nil and our maneuverability would only be possible by the credit we received by our liquor vendors. My father would arrive every night promptly descending to his hands and knees to help us install the marble top and the tile on the face of the bar. His drive was unforgiving and when necessary kept us all working while he went out to buy chili cheese dogs from the Dog House, barbecue from Powdrells, or tamales and burritos from El Modelo.

When Miguel's mind was spinning with the enormity of the task and the realization of our handicap, Phillip would spend time with him when no one else was around, encouraging and pushing him to stay steadfast. It was beautiful, wonderful, and unknown to me at the time, but this was about the work and thankfully no one better to have on our side than my father to get it done.

A connection was made and as soon as it appeared it quickly drifted off when The Dingo Bar opened on schedule with no room to spare. Named after a bar Earnest Hemmingway frequented in Paris, and christened on opening night with a staff hand-picked by Miguel with little or no training but enthusiastic to an idea that pushed the artistry of music and more importantly the musician to the forefront.

It was smashing success on day one, witnessed by the fact very few of us knew the prices of the drinks continuously flowing but that didn't seem to be the point anyway. In fact, the point was made clear on a t-shirt made as a marketing tool and a snub to all the naysayer who said we couldn't make it based on our business model of music first, profits second. The front of the t-shirt read: "Don't You Fucking Get It Yet" and the back listing who had roamed the stage: Mose Alison, Alejandro Escovedo, Marshall Crenshaw, Blue Rodeo, Wilco, Modest Mouse, Warren Zevon, G Love and Special Sauce, Maria Muldauer, Earl Thomas, Dick Dale, Yo

La Tengo, Julian Lennon, Mike Watt, Son Volt, Eddie Vedder, The Shins, The Foo Fighters, Eric McFadden, Clarence Gatemouth Brown, Phillip Walker, Joe Louis Walker, William Clarke, WC Clarke, Sam Lay, Magic Slim and the Teardrops, Tab Benoit, Leon Russell, Leon Redbone, Johnny Clyde Copeland, Eddie Harris, Phil Guy, Ian Moore, Iguanas, Jimmy Thackeray, Bob Margolin, Southern Culture on The Skids, Dandy Warhols, Paul Kelly, Ben Folds, Mekons, Swans, Jayhawks, Tommy Stinson, John Spencer Blues Explosion, Foghat, Mermen, Keith Urban (in a band called The Ranch), Cake, Billy Joe Shaver, Roomful of Blues, Duke Robillard, Charlie Musselwhite, John Hammond, Dirty Dozen Brass Band, Big Bad Voodoo Daddy, Guitar Shorty, Junior Wells, Jimmy Rogers, Long John Hunter, Kenny Neal, Lucky Peterson, Sam Meyers, Marcia Ball, Rod Piazza, Poppa Chubby, Gary Clark, Sleppy La Beef, Nashville Pussies, Crash Worship, John Cale, Flake, Alien Lovestock, Apricot Jam, Hovercraft, Calexico and many, many more…

Between Austin and Los Angeles, we built a reputation of being the spot to play when on tour. International acts, indie bands on their way up, country alternative, blues, and jazz artists flocked to our establishment to seek sustenance and artistic freedom to stretch themselves and their dreams. It wasn't a bar. It wasn't a live music space. It was a home to those searching and reaching for dreams that otherwise would not or could not be realized without this venue—and that included Miguel and I.

While I was basking in the relevance of the Dingo Bar in the national music scene as far as musicians were concerned, the light, I was churning out the hours and customers at Contract Associates, the dark. Strangled by the trappings of financial freedom provided by the business world and the opening of a whole new lens on life by choosing my passion, I found myself wavering on my tightrope, trying to find balance but unable to reach out to another to discuss this dilemma. I was out of balance. Not a good place to be when navigating sans net.

I was christened at birth with the blessing and curse of being a hard worker, and when the responsibility required full measure it was applied to completion and then abandoned. It was more than the hours I was compiling at both venues, it was the ingrained state of mind developed by wearing the top hat alone that nothing was outside of my capabilities if I so desired. I could do it all. It would be worth it someday. The challenge is to gauge what level of energy is necessary to keep all the desires in play when one is faced with multiple options and unable to cut away the remaining contenders. So we keep it all going, hoping that the Darwinian laws will select the path we were intended to traverse all along, tragically eliminating the essential human trait of the power of choice. We want it all, not knowing what is really at stake. Our humanity. The ability to be who we really are is jumbled in the tyranny of what we portray. Smoke and mirrors.

I loved the Dingo Bar and what it provided to my soul. The other business was providing sustenance, but its weight waned heavy on my freedom. I was afraid to exercise what was calling out to me since my earliest memories. I was good and some even thought gifted at the whole selling process, but it was another game within the games I had been playing since a child, hoping to keep what I had and get what I wanted. I wasn't passionate about it at all, finding myself frozen in indecision between what my soul needed and what my physical being thought it needed to keep the show going.

With the inability to have any real intimacy with another, and the only experienced safety in life was to turn within and keep the fantasy alive, creating the perfect conditions for the dark of my life to take root like never before. I had a foot in fantasy and a foot in reality. I was unable to cut away from either. The recreational urban spices became not so recreational to keep my human frame in play.

With money in my pocket, cocaine became a welcomed friend so I could make it all happen. The show must go on! The ego is relentless.

My soul was tortured, trying to find a balance between the light and dark in my life, and even though from the outside perspective it might look enviable to own two successful businesses, it was not. I was in the limelight, surrounded by amazing people while currently exercising my circus performers on all cylinders, and at the same time the depth of my loneliness and isolation was immeasurable. I was searching, not sure for what, but I was searching. Maybe I was looking for something to distract me from the pain I was feeling inside of not being able to reconcile this whole dilemma. I wanted to connect to someone and the wake of women I had left behind obviously didn't seem to fit the bill.

Everyone around me had a significant other, and some were in fact getting married and moving on in life, and wasn't that what I should be doing as well? Now it wasn't their fault it didn't work out because the cause was plain and simple. I didn't have the ability to maneuver outside the circus, stripping off some layers to have a chance of developing any type of genuine relationship with the other sex.

With no real examples when growing up and with no real connection to anyone to get some insight on how to maneuver in this most intimate arena, I was doomed. The current prescription of success, alcohol, drugs, ego massaging, tightrope dancing sans net, and sex was not enough to keep me above the pain I was feeling inside, so as any good addict of the self my reasoning informed me that more of all that had to be the answer. Right?

This inability to navigate outside of the circus of one had me on a self-destructive path internally, but externally I was able to keep it all together for the next two years with none the wiser. Gregg (from London) had moved in next door at the Eller Building, and let's say kilos of cocaine and Uzis and other assorted weaponry to protect high stakes distribution were the instruments used to subdue the pain of participating in a life enviable to others but was boring because it impaled my soul. The unknowing introduction of heroin in a pipe passed around the room was the ultimate high, overwhelming my euphoric taste buds and gladly scaring me because the desire to replicate was so strong I never consumed again. I knew I would be unable to free myself from this heavenly demon and I trusted that feeling like I never trusted before.

I was frozen in indecision, unable to proceed with intent on any path, since releasing any option was inconceivable for fear of missing out on another experience. I was a glutton. It's a common human interpretation of the facts, which precede our next decision or non-decision when we feel capable of doing it all and at the very same time unable to do justice to any of it including my withering soul. The walls were closing in on me, and I couldn't wait for all this silliness to pass so I could finally have some peace in the perceived thought of what death would be like. I was unstable, but no one knew. I knew but ignored the feeling in my gut. Delusion.

I was masterful at perception manipulation, a skilled learned early on in childhood while navigating around my household eventually to be projected on my voyeurs. There was no open dialogue or ability to share what was really going on during childhood because the familial desire to portray a shroud to the outside audience ruled the lectern. It was a tragic tool to my navigational paradigm of being alone at the top of my circus pyramid, and even though there were those who surrounded me at the time that could help they couldn't, because I wouldn't let them. Maybe I could let one?

Exhausted physically, mentally, and emotionally, I was quietly hoping that this sordid path would lead to the short stay on this earth I had been so comfortable with since my earliest memories. When out of nowhere an angel appeared draped in human flesh with a childhood experience that was as broken, as mine seemed to be, while interviewing to fill a sales position at Contract Associates.

I clearly remember watching Leigh Ann walk through the doors, wearing a dark blue suit with long, straight, blonde hair pulled back. It became difficult to breathe in her presence, a first for my circus and me. An overall sense of nervousness moved through my frame. I was unsure of its origin, since I had never experienced this feeling before with so many performers to fall back on when faced with uncertainty of my next step. Baffled.

I was struck by her all-natural beauty accented by the angel kisses sprinkled on her face framed by these green/blue eyes sparkling life. There was something deep within her beauty that touched me like no other woman had done before, unsettling the stoic foundation crafted by the circus of one. The connection was instantaneous as butterflies welled in my belly and sweat dripped from my palms. And even though her stay was brief, we were now tethered to each other, hoping we could navigate our way past the obstacles from outside sources, but more importantly from the ones altering our own experience by the dreaded self-will.

Leigh Ann was in a relationship, and we became friends, seeing each other when it was appropriate, hoping to uncover the connection that dwelled in our beings for one another slowly. Her faith was deep, and on more than one occasion while we were having lunch talking about our life experiences, two old souls intertwined in an erotic dance, she would boldly reach out and ask me if I wanted to go to church with her on any Sunday I was available. This was risky.

Now Sunday was the only day I was not working, and it usually consisted of an early breakfast to cure my hangover and lots of sleep the rest of the day. I was interested in Leigh Ann—not so sure about the church thing—since my early childhood experience with our traditional faith of Catholicism was shallow and of the ritual variety. With a forced altar boy experience and no real practice of faith at home the sit, kneel, stand spiritual experience was empty and quickly abandoned when I left home for the first time. I guess abandoned would be a stretch since that would mean I had some type of understanding, but in all reality I had more questions than answers about spiritual matters. I wasn't interested in going to church, but I was interested in getting to know more about this woman who suddenly appeared in my life, so I relented and we planned a church date.

At that time, any type of religious identity in my life was nonexistent, but Leigh Ann's approach and genuine offer was more than enough to quash my disdain for the extreme religious fervor regardless of the denomination or tradition that has swept our global landscape over the past century. Every faction grasping for perceived lost souls quietly crossing their fingers, hoping their choice would be the right one when death came a-calling. The basic human desire to resolve the life after death dilemma scares or lures the human being to wrestle with these profound life questions. What should I believe and whose side should I align with?

Personally I wasn't scared to die and I knew about this God feller, just didn't see how he would fit into the management structure of the circus of one. In one way or another I was always grappling with the light/dark, life/death questions, stirring somewhere deep in my being a desire to unravel this dilemma. It was of high importance, although not sure why all the effort and energy was necessary.

The circus was performing to sold out shows twenty-four seven, and I couldn't be more lonely at the top or was it the bottom of life? I couldn't tell. All I knew at the moment was my butterflies and sweaty palms were telling me something was radically going on inside the circus of me and possibly this revelation needed some investigation.

Leigh Ann wasn't taking any chances, intuitively knowing I was walking on troubled waters and the possibility of me opting out on the date so she insisted on picking me up and taking me to Hoffmantown Baptist Church. I was going to rehab in a way, just didn't know it at the time. It was the same exact church where Norm was once pastor and where Bob Jefferson was an elder. I was mesmerized by the singing, sermon, and lack of ritual wafting through the cavernous space, missing were the replicas of religious icons except for the baptismal bath high above the pulpit the size of the horse trough we used to play in the Stones' backyard.

I found myself comfortable and intrigued by the relevance of the sermon. Feeling the contemporary connection to the scripture being discussed and how it applied to my life was a breath of fresh air. My previous experience with the Old and New Testament seemed so distant and garbled with tricky names and hidden meanings unable to be deciphered without intense teaching, which wasn't a tenant in my childhood religious tradition. I guess I was searching without searching and with the gentle hand lead by an angel who knew my struggle without knowing its true nature—I submerged in this experience ankle deep.

It didn't take long for Leigh Ann to fade to other matters over the next several Sundays, but intrigue and my resolve to get a better understanding of what this feeling was when I went to church willfully had me gladly attending alone. The heart of my own troubled matter. With the spiritual door wide open, I walked through to see if I could do some business with this God stuff, hoping it wouldn't interfere with the evolution of the circus, which would be a deal breaker. I was bending to the idea of being willing to be willing to work with this God character with one important caveat, that I alone would be the wearer of the top hat pulling the strings on the active ingredients in my life. The counsel would be considered at the very least and that in and of itself was a major breakthrough. A copilot?

Meanwhile the circus was flexing its muscles, having me spinning plates with two businesses, an awakening spiritual thirst of which I couldn't understand, a drug infused secret to keep the tent inflated, and a desire to further this friendship with Leigh Ann into something more without really knowing how to do that. I didn't have anybody to turn to or better stated, wanted to turn to. I trusted no one with these deep questions and better yet how to unravel my current unsustainable situation, which surely left unanswered, would lead to the dark end I was expecting just not sure of the final solution.

Interesting things happen when one works new muscle, and with one perceived angel in fold another soon followed. Ann Campbell, Leigh Ann's mother, was aware of one aspect of my spinning act and had asked me whether I wanted to further an understanding of my spiritual thirst through discipleship. I wasn't really sure what that meant and was not sure if I wanted to exercise the energy necessary to fully understand the spiritual life. I was willing at the moment to try anything, even though I wasn't fearful of an early departure physically from my frame. I was hoping I could at least find a morsel of peace while on the way out. Maybe this was a way?

Ann was beautiful and broken in her own unique way with a desire to sustain life like no other human I had personally experienced as she battled two bouts of breast cancer, surviving to share her experience with others centered on a deep connection with her God. Born and bred in Kentucky from a long line of strong women who kept tradition and faith as the cornerstones of their lives through the tough times in life. She was on solid ground.

Her sweet Southern accent and brilliant blue eyes twinkled hope no matter how difficult life obstacles surrounded her and the troubled lives she touched along the way. She was so honest about everything, and sometimes her words hurt you as they rolled off her lips, but it was the only way she knew how to communicate her love for you. Without asking, she would take me in under her spiritual wing even though my relationship with her daughter was tenuous at best, seeing a higher calling at hand with a desire to have me find my own spiritual experience. She would lay hands on me and pray for me and I would feel a love that even to this day is difficult to explain. Little did I know, Ann was using all the tools in her spiritual quiver to help me.

At a dinner party hosted by Ann, I was introduced to Bob and Ann Jefferson. While sampling some homemade chicken potpie and a few deviled eggs, the topic of a weekly meeting held at the Jefferson's household came up. It was a question and answer discussion held every Tuesday night for those who had questions they wanted answered about spiritual matters. The attendees would ask the questions, and Bob would answer them to the best of his abilities. Sounds safe? I had a lot of questions and an emerging desire to get to the bottom of this spiritual well that had gone untapped my entire life, so with Leigh Ann close by for safety purposes we showed up on time the following Tuesday with a personal desire to sit passively and listen to the dialogue. I didn't want to engage. I wanted to learn. Up to my ankles.

The desire to have some basic knowledge and an overall better understanding of certain spiritual matters was a sure remnant of my lackluster previous training and at the same time, an equal opposite desire to leave these matters uncovered for fear it might change everything. I was in the crosshairs now with an uneasiness that wanted me to crawl out of my skin and the room, but I was safe as long as Leigh Ann was there, and this proved to be the case when we attended church for the very first time. Ann and Bob sat in two high backed chairs while Leigh Ann and I shared a small sofa, waiting for the other attendees to walk through the room to hopefully get the spotlight off of me. I wouldn't be so lucky.

Ann suggested we start and let the others join in when they arrived, and instantly terror rushed through my veins. Suddenly all eyes turned on me, waiting for a question to get the ball rolling. I had no idea what to ask with a previous plan of relying on the other attendees' questions to mask my attendance. My intent was to get some insight into this spiritual world I was currently experiencing and then be done with all this searching. The spiritual life seemed so complicated. Too much trust. Too much faith. Not in my circus. Not cerebral enough for my taste.

At that moment I had so much going on with a steadfast intent of paying attention to all the plates in motion, leaving me apprehensive of the effort it would take to understand this spiritual stuff if I submerged any further into these waters. With no plan of escape formulated beforehand, I gazed down at the coffee table, separating the space between the sheep and the shepherd, and in front of me was a gargantuan Bible splayed across the table, and out of nowhere burst out past my lips my first thought.

"I want to know what is true and what was not true in the Bible?"

I couldn't believe I asked that question, but it's the gem I spat out when under the gun. I uncomfortably nestled back in my seat and for the next two hours listened as Bob spoke with intellect and an unmatched passion about the amazing attributes of the Bible. I was having my first sober spiritual experience. I just didn't know it at the time.

Bob would weave together a story that portrayed the Bible in a light that was more than God's word, it was about archeology, philosophy, poetry, sociology, music, mysticism, war, peace, death, addiction, betrayal, love, and every human experience fathomable. I was transfixed by how Bob taught with such a deep passion and detail of the provenance and history of the languages, traditions, and cultures of the time. He would take us on a wild magic carpet ride through the text, and at times when his passion overwhelmed his emotions, huge pools of tears would well in his blue eyes with not a tear leaving its safety.

I was tingling and high like never before, and I don't think I touched ground for several days thereafter. I was amazed at what lay beneath the covers of the book sprawled out in front of me that seemed so archaic and out of touch with our current times, and in two short hours Bob brought it to life like I've never witnessed even till this day.

Something happened to me that evening. I was finally tapped, and the turmoil residing in me had a release valve and if massaged correctly, the pressure welling over the past twenty-nine years could be managed in a slow methodical way. Maybe living was in the cards for me after all? The only question now was how can I preserve the circus of me while mining this new fountain of understanding?

Over the next week I floated around from one plate to the next, focusing in on Tuesday when I could resume the question and answer dialogue with Bob. I didn't need Leigh Ann with me this time around as I experienced safety and honesty, and above all, I knew I could learn from this man of high reason and intellect. He was heaven-sent.

Bob was from Texas and was raised in the church, studying the Bible when commanded and the books of reason more intently after his stint in the military. He earned a degree in nuclear engineering and found a career at Sandia National Labs to steward our nuclear arsenal of which all was highly classified. His career had him traveling the world as an expert in his field, positioning him face to face with our formidable adversary at the time, the Soviet Union and their secret KGB spy network.

Adept at spinning his own plates with a growing family, professional career of global significance before that word became passé, a gift of teaching the Bible, a desire to fly planes unquenched after not passing the eye exam to become a fighter pilot, and most of all wherever he went a "Try God" pin on his lapel. He was bold and strong in the knowledge of his faith, holding tightly to his chest a little known secret reeking of blasphemy. Thousands would flock to Bob's Bible study teachings throughout the years as he enriched others in the word, laying a solid foundation for spiritual understanding, but his struggle was internal as the power of his reason and his faith would not be reconciled until his late forties as he himself struggled believing what he taught. He had all this knowledge in his head he just hadn't transferred it to his heart, yet.

My spiritual storm was building, and I would be the only patient who showed up the next Tuesday, finding myself free to ask questions which were boiling inside me for decades. He would listen and then answer each question in vivid detail. He was speaking the language of reason combined with faith, resonating with my own way of navigating through life and our union was perfect—well, almost. The only difference was, the faith I had solely rested in was my ability to make life happen. A sordid faith of one. Toward the end of our three-hour instruction, Ann asked if I would consider being discipled and I couldn't answer yes quickly enough. At that moment she turned to Bob and informed him with her eyes only, that he would be the one who would disciple me.

Higher powers were at work, and I was right where I needed to be with Bob being the perfect teacher, beginning a relationship that would change my life in so many unexpected ways. I would spend the next year, one on one, with Bob every week studying the Bible and more importantly all of life. He would teach me about having balance in life and that too much weight on any area of life would be troublesome including my spiritual life. I would share with him respectfully my circus shenanigans, and he would listen and love me even more. We researched my inability to connect with my father, and he encouraged me to understand the man, not what had been missed.

It was the first time in my life I consciously realized I had missed out on a vital relationship. I was wrong as a child when I responded to the other kid's questions of what it was like not having a father. I had missed out on so much. A vital relationship missed between a father and son illuminated only by the example Bob was showing me without condition. It was the first time I trusted another human being completely as we laughed, cried, and learned from one another one precious moment to the next.

What I was yearning for and missing with my father had been quenched by my relationship with Bob Jefferson. My desire to fill that void was gone because I now felt he was my father in the ways that really mattered.

Over the next several years my life changed drastically, as my participation in The Dingo faded and my responsibilities at Contract Associates increased. Along with these changes came a reprieve from alcohol and drugs while I researched this spiritual life that needed all of my attention. I would move on from Hoffmantown, finding my own church at Calvary Chapel, Albuquerque a non-denominational evangelical place to study.

I submerged completely, knowing that if one hair on my head was not under the spiritual waters I would be susceptible to my own will. I was being led, but I was unsure of my destination. And all the while something in me didn't feel quite right.

14

HYDE IS A JEALOUS LOVER

I pedaled my beach cruiser down Rosemont Street toward Windansea to parallel the coast, passing on my left Big Rock, Windansea, Simmons, Rock Pile, and Little Point surf spots, sprinkled with early morning surfers bobbing in the water and waiting for the next set to come rolling through. I wound my way through the Barber Tract manicured neighborhood to Prospect Street, with a final destination of the Contemporary Art Museum's outdoor café. The ritual of hopping on my bike to get to my next destination had developed into a practice, soothing my weary soul that always seemed to be wracked by fear, no matter how good or bad things became in my life.

At first, this mode of transportation was a vehicle to slow my life down to a point where I could see, hear, and finally feel what had been surrounding me all along. It would change.

The landscape of La Jolla was comprised by the sacred grounds of the mountain to the east cascading down the cliffs to the sea below, held together by the whisking palm trees swaying in the light breezes. It was as if you could taste its medicinal value if you slowed down enough, and then and only then, could it be recognized by the human soul. Its physical beauty was second to none, projecting a mystical feeling that would rattle your bones if you moved past the fancy cars and fancy seaside homes to the true nature of this small dot on the planet.

The combination of the landscape and people stewed a unique cauldron of hope where anything was a possibility if you listened to the beat of your own heart. It was my slow-beating heart echoing to the heavens when pedaling up and down these streets, moving past the physical nature of my surroundings and drifting off in moving meditation to a mind no longer held captive by the confines of space and time. I had found my spiritual vehicle, and it wasn't me, more and now…anymore.

The spiritual awakening I experienced after returning from New Mexico produced a sense of being connected to something other than my own will for the very first time. It was a strange feeling, as if I was losing control of my life in a way that provided a sense of grounding.

The reins of life I always gripped so tightly gently fell from my hands as I closed my eyes, soaking up the freedom and separation from my past, trusting *my* way was no longer *the* way.

I was unsure of this newly poured foundation, instilling in me a desire to connect with Jerry as soon as possible to share and go deeper with these feelings, so I could get a better understanding of what was happening to me. At the same time, I was approaching this discussion with caution, knowing I had manufactured this feeling in the past with a sole intent of keeping what I had or getting what I wanted, the active ingredient. The self-truth is complex.

The battle of my will versus God's will for me turned out to be another act in my circus. I desperately wanted to be feeling what I was feeling and for it to be genuine, but I couldn't trust what I was feeling inside when it came to spiritual matters. I'd experienced numerous changes over the last several months, proving a desire to do things differently, with honesty the heart of the matter. I was only hoping Jerry could shed some light on the feelings residing in me while I navigated through life at the moment without a plan, without expectations, waiting patiently for the next thing to happen.

The above-ground maze of walls constructed willfully since exiting the womb forty-four years ago was now gladly tumbling down Jericho-style. They'd never protected me from me. Tragic. I was now exposed to the enormity of life for the very first time, unsure of where to lean next. All I had trusted to get me through the light and dark of my life over the years was now falling away as what I feared most in the past, trusting in another, was all I had left to confirm this feeling inside my being. I didn't know if it was real or circus driven.

What had frozen me in fantasy and delusion for four decades, the inability to connect in an intimate fashion with another human being, was now flowing out of me so naturally, leaving me baffled by these new events. The nature of our selfishness is cunning, baffling, and powerful, only trumped by the power of ripping open your chest and honestly sharing your life with another. It was surreal looking into Jerry's eyes, sharing with him my experiences over the past few weeks without altering the truth that had been ingrained in how I navigated since my very first breath.

The ability to sit down with those whom I had harmed over the years, how each experience healed me in unimaginable ways and the freedom it created for a new relationship to be nurtured with my voyeurs in the future, was an unexpected bonus. No expectations of what might come next was the mortar now binding these relationships going forward, freeing myself from the need to start building walls for safety. It felt like anything was possible.

While listening, he leaned forward and smiled, knowing full well my experience released me from the bondage of self. He would read a passage confirming the promises I was experiencing if I worked these steps with full measure and honesty. And then he would lay the book down, sharing his own experience of when he had moved past the bondage of me, more and now to a freedom unchallenged by fear. Or should I say the real fears in life, not the ones fabricated in our mind.

It was the first time in life I felt as if I was not alone, connecting to something much larger than myself. I was beginning to understand the connection between myself and what lay beneath all my flesh and life experiences I had mined over the past sixteen months, one painful, exhausting, life-draining spadeful at a time. I'd trusted my gut feeling over the past several weeks in ways that, for me, was not my normal mode of navigation, prompting Jerry to smile from ear to ear as he instantly recognized what had taken place in my life.

I was like the shifting sands at Windansea revealing what was beneath all the self-willed, ego-driven experiences piled on top of each other over the years. I had finally exposed my beautifully mangled and twisted roots, which had given me life all along. What was critical now was to keep digging in order to have sustainable change in my life keyed by understanding the provenance of the feeling residing in my belly. The roots were exposed, but the digging had only begun if I wanted to move beyond my self-imposed institutionalized fear and anxiety for a chance at peace, which I had been longing for since my first memory.

Jerry knew the importance of my question, as he too faced this dilemma in his own journey, sharing with me a story from his sponsor's sponsor, Bill W., one of the founders of the twelve-step movement. The discussion centered on our current topic of the "gut feeling" and what in fact was that feeling. A feeling stirring in every human being, comprised by a mystical formula, since reason or science cannot explain its germination. Our intuition, gut feeling, according to Bill W., was God speaking directly to him. It was a conversation with the God of your own understanding, possible only when we quiet the mind to listen to the space deep inside our being. It's the feeling inside us knowing the coordinates to the decision approaching us before it has entered our consciousness to act upon.

At that moment, it was as if a sledgehammer crashed through my cranium, smashing the navigational device I had sieved all my decisions through my entire life. When those words seeped into my head, they mysteriously didn't bounce around this time until I could devise a first thought. This time, they went directly to my heart. I understood for the very first time the definition of the word "intuition," even though you won't find this version in Webster's. The result of this enlightenment would be the abandonment of fear in all its forms, whether perceived or not, with peace in my life, regardless of my state of mind. I would never be alone again…the heart of my matter. I'd been connected the whole time.

Suddenly, a wave of sadness rushed through my bones. I had been lost for so long. I only wished someone had shared this with me years ago, possibly limiting the wreckage to the unsuspecting voyeurs of my circus and the untold damage to my own well-being, but now thankful for all the experiences residing in my jewel box of life. I was ready to move on with steps ten and eleven. I wanted to look back, but regret was coming on strong. I leaned forward.

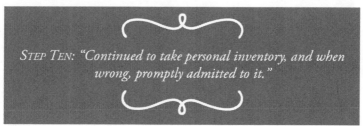

STEP TEN: *"Continued to take personal inventory, and when wrong, promptly admitted to it."*

The process of self-analysis was over, moving into a practice of examining our behavior on a daily basis. This "one day at a time" stuff I'd been hearing about and bored with over the past year and a half was now making sense. I now had the opportunity to actively participate in my humanness, my broken nature, within a time frame I was capable of working in to adjust my actions or inactions. What was insane all along was for me to believe I could drag the past into today and at the same time manipulate and control what may come tomorrow, all while not giving my best efforts on how I was destroying what was around me in the here and now.

One day at a time was not about drinking—it was about living within my human capabilities. It was the relief valve for my daily existence if I practiced it, with the benefactors being myself and those surrounding me, since now I had a practice allowing me to patiently correct what was wrong with my actions and inactions one day at a time. In the human condition, we are imperfectly perfect and in desperate need of a practice to recalibrate, push the restart button, adjust the sails before we get frozen in life's trivialities.

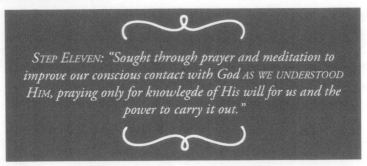

STEP ELEVEN: "Sought through prayer and meditation to improve our conscious contact with God AS WE UNDERSTOOD HIM, praying only for knowlegde of His will for us and the power to carry it out."

A shift in the me, more and now paradigm of how I navigated my life through my reason, redirecting that energy in a spiritual manner, seeking guidance in my current direction, with the added benefit of subduing my willful nature and connecting to something much grander than I. This new navigational approach allowed me to recalibrate my compass, my will, on a moment-by-moment basis if needed, which may in fact have other plans for my day. Even though my will had been strong and guided me to so many wonderful experiences, it was now clearly understood that my gluttonous will had done much more harm than good.

It was now upon awakening, when I would start my day not focused on my will, but God's will for me. I didn't want this to be a ritual like it had become in my previous life experiences, when trying to tap this well of truth, but rather I wanted it to become a practice that I grew with one day to the next, cognizant of my imperfect humanity. The reality is that some days were connected and some days were not. Human. What a relief. I was relieved.

The arduous task of moving through the steps with full measure was almost over, and I knew my life would never be the same if I kept moving in a direction that fostered a continual changing of everything in my life. I was ready to tackle life again, but with one vital ingredient that had been missing all along. Trust.

The circus of one was now soliciting counsel on vital life decisions with the desire to reach out to another when I became confused or unsure of my next move. This new vein in decision-making became critical as to how vital nutrients would be delivered to this old, but newly refurbished vessel, since now I actually could move past the first thought to entertain as many thoughts as I wished before deciding where to navigate next.

This new desire to reach out to another would serve me well over the next several months, when I was approached to reenter the corporate world with an offer solving all of my financial woes, which were mounting when my gamble to sell my home one year earlier had come up snake eyes. My precarious financial position had me leaning into old patterns of navigating, culminating into a state of mind that a triumphant return to sales would be the final thread to a new tapestry of how I lived my life. At this point, my resources were exhausted, forcing my hand to ask for help financially from some family and friends. This new turn of events was unsettling and essentially the kiss of death to my circus.

Being financially tied to anybody for anything was rule number one when wearing the top hat, and now with this last refuge of my circus soiled, my life was exposed to all. Maybe it was what was needed to nurture new muscles that otherwise would have never occurred if my plan of selling my house would have come to fruition. If my home had sold, I would have been primed for anything in life with sobriety in hand—an awakened spiritual condition, a desire to develop intimate relationships, and a bounty of cash and no debt, which would allow me to step into uncharted waters. I was lucky it hadn't sold. I was still on the razor's edge.

I could chase any desire I wanted to in life supported by a newly inflated ego that had undergone some adjustments, but for all intents and purposes was very much still intact. There is a saying in the rooms: Don't get healthy by Thursday, because you might find yourself drunk on Friday. In other words, don't be in such a hurry to tighten up all the loose screws in life. Let things progress naturally in their own time. Funny and not so funny, every part of my plan I'd manufactured over a year ago had not panned out, but that didn't stop me from putting on a suit and tie, clipping my locks, and shaving to see if I could land this opportunity and make life happen once again.

The circus was salivating for a comeback as I reached deep into my archives, rustling up the very best of me, blending that with the new and most powerful weapon ever availed to my arsenal, the ability to be honest under any circumstance. Honesty is the most powerful tool available in the human condition. Even love comes in second if honesty doesn't precede it. The light of life was blinding...I was ready. I hoped.

Finding myself in a high-rise office building in La Jolla, sitting in a stately office, with bloated ego just waiting to out-duel my potential employer. Ten minutes deep into the interview, after all the formalities were dialogued, an open-ended question was asked, and without hesitation,

I undressed to disclose my trials over the past year and a half, with no deletions or add-ons included. It was the simple truth of how I'd lost my job, what came next, and why I was here today.

The words flowed with an ease and strength I had not experienced before when sharing the truth, expressing how my recent past changed my life in so many unexpected ways and how like never before, I was prepared to truly serve another with all of my life experiences in fold. I was at the height of my game, and the opportunity was in the palm of my hand. I was steadfast in my approach, determined to not hide behind my past in order to get what I wanted, and if honesty was a deterrent to getting the opportunity, then so be it. My soul was alive. I was no longer dependent on my reason.

The formal nature of the interview flew out the window as our discussion became more intimate, with an uncovering of both our life experiences. I was moved by the energy flowing in the room, and so was my potential boss, knowing we had laid a foundation of a relationship that could be built upon without limit, based on honest, open, and respectful communication. I was connecting in a meaningful way, overriding my initial intent of getting all gussied up to ease my financial woes. I was changing without intent. Life was happening without alternation based on fear.

The opportunity was ideal, but my desire to fly solo on this decision was in the past, so I sought out a second opinion before I accepted the offer. I reached out to one of my fellow *Sunrisers,* Jim, making sure not to edit my feelings and financial information with the purpose of molding his response. I asked him point blank what I should do. Jim listened intently and queried me about the opportunity, wondering how long it would be before I expected to be back on a solid foundation financially if I took the offer. Those were important questions, the trivial, but what he asked me next was absolutely brilliant and an angle I had never entertained before in my life, the heart of the matter. He wanted to know how I would feel inside if I were back on solid ground under these circumstances.

Ahhh! He hit me with a dagger to the heart, questioning my honesty with what mattered most in my life, safety and comfort through financial means, or passion for what lay within, which I had abandoned so long ago and was now unsure of what that really was. I wasn't ready for his question, but who really is when our nature tells us to identify the pain and a solution to the pain being the weight that tips the scale in our decision?

Now, Jim was speaking from his own life experiences when he asked me this question, as he had sourced his own pain and the decisions he had made and now with hindsight as his ally, he could ask the question no one asked him.

"What you don't want to happen in six months or a year from now is to look back and realize you have solved the short-term pain, but your heart still hurts. Trust me, you don't want to waste the energy and effort, when all along, you could be following your heart."

My synapses were firing with all this information sinking in deeply, reflecting on my past and realizing I had repeatedly made this mistake so many times in life. I was now recoiling from this light illuminated on the landscape of my life, and before I could regain my form, Jim delivered the crushing blow, propelling me forward and giving me the courage to change tack in life and chase my dreams.

Up to this point in your life, not one of your life experiences has been wasted. But please hear me when I share this with you: you have no more time left to waste!...Jim.

My decision was made, and even though I had no idea what dreams were available to me now, what I was now sure of was I had no time left to waste. I would forgo the offer to see what in fact was in store for me next. I was at peace with the decision, although challenged financially, a vital ingredient to a highly functioning circus.

With a fire burning in my belly to further my spiritual walk, I agreed to host a men's Bible study at Contract Associates starting at six a.m. every Friday morning. Its intent was to be a refuge for those who attended. A sort of port where we could dock to refuel and recharge for what was to come our way as we crossed the daily intersections of life. Our group had no formal structure, other than reading some scripture and discussing it amongst each other, and as far as spiritual maturity goes, the participants were infants except for Steve. Steve had a family of four and a thriving business, with a past consisting of being the youth pastor at Hoffmantown and a college football career at the University of Oklahoma, with a national championship ring proudly displayed on his right hand. At our first meeting, Steve suggested we go around the room and share a little personal history and why we wanted to be a part of this group.

Now, David — who I actively practiced the dark of life with — was in the room, along with Brent, a co-worker, and a few other cats. But Tim, whom I'd never met before, stood out from the rest, literally.

Tim was a six-foot-three, two hundred twenty-five-pound professional steer wrestler, fluent in French, from the town of Clovis, New Mexico, all gussied up in a suit and tie masked as an attorney. We were complete opposites, with the same exact experiences except for the details. I was so thankful he preceded my oratory, as it allowed me the space to not be so intent on editing my own story, even though I did. He was better at being himself and honest with his shortcomings than I ever hoped to be. At least, that's the way it felt while listening to him share his story.

What I never quite grasped before when juggling the truth was that ninety-nine percent honest was one hundred percent not the truth. The one percent bridge was killing my soul. A life-long barrier I was unable to traverse on my own. The reality was I wasn't ready to really uncover and reveal what stirred deep within the circus. Although I was moving closer to that ideal — I just didn't know it at the time.

Now, I have no idea how deep he went at exposing his secrets, but what I came to respect and love about Tim was whatever he was feeling at any moment was about to come rolling off his lips. The bull in the china shop would frame Tim well when describing his ability to keep in what he felt about a subject. I was assured that, when in his presence, it would be real. For someone who had danced with delusion and fantasy for so long, it was refreshing. What struck me deeply and drew me near was his ability to speak about the dark in his life so openly. And even though I had no idea the depth of his darkness, he at least was being honest as best he could.

I have no idea if Tim felt this way, but we were connected deeply, and I would hold his hand tightly over the next several years while we both sunk deeper into the spiritual waters. I knew he was like me and I needed him by my side, unsure of the others I might encounter in this new environment.

It was a connection not unlike Gregg, Kevin, and Miguel, with common interests the backbone, except now we tiptoed in a foreign land of our own choosing. If Tim could do it, I could do it, I constantly reminded myself, even though I never told him as such. I kept close while I pushed down the dark in my life deeper and deeper into the caverns of my being, hoping this would all pay off in the end.

We studied together, soaking up the book-by-book, verse-by-verse, and word-by-word intense Bible lectures indicative of the teaching style of Pastor Skip at Calvary Chapel, fitting in perfectly how I wanted to absorb this information in my head so I could rest in the safety of the light provided while in this arena that had a high value on being good. I wanted to be good; I wanted to be in the light. I didn't want to be drawn to the first thought in my mind that positioned me squarely in the domain of me, more and now, I, self and me. I was safe as long as I was studying, memorizing scripture, attending church three times a week, and going to the Toliver's house on Thursday nights for Bible study, homemade pies, and ice cream.

The draw to me, more and now was powerful, forcing me to grip tighter to this new life and never, ever look back. My reason was strong and my will determined to fill this seemingly unquenchable draw to the dark while this new light surrounded me. If I was successful absorbing the light while smothering the dark, I would be able to withstand the desire to unchain Hyde, who, by the way, was doing push-ups and pull-ups in the basement of my life, waiting for an opportunity to take center stage. I was tapping new sources, and Colonel Toliver would spring forth a new vein of direction sorely needed.

The spiritual and life guidance Colonel Toliver provided was providential, taking me under his broad spiritual cover, teaching me what had been missing in my childhood and, when necessary, escorting me up to his study to get to the heart of a matter, whether I wanted to or not. His deep resonating voice would be intimidating to some, but to me, it provided comfort of direction and integrity that had been missing all along.

He was of deep faith and military structure, which I clung to, but what moved me most was his ability to undress his ego and pride while openly examining the battle between his will and his faith that consumed him as a brash young Tuskegee Airman flying the world's greatest fighting aircraft while doing two tours in Vietnam. He would have his own perfect storm high over the Arizona desert while testing F-15s, rattling his will to surrender to the God he acknowledged but rarely followed when his reason and ego took the reins of life. He would share all his trials in life, unfortunately for this wearer of the top hat unable to see the common connections that I too had been battling, as I sourced only the desire to quench the spiritual thirst being provided shown by his unconditional love and honesty. I loved being in their home and being a part of the enormous extended family. Being part of something larger than me that in time became a vital and necessary refuge for me in my weekly circus of spinning plates.

Sobriety at this point in my spiritual awakening was nothing short of what is described in the rooms as "white knuckling it." It was a hiatus, not a reckoning. I was helping out one day a week at the Dingo without the drink, finding the environment still attractive to my soul, but not sure why. My new religious training was emphasizing the importance of following the narrow road less taken, and that was always my navigational route since childhood, so why not knock off the rough edges and be a shiny penny standing out from all the random change walking this planet?

The coordinates were simple. If I distracted myself with this light looming in my life, it would keep me from willfully descending to the basement, where Hyde was now residing. If I could make this fantasy come to fruition, then I could have what I longed for, what everybody in this new Wonder Bread environment was experiencing, what I never felt when growing up…a family. At least, that's how I felt.

The draw to a family lifestyle was foreign to my experience and never really a conscious desire due to an expected early departure from my earthly vessel, so why all the bother? Those feelings had changed over the past several years when enlightened to a new way of life by the examples laid at my feet to witness: the Jeffersons, the Tolivers, the Campbells, and the Kunkles. An array of families rife with their own imperfections but held together by a web of faith I wanted to emulate. It was time to roll the dice.

I would make a deal with this God fellow. If I did all these things he asked of me and pushed the dark of my life away for good, filling this earthly vessel with as much good as possible, then I too would be afforded a family life like those now surrounding me. A crafty but potentially tragic deal-making, having very little foundation to rest upon if the tides of life washed away what I was bargaining for. In the human condition, you'd better be prepared for some turbulent seas; it's an essential part of life.

My resolve to this way of life would become my sole desire buttressed by my strong will and a tested friend; my capacity to absorb as much knowledge in my head as possible to get what I wanted or keep what I had, and in this instance, it was to attain a family of my own. This fantasy would move to the center stage of the circus, knowing full well I could pull this off with some examples to follow and a chained dark life in the basement. My heart was aching for a connection, a connection that in my mind and heart could only be filled by one person who had shaken my foundation several years earlier, jettisoning me in a whirlwind of experiences surely heaven-sent.

The bar was raised high, and I couldn't seem to find another to replace Leigh Ann, as she herself was navigating her way through the tricky landscape where the matters of the heart are concerned. We were friends as I was learning to love another from afar, hoping the currents in her life would change, forcing her to see the change in me, with our union only a matter of time. At the moment, I had plenty of time to right the ship for her to see, but my ego always took the lead, pushing my desire to get what I wanted with immediacy, regardless of God's timing. I want what I want when I want it!

Now, at this point in my life, there was a storm building outside the walls of my circus, centered on my new direction in life. With a history of never really caring what anyone thought of my actions or inactions in life regardless of relation, a change was slowly occurring, causing some movement in that arena.

The new light burning in my soul exposed a desire to share this new understanding, and with more than a little encouragement by Bob Jefferson to reach out specifically to my biological family to share my new life. His counsel was loaded with wisdom, explaining that we are fearful of things we don't understand, especially when it occurs to loved ones and even more so when the change in you stirs up the feeling in another, if they too should be making some changes. Change evokes fear, not only in the one changing, but also for those witnessing the change. Tricky emotions. Not always easy to recognize.

It was evident my biological family was in the dark when it came to my life, so with a heaping dose of compassion and honesty, if I could communicate my new coordinates without preaching my new way of navigating, it would be a good starting point.

Bob continued, "It is not possible for anybody to understand if you don't communicate in a respectful way the changes in your life."

The marching orders were understood, and my story was simple. I was a born again Christian attending a non-denominational evangelical church and happy.

Bob suggested meeting with each family member individually to allow for direct discourse, and overall, it went well, with some sharing their own experience, while others listened and moved on. I know I have mentioned this before, but in the human condition, we exert a tremendous amount of energy wrestling with what others are thinking about us, draining our precious energy for positive endeavors, oblivious to the fact that if they are anything like ourselves, we are not thinking about them at all. In my biological family, the "I" always came first, even though it was deceptively cloaked with all the right words, leaving little room for another inclusive of blood when the push came to shove.

The explanation tour was over, and I was hoping I could reengage with my family in a meaningful way, since in my mind I had reached out and back to connect with everything on the table. Well, almost everything. I wanted to be a part of my biological family, and I also wanted to have my own family, and without really knowing how to do either one individually, setting in motion the plan of melding the two together to strengthen the probability of having at least one and, if really lucky, both. Make no mistake, I would sacrifice the former for the latter any day.

My will was strengthened by the idea that if I was really good—I mean *really* good—I could still get what I wanted when I wanted it, and now with regard to others if necessary. It was a shift in the coordinates of how I navigated, but the intent was the same as before. And even though my friendship with Leigh Ann was just that, with no commitment on either part, we were connected, trying to hold on to a feeling welling deep within our souls. The battle to hold on to that feeling was never present when together, but always lingered when apart, as outside influences and options would weaken our bond, tearing us away from what bonded our souls upon first sight. I needed to jumpstart our connection. I needed to make it happen. I needed to alter my course. I knew of no other way.

This new plan of melding my family desires had me leaning into some uncomfortable territory with my mother, who was single-minded in what went on in her children's lives. I was defiantly manipulating the situation when I invited Leigh Ann to join me at my brother Mark's birthday party, with the intent of cross-pollinating these two desires, hoping acceptance of my new changes and whom I desired would be the answer to my new fantasy of having a family.

In the recent past, I had relied upon Leigh Ann for support and safety when in a new environment, and now the roles were reversed, this time with me being the provider of safety and protection. My spiritual growth had the circus on a new plane, but what came next drove my spiritual emersion to new depths and simultaneously deeper and darker into me, more and now. The battle lines were drawn.

It was always uncomfortable for me in the family environment, finding myself giving full measure this evening to make sure nothing went wrong, hoping Leigh Ann would not feel what I always felt, an outsider. It didn't take long for that wish to unravel, as my mother decided to pass around a photo album with pictures of me in a past relationship. Whether it was with intent or not was beside the point, and at the very least, it was bad form. I could see the discomfort and pain in Leigh Ann's eyes, knew this type of reception would only drive the wedge between our desires of the heart and what our minds would assemble of what our future together may hold. It's one thing for rifts to arise between family of biology and family of your own after marriage, but it's more devious when you're still trying to solidify a relationship while outside sources are intent on altering your experience.

My mother's stoic nature, long face, and short responses when engaged by Leigh Ann were more than enough to boil my blood, throwing a wrench in my plan of creating a family of my own. Non-verbal communication can cut deeper than words. Directed silence is debilitating. The event was gladly over, and I made sure to keep Leigh Ann safe from any other harm, regardless of our future together, up until I pulled my mother aside to voice my displeasure on what had just occurred. A defensive posture was taken, and we both dug, in wanting our own way.

As the fear of losing control of the situation escalated, my mother reverted to old patterns of problem solving by cutting deeply at our connection. Whether it be punishment or the dreaded silent treatment to get her children to conform, it was becoming obvious that drastic measures were needed to get what she wanted, and that's when the real source of her displeasure with my choices in life came roaring out.

"You have denied your culture and your heritage by going to that church, and if you decide to keep company with your new friends, then you are not welcome at my home."

It was the ultimate slicing, dicing, and manipulation of another to get what you wanted when you wanted it. It was love with condition, a fatal blow to any relationship. A formula I knew too well when collared with the Darwinian mindset fostered at home.

Even though my connection with Leigh Ann would continue and my desire to pursue a family with her remained, the obstacles to our union pushed us further away from that reality. This realization drove me deeper into the spiritual waters, seeking comfort and direction, and at the same time wondering if all this good was worth it if I didn't get what I wanted or keep what I had. The constant battle running through my mind of what lay in the basement of my life was starting to compromise the strength of the links to the chain that kept Hyde from coming out to play. I kept asking myself, was this all worth it?

In the human condition, the suppression of a desire without it being fully reconciled only leads to the escalation of that desire. In most religious traditions, the line between good and bad is drawn clearly, setting in motion the tightrope act of toeing the line with those one has chosen to be like-minded.

I wanted to be with my new friends, and I loved the spiritual training and family provided in this new environment, but Hyde was isolated, angry, and needing some attention. I was holding on to the good, hoping this ban from my biological family would not curdle my desire to have a family of my own, and with providence, Ann Campbell and Colonel Toliver would fill my parental roles, with God as our marrow.

My new idea of family expanded beyond the confines of DNA, providing the nourishment to continue down the road less traveled, but leery of the fact I hadn't reconciled what lay beneath the topical skin of how I navigated my life. The circus was in complete control, hoping my new religious training would be enough to keep the performers of my circus that were foaming at the mouth to take the stage by this time while being currently chained in the basement. A spiritual battle was underway, causing emotional and physical turmoil.

I didn't know it at the time, but my foundation was starting to crumble, with my reason in full control. I was in deep trouble, ignoring all the signs.

The Dingo represented who I really was in so many ways, based upon the formula of creating a space that fostered dreams first and monetary gain second. It so happened in the cosmic shenanigans of the universe the choosing of our business model drew two friends closer together and at the same time became the spark igniting a fire that quickly incinerated the other friendship. A higher purpose was clearly our emphasis, but when ego, pride, and wanting your own way supersedes a common goal, the ability to stay the course collectively can shatter what bonded a connection in the first place. Blood, long-term friendships, business relationships, and marriages are not immune to the power that can be wielded when our way blinds us from the bigger picture of communion with another.

My partners were more than friends, sharing an intimate life experience when Miguel's father, who had been suffering from a long battle with cancer, decided the fight was over, choosing to exit life in its physical form. It was a time to lean on another, and Miguel leaned on his best friend, a life experience for both parties that would surely be able to withstand the desires of the self. But little did I know at the time, what was at the foundation of our business model, paying the musicians one hundred percent of the door proceeds would be the start of a disagreement that would tear a friendship apart. It didn't take long for ego and pride to show its ugly face in other areas of our partnership, as unknowingly to me, Miguel had made a stand, as did his friend. The inability to communicate beyond the disagreement would eventually send their relationship into a tailspin, forcing Miguel and myself to defend our business foundation when sued by our third partner.

It would be the first time in my life I would be challenged to choose between the betterment of the circus and a friendship I trusted without really knowing why. In a legal setting, I was approached by our third partner and asked to choose his side, essentially pushing Miguel out of what was his all along. The sell was financial gain for me, with a suspicion that ego, pride, and greed were at the heart of the matter for Miguel's best friend. It was the dissolution of a friendship, a marriage of sorts, and I happened to be the child in the middle. I guess this experience already resided in my jewel box, even though I was oblivious to the details, but this time, I was afforded the luxury of choosing between right and wrong—or better yet, integrity.

Now, don't get me wrong, money is great, but friendship every time is better. I would do the right thing and Miguel would do the other, settling out of court by cutting a monthly check to his best friend, essentially draining the capital needed to sustain our den of dreams. Miguel would harbor this weight all by himself over the last two years of the seven-year lifespan of The Dingo Bar, until the doors were shackled, ending our dream, but also for those who hadn't yet realized theirs as well.

While The Dingo was playing its last round of shows, I busily ground away at Contract Associates, shuttling back and forth between our office in Albuquerque and our office in Los Alamos, New Mexico. We successfully won a contract to provide furniture and design services to Los Alamos National Laboratory, the same place where Oppenheimer and the boys developed the first nuclear weapon, changing our world forever. It was fun and exciting, dealing with high security areas and million dollar projects, but never enough to keep my interest.

The seven-year itch was creeping up on my professional life, if you want to call it that, and I found myself searching for a higher level of game to keep engaged, when we were approached by our main supplier and General Motors to open an office in Juarez, Mexico, to service their plants in Mexico. I was intrigued, but more importantly looking for a way to run the whole show. It was always all about me, more and now! My ego was insatiable.

In no way was it a replacement for what I'd abandoned some ten years ago, piquing my interest to keep me around at least for now. I would spend the next nine months, four days a week, in Mexico, learning about the import/export business along with the demands a large corporation expects out of a small business, while leaving little profit on the table to show for all our diligence. There were numerous business lessons to be learned, but it was the lesson learned outside the walls of commerce auguring insight not only regarding the light in my life, but the dark as well.

The airport would become a weekly welcomed suspension of reality. I love the airport on an early Monday morning to see what costumes humanity had rustled up to get to where they were going. It was a constant in my life to examine each and every surrounding to see what would add spice to my circus. As the Ferris wheel of life spun round and round, I consciously took mental notes, hoping this current experience would deliver what I was missing. The only problem was I had no idea what was missing.

No one knew what I was doing when I rolled my luggage up to the skycap, and neither did I for the most part, but by this time in life, I was a master of creating something out of nothing, fortifying my ego to dive into anything capable or not.

I would move around the cabin each flight to listen to the conversations by the same faces setting out on a weekly excursion to sustain a family at home. I would never utter a word; rather, I was learning what I was missing. This was a way of life, a way to grind out a living to provide for loved ones, a way to climb up the ladder of profession, a way to develop business contacts for the next deal to secure their place in the world. It was all the things I wanted and, at the same time, detested out of life because it seemed so boring. It was a weekly reminder of the battle raging within my soul, grateful for a flight duration lasting only forty minutes, knowing in only a few short minutes, I would be driving across the border to an opportunity bounding with challenges I was unsure if I was capable of handling.

My Spanish was of the educational variety and far from conversation ready, especially when trying to explain the nuances of our industry in a second language. It was an obstacle always rumbling in my mind, but it never stopped me from trying to show my earnest intent on speaking the native tongue, even though most everyone spoke English. I was thanking Goose every time I crossed the border for the lesson he'd served so long ago, leaving home at home when away if you desire to be a part of the culture you are visiting.

For the first several weeks, Javier, our salesperson, would pick me up at the airport and take me across the border to our office in a ten-story building nestled up to the Country Club of Juarez. I would watch every twist and turn, every landmark, every *Fonda*—family owned restaurant—serving up delicious vittles, as if I was creating my own visual map of the environment. I didn't like being dependent on another, and I wanted to be able to move around my new city to scour its delights without limitation. It was the same feeling I experienced with Kevin and Gregg when moving about London in the early hours, crisscrossing our way through the neighborhoods to find home. I would be a visitor, but not for long.

Our designer/office manager, Gabriela, a young architect by trade, studied at the prestigious Monterey Tech, a sister school to Harvard. She was married to another young architect, whom she met at Tech—Octavio, the lead architect for the largest developer/construction firm in Northern Mexico, specializing in the financing, design, and construction of manufacturing plants. They were an amazing couple, extremely talented professionally, well-traveled, a high sense of fashion, art conscious, loved great food, and for Octavio, a self-taught proficiency in six languages. I was soaking up my new surroundings of a country I'd thought I had a grasp on, but in fact was oblivious to the deep wealth of its people and culture.

I wanted more, needed to know more about this culture and its people if I was going to be useful to my fellow co-workers and potential customers. I knew I could teach them about the products and business strategy to have success with our clients, but strategically, I was lacking a vital ingredient necessary to pull this fantasy off.

In all reality, I was an outsider who somehow needed to be seen as one of them if success was a possibility. It was the lesson I learned early on in my sales career when calling on my Native American brothers and sisters when trust and integrity would be the key to opening the door to the hearts of people shuttered by double talk and dishonesty. How could I do this dance with a new culture and at the same time develop relationships with my co-workers and potential customers with the constant weight to make sales? A formula was devised, although unconventional. My sweet spot.

I leaned on my old tracks from childhood and would eat my way into their hearts, which so happened to be an important part of their cultural make-up. Eating was not only for sustenance, it was a time to build on family, friendships, and to solidify business opportunities, all while singing a sweet ditty to a belly without boundaries. Now we made calls, developed proposals, introduced new products to the marketplace, navigated the importation of products over the border, and gave hour-long presentations to architectural and design firms to nudge our way into any opportunity. But nothing really happened until it was time to eat.

With no aversions to any cuisine and a willingness to try anything at least twice, nourishment played perfectly in my desire to further my new friendships and, at the same time, business success as well. When you're willing to try anything, it was much easier for my voyeurs to think of me as one of them, rather than the *pinche* American down here to make some money and go home when it's all done.

In no time, I was eating at three-table family restaurants, where the grandmother was making the food and the grandkids would bring the hot plates of cow brains, tongue, tripe, and goat heart and liver to our table. To the more refined restaurants, where the eclectic food of the Aztecs were served, including worms, corn mold, ants, pigs ears, grasshoppers, and some stuff that they dared not tell me but encouraged me to try, and try I did.

The transformation was instantaneous. I was a local navigating my way around the shantytowns and cardboard shacks that housed the majority of the residences of this town of two million, sitting side by side, breaking bread, and practicing my Spanish with people no matter their station in life. I would go to areas of town my friends would not go to for fear of safety, but for my circus, it was an opportunity to be comfortable in my own shoes.

Knowingly, I was releasing the grip on my Wonder Bread life. It would be only a matter of time when the completeness of me would come crawling out of the basement of my life, well-rested and fit for some showtime. I was comfortable in this new environment, yielding a freedom to get closer to the completeness of me more than ever before. It felt like home in a sense. A feeling that was foreign to my circus. Home was always the next show.

I was across the border, in a different culture, with the intent of growing a business while nurturing my circus, and if having some cocktails with my new family was necessary, then so be it. But it was more than the controlled drinking mindset I realigned myself to; it was the emergence of Hyde from the basement of my life, waiting patiently for the night's adventures to commence every time dinner approached. It was much grander than the drink being reintroduced back into my circus. It was the self-imposed celibacy I had endured for the past two years as part of my deal-making with God that now needed some serious oiling to unloosen the tension in my spine.

It didn't take long for old patterns to emerge, pushing me deeper into the abyss of me, more and now. It didn't matter whether it was a hotel lobby, reception area of a manufacturing plant, restaurant, museum, or my favorite place to play, the airport terminal. I was engaging again with the opposite sex for the purpose of the only intimacy I knew how to engage in. It was a dance I knew too well, and now, seasoned with money and a tempered ego, not to mention the illusion of refined drinking, it allowed me to entertain in a way that soothed the emptiness ever-present in my heart. The perfect pairing of great food, great wine, and a beautiful woman was now on stage.

It was a tale of two cities only distanced by two hundred fifty miles, but necessary to release what was inside of me all along. A desire to be connected to another, to run my own shows professionally, to realize the chaining of a vital part of me in the basement of my life was obscene. This shackling never felt right without really knowing why. The only problem with this new freedom was the fact that a mere two hundred fifty miles separated my actions and inactions, when in reality, they were a million miles apart, since what went on in one environment was not going on in the other. Living two lives was an accurate description.

The inability to reconcile these polar opposites was now staring me right in the face, and I had no other option than to alter the truth to myself. I had changed in so many wonderful ways over the past several years, with a spiritual awareness benefiting not only myself, but also those surrounding me. I knew what was going down, what was happening to my life. The inability to halt a war that was just starting to unleash the heavy artillery at one another was my reality.

What was at stake was peace in my life, physically represented by the inability to now sleep through the night. My mind never rested again, knowing consciously I was moving the dark and light of my life into two separate corners of me to keep the circus tent from crumbling. The show must go on!

I was ready for anything with the circus leading the way. Saddled with an emerging spiritual foundation to bolster a bulging ego, I was left with no other conclusion. My navigational settings seemed sound, when all along, my soul was being ravaged by my actions and inactions in life. There was good and there was bad. At least, that's how I viewed it at the time. But what came next was beyond my wildest imagination, culminating in drastic measures if the circus was going to live another day.

15

TORN TO PIECES

The landscape of *Sunrise* was changing with the absence of Joseph, Eric, Franz, and Sung, and now Tawny was moving on.

I missed her arrival at *Sunrise* while attending my court-imposed sanctions of community service back in the spring. She would generally arrive shortly after the readings had been completed, with hair not fully dry, looking as if she had other matters on her mind but glad to be where she was at. I would save a seat on the bench next to me, extending the daily reflection in her direction. We always smiled at each other, knowing today would be another great day if we could find some semblance of balance in our lives. This was her place of refuge from all she was attached to in life. It was a place where she could let it rip and feel safe while challenging the origins of what was causing her imbalance.

It was nice to have her intellect in the room, to have another female voice challenged by the modern pressures of profession, relationships and, in her case, the reconciliation of spiritual matters hampered by a life dedicated to science. But it wasn't any run-of-the-mill science she was practicing, finding herself engaged in high stakes research where the cure for people with debilitating diseases was the end game.

As far as influence on the cutting-edge work in her field, she was at the top of the profession. A precarious position when the potentiality of saving not one life, but also possibly millions of lives was within her reason.

I never had the impression she was overwhelmed by this heavy load when it was her time to share, as the expectations awaiting outside the room were left in their proper place while she tended to what she could not engage in anywhere else. It was safe and she could be honest about everything at *Sunrise*. I was glad she was my friend.

Now, I had been examining my own spiritual condition and foundation over the last several months, diving head first into the spiritual waters not guided by tradition, but rather to have a better understanding of my own experience and beliefs. I had years of study under my belt, clearly toeing the line when the defined road to salvation in my tradition of choice was being proselytized. Even though I tacitly believed, something was always gnawing in my gut about our way being the only way. It never felt quite right. I needed to do some more investigation and, in fact, was commanded by my own tradition to investigate the findings of man when it came to representing God and His intent.

I would seek out and read Bart D. Ehrman's *Misquoting Jesus*, the story behind who changed the Bible and why. A sobering reflection on how man in his infinite brokenness influenced the versions of the Bible as it made its way through time, altering the true intent, while at the same time enhancing a particular strain of power or need at the time. With this new freedom, my desire wasn't to throw out the baby with the bathwater when it came to the whole text. Rather, it allowed me to be freed from certain things orchestrated to narrow in my focus on the possible outcome if you believed in a certain way. The scent reeked of man, not providence.

There is an all too familiar need in the human condition to edit the original intent when we are unsure of an outcome, so we hedge our bet, only allowing one choice for all to choose from, hoping uniformity will bring strength and purpose when in fact, it shutters the opportunity to honor another's way. At *Sunrise*, I was witnessing people from all walks of life and traditions gathering to find a spiritual experience without the tourniquet of having only one way to change their lives from the inside out. The common denominator was the spiritual experience, not what vehicle you experienced the transformation on.

The freedom to explore and challenge what never quite felt right in my gut, which had to be implicitly agreed with if I wanted to belong with my chosen religious tradition in the past, was now on the table. The freedom to weed my own spiritual garden of life was what was at stake here and the last wall still standing between the chance of having sustainable peace in my life and certain death of my soul. It was time to uncover sacred ground, and I was digging like never before.

I would devour two works by Karen Armstrong: *A History of God—The 4,000-Year Quest of Judaism, Christianity and Islam* and *The Battle for God*. These works allowed me to see the strain of man interweaved in our understanding of God through our traditional lenses and how in fact the possibility of clouding the true intent of a power grander than all can be colluded by this intervention. The fact all three of these great traditions arose from the Abrahamic tradition, splintered away from each other for reasons having to do more with man's will than God's will and now sadly oblivious to our shared beginnings. A rift tragically widening as the fear of tomorrow only becomes less sure, ignoring our common ground for the sake of wanting to be right.

In no way am I drawing conclusions for anybody with regard to a specific understanding or tradition one should be leaning toward, knowing now the freeing element for me is to have my own understanding and to honor those not of my own.

All of this searching and enlightenment I was experiencing could be summed up by a single physical act at the end of every meeting at *Sunrise,* when people from all walks of life, spiritual understandings—or lack thereof—stood together, holding hands, and prayed for one another and for those still suffering outside of those rooms, not inclusive of alcoholics. Whether one prayed out loud or meditated in silence while in the circle was irrelevant, with the importance being an ability to see beyond our differences, the trivial, bonded by our common brokenness as human beings to reach beyond the self to seek guidance, the heart of the matter.

And maybe it was easier for me to see and absorb this insight into the thread weaving itself through all human beings, a common connection of being broken and the freedom attained when we honor not only our own way, but also those of others. My palette memory with the dark in my life had me snuggling with the thought of death at an early age; reconciling this element of our human condition without the walls driven by spiritual tradition left me unafraid of death and to what lay beyond life if anything.

If death and the afterlife is the defining element separating one tradition from the next, then the possibility to honor another's way is clouded by the certainty your way is the only way with regard to what happens to our human frame after life. One day, one moment, and now one breath at a time allowed me to have peace with my own struggles as a human being and, at the same time, allowed me to have compassion for others afflicted with the human condition. If you had found your peace, then I honored it while practicing my own. If you are searching, then I honor your journey, making sure not to alter your experience intended for you all along between you and your spiritual experience. The most sacred of grounds.

On the day of Tawny's departure to greener pastures professionally, she rolled into *Sunrise* after the practice of standing to hold hands had been completed to say her goodbyes. As she made her way around the room, a warm feeling flowed in my belly, knowing something precious was forthcoming.

We would sit on the bench together once again where we had shared so many wonderful experiences, talking about the logistics of her move and if she was excited for the new opportunity. While in conversation, I watched her bend from her waist, reaching into her bag to retrieve a book she had wanted to share with me for some time now. I was unaware of the depth of her own spiritual battle residing in her being. It's impossible to know another's depth — only our own. In one form or another, we all have a deep desire to research and possibly reconcile this thirst unquenched for way too long. In the human condition a vital journey.

The need to search beyond the reason to find what was possibly missing, stirring inside, and unable to pinpoint the source, the heart of the matter, the heart of all that matters. It's funny, but when one finds themselves in this uncomfortable dilemma, the tracks of our old ways of navigating life rush to the forefront to calm the waters. It would not matter if your life experience maturity was developed enough to find a different way to unravel this dis-ease, as Tawny retreated to an environment providing the nourishment to make it in life this far: the library. It was one title that caught her attention, giving her the freedom to check out the piece and, at the same time, no commitment to anything regardless of what was uncovered in this investigation. It was research, plain and simple.

The book was Neale Donald Walsch's *The Complete Conversations with God, an uncommon dialogue.* It was a text stretching the boundaries of my own spiritual tradition, while at the same time allowing me to remove the last barrier of melding the mystical life with my spiritual tradition. It was the enlightenment my Nana knew and practiced without hesitation. A spiritual practice that today is losing favor with the demands of being a part of a believing tradition. It opened opportunities for me to practice my own daily, hourly, minute-to-minute, breath-to-breath conversation with the God of my own understanding without regard to the finality of life and the unlocked treasure of what lay beyond the beauty of death.

The battle between the sovereignty of my reason and the sovereignty of the God of my own understanding was reconciled. I had uncovered my own sustainable spiritual peace, residing the whole time no farther than six inches due south from my chin!

It was time to finish the steps and see what would happen next.

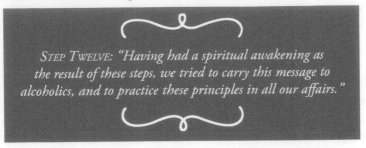

STEP TWELVE: *"Having had a spiritual awakening as the result of these steps, we tried to carry this message to alcoholics, and to practice these principles in all our affairs."*

The last place I ever thought of looking for peace was within my broken vessel, when all along, it was just waiting for me to unlock the door. Our world and religious traditions tell us to look in so many different places, confusing a sacred walk of finding peace, no matter the ebb and flow of happiness in life, and if you happen to be a human being, you are going to have fluctuations in the degree of your happiness. Being confused and unhappy makes you human, that's all. Nothing more, nothing less!

It was now time to stand up and walk out of the rooms and go back to one's family, church, community, and profession to apply the principles of what we have learned while trudging through the steps. Much has changed since we crawled in on our hands and knees, hoping relief was possible for a life that seemed too much to bear. The shackles of our lives had been released, and now sole responsibility of our actions and inactions in life rested with us.

I was beginning to trust the light and life source within myself, freeing the shackles surrounding my spirit once and for all. I could finally be released within my own vessel to be what I was intended to be all along. No one has to tell the acorn to become an oak; we provide nourishment and let it be what it is. What I had been searching for my entire life was within me the entire time, and my new mantra was to pray for it to be exercised before I ran out of fuel.

I was no longer devising an early exit strategy. The beauty of life now was the ability to find out what was within me all along, without expectations one moment to the next. The best show on Earth. No circus needed.

In my early thirties and currently in circus heaven, straddling the two worlds of my life and unable to make sense of this feeling roaring inside of my being. I was studying and absorbing the culture of my ancestors while navigating the world of international business, with not a clue how to make it happen, but it happened. I could see myself living in Mexico, building this opportunity into something I could call my own, but instinctively knowing I would always be the third wheel in ownership and decision making if I trudged forward. I never liked taking direction from anyone, and even though my role was plentiful at the moment, it would never be what I wanted, what I needed to sustain my bulging ego.

The world of business and circus tent stuffing was trivial in regards to what was going on behind the curtain of me, the heart of the matter. My spiritual awakening over the past several years had ignited a sense of delivering the best of me to my voyeurs, rather than the ability to blow your mind with wild debauchery. I wanted to make a difference on this blue planet, and I couldn't see it happening by moving products from one link in the food chain of business to the other while skimming off my portion. I was bored, with more of the same in store for me if I just kept on making it happen. I could make anything happen. Always could.

As much as I loved being in Mexico, I had to abandon the opportunity and my connection to Contract Associates if I was going to be able to reconcile the war residing in me since my first breath. My survival was on the line.

While wearing my business costume, I had developed a relationship with the business manager at Calvary Chapel, Bob Church. We quickly became friends as he became a bright light in a world where I was unsure of its followers and their intent. We would run along the large concrete flood channels crisscrossing the Albuquerque landscape, sharing our lives with each other one step at a time. I would share with him the battle raging inside, and he would share his own experience backed up by some scripture to research on my own. I let him know I was done with the business world and needed to share my life in a way of helping others who could not help themselves. I had no idea what was available, but Bob had a wonderful idea that touched all of me.

Now, Calvary Chapel, in Albuquerque, started some ten years earlier in the community room of an apartment complex, surging quickly on a foundation of sound teaching to a reported ten thousand worshippers. It was a mega church, with plenty of people tithing, allowing the ministry to reach out beyond the local community and into the world. The national and international reputation of our spiritual leader, Skip, would attract spiritual speakers and missionaries of the highest regard.

In fact, one of the church's board members was Franklin Graham, Billy's prodigal son, who had massaged the pastor's kid lifestyle to its fullest until the call within himself pulled him to the pulpit. He would lead his father's ministries and create his own, reaching out into the world, with one of those efforts being a little-known offshoot of the highly successful Samaritan's Purse. It was the medical mission's arm of that ministry, a sister to the more well-known Doctors Without Borders. A group comprised of professional volunteers placing themselves in harm's way to serve the war-torn and natural disaster areas of our world.

With my recent departure from the business world, my till and available time was abundant, and that was a problem, knowing full well if I didn't do something soon, the turmoil inside would show its face once again, unleashing Hyde to play at will and sapping a golden opportunity to change my course once and for all. I had a plan—or should I say a thought.

My entire life, the desire to push the dark away for good was a constant, hoping I could find a semblance of peace to shield myself while this battle raged on. I had a plan of accomplishing this feat, with an equal desire to help others, and if I could do both at the same time, it would be ideal. My plan was simple: ask Bob Jefferson for his counsel and, more importantly, his blessing to further my spiritual knowledge with a stint at The Dallas Seminary to eventually have a pulpit of my own. It was a homerun in my eyes, and all would benefit from this decision. I thought this news would bring joy to Bob, but his reaction was far from what I expected.

Bob didn't want me to move in that direction and was stern in his feelings of my role in helping another.

"If you attain the credentials and then your own church, it will not be the best use of your gifts. You have a gift of touching people outside the confines of church, not possible if you directed your energy toward a controlled group. I believe your impact will be most valuable being in the world. My wish is for you not to go that route."

I had trouble understanding his reason, and maybe it was because it was not my way, but another's, or maybe I didn't understand what he was saying. In all reality, I had not reconciled the war within, and somewhere deep in my consciousness, I believed total emersion in the pulpit would keep me safe from me. I heeded his counsel and kicked forward, never to let the thought wander again in the battle within.

The pastor plan was out. How about a missionary? Bob Church's plan was to contact the person who headed up the medical missions program for Samaritan's Purse in Africa and offer my services for a year. My résumé was dusted off and sent with the blessings and recommendations of Calvary Chapel. A position was opening up in a couple of months in Uganda, with the responsibility of coordinating shipments of supplies to the hospitals in war-ravaged Sudan. It wasn't my plan, and maybe that was the key.

The opportunity to really help another was within reach. The opportunity to shed the monetary yoke for a higher calling while supporting myself at no cost to the mission, positioning me in the world where I could make the most impact as Bob Jefferson had advised. I was excited like never before, feeling like all of this torment over the last thirty-four years was finally coming to a head to benefit another. My internal war would be overcome by the war I was going to help fight. It was about the greater good. It was not about me, I thought. It was perfect. I hoped.

An interview was conducted via satellite telephone with the man who would make the decision whether or not I would be packing my bags for a life-changing experience. He was deep in the jungles of Africa, and I was hoping to be with him soon. In his mind's eye, everything looked like a go, but he wanted to pray about it first to make sure it was the right thing for all. It was in God's hands now, and whatever came about would have me where I was supposed to be at the time. I experienced a rarity in my life — peace — for a brief moment when exiting the church offices, unaware of the new battle that lay ahead.

My oldest brother, Juno, had navigated his way back to New Mexico from Chicago with his wife Julia and a growing family. He left New Mexico at the age of seventeen, hoping to further his insatiable desire to further his knowledge academically, but also to free himself from the ties to his own experience when growing up in our family. It's ironic, but in some way, his survival was dependent upon leaving his biological family and his return to create a home for his own family based on a perceived environment of safety in New Mexico that went underserved as a child.

He was lured back by an offer from my brother Ralph-David, who himself decided his safety would be best served by being in business with our father. Juno would come on board to add his intellect to a business suffering through some tough times with no profits to show for years. They were holding on, looking for some new blood to right the ship, and Juno had had his fill with the high finance world. A shift in his coordinates was the heart of his matter, as it was about his family, not himself anymore. Promises were made and a deal was done.

For all intents and purposes, Juno and I were strangers. We were alike in many ways biologically, sharing an abundance of DNA and, at the same time, miles apart on so many deep-seated ways of survival. Independently, we had created our own islands of safety as children and then as adults, with his most recent and highly protected sphere of safety composed of the family he would raise with Julia.

Time and distance freed Juno from the dysfunction of our family unit. However, he unknowingly was placing himself and his family in harm's way by being unaware of the potential minefields strategically placed for survival by all the family players when their survival was at stake. With his reason alone, he tried to clean up old family ties when it came to business dealings and for the most part was successful.

What he didn't know was the potential partnership he was counting on to sustain his family would be the foe he would struggle with the most. Sometimes in life, being with those who you're most like doesn't necessarily mean unity of purpose to achieve a common goal. The goal was to make money with no disagreement on that front, but what was at stake would be the sharing of the bounty, if any. The stakes were high and the dice were rolled.

Meanwhile, I was biding my freedom, playing golf and nourishing my spiritual condition. I was residing in one city at the moment, feeling relief from the duality of my circus act and patiently waiting for a phone call to open up life to an experience containing the potential to change my course forever. I was calm, knowing the decision was in capable hands, testified by the fact the man making the decision was praying for guidance as well. I expected a decision around the end of January and was feeling a sense of calm in my troubled waters for the very first time in my life, even though I had trouble absorbing the feeling.

One of the underlying currents in the human frame when feeling this feeling is to understand its genesis. The desire for me to control each and every moment in my life always took precedence, causing the turbulence I always flew in, but by releasing expectation and the attachment to an outcome, I was now having a sense of peace. It didn't last very long.

The peace I had desired my whole life slipped slowly away when approached by Juno to query my plans on what was next in my life. He was the only family member who asked me this question and by this time, the only family member I had any real communication with. The biological lines were drawn several years earlier, and my life seemed to be all the better for it. I spoke frankly with Juno, sharing with him what had transpired over the past several weeks and my desire to travel the road less taken while helping another along the way.

It was the most vital element in me needing to be exercised. I would try to explain, but what I was unable to share, what I hoped for in silence, would be the end of the war raging inside. I wish I could have expressed those feelings out loud; sharing what was at the core of the circus with anyone regardless of my new spiritual foundation was tricky. I trusted only skin deep, including my growing relationship with God, knowing this whole spiritual walk stuff could crumble due to my deal-making with God years ago. I was the only active ingredient in my life, tragically leaving me standing alone if it all came apart.

He would challenge my spiritual foundation, asking me if I believed literally what was in the Bible. I was stumped. I knew something never quite felt right, but I was committed to my tradition, and to be a part of it, I had to believe in it all. My answer was a tepid yes at best, twisted with some logic to convince my audience of one.

We would wrestle over the reasoning of my desires several more times over the next several months.

I'm sure he was concerned for my safety in some regard, the trivial, but if it didn't work out, "Why you don't start your own company and we can be your partners? We will run the back end of the business."

It made perfect sense business-wise. I could do what I do best and leave all the details to someone else. Half measures. I loved building things, taking risks, while I despised the monotony of running them when they became successful. Boring. Suffocating. The fun was in the risk of flying through the air without a net, and unknowingly, it was a button he had pushed. At the very least, it was an option if God had other plans for my circus and me.

Waiting. Patience. With reflection, I wished I didn't have a second option to sift through while my higher power delivered the verdict. Cutting through only one option at a time was my forte. The heart of the matter was to change the tides to the internal war one way or the other, hoping the light would intercede on my behalf, with sustainable peace the end result.

As one month turned into two with no phone call, I began to prepare for what may lie ahead. Maybe it was time to reconnect with my brothers and father in a new way. Maybe my missionary field was a lot closer than I'd anticipated. Africa would be the easier, softer way compared to the challenges of being yoked with my new business partners, whose heart of the matter was self-survival based on material wealth. Money meant a whole lot more to them than it did to me, and I knew this going in. How could I shield myself in this arena if our union was meant to be? I had been wearing a W.W.J.D. (What Would Jesus Do) bracelet on my wrist for the last several years as a reminder to a higher calling, and if my destiny were to be yoked with my brothers and father, I would need a reminder for myself. The corporate name would be W.W.J.D. LLC. I was only hoping that would be enough. I was building another wall.

No call! Time was running out, even though it really wasn't, but I was the active ingredient in my circus, and something needed to be done to start the show. Everything in my being, my heart, the survival of my soul and the potentiality of peace in my life, rested in Africa, with staying in New Mexico and starting another business a distant second. I was isolated in the decision without reaching out to Bob Jefferson or Mr. Toliver for spiritual direction. In my heart, I believed I was ready to thoughtfully, with God leading the way, come to a sound decision. It was a tragic mistake. I was truly a circus of one.

The draw to the old tracks of making something happen slowly crept back in by setting a date of moving forward with option two if I had not been summoned to a distant land to save my soul. The date came and went, and I committed to option two, reasoning no call was the answer from above I had been waiting for all along. I'd learned about the essence of integrity over the last several years, with the vital ingredient being my yes is my yes and my no is my no. The ability to stick with a decision if the circumstances change, even if that decision could be revisited, was not an option, especially if the revision would only be to my benefit. The Dingo Bar was instrumental. We never know where and when the lesson for growth will be served.

This new way of navigating my circus would be tested within the first week of my new enterprise, as the phone call I had been waiting for, although not patiently, would finally arrive. Africa was calling and my services were needed as soon as possible. My integrity was on the line, and I had no other choice but to decline the opportunity and follow through on my decision, no matter either the outcome or the pain inflicted on my soul already realized. I was unequally yoked with my partners, and I knew this from the very beginning. We would never be able to till the line of honesty and trust, the heart of any relationship.

It was the right decision, I kept reminding myself in the first year of business when trying to execute a business plan written within the confines of my mind only. It was fun flying solo, making strategic decisions, developing a team, and setting the tone of how we did business with integrity. It was a business model foreign to my partners, as they were hoping I could make magic once again with certain windfall coming their way, the heart of their matter.

A strategic alliance with a major manufacturer would develop and a courtship commenced. I knew I needed a differentiator to separate my model from my competition, and in my mind, my decision was being blessed from above. It would be the first time I would lay eyes on Harold, an instant connection on a shared way of doing business, with integrity and humor being the ties binding us together. If I needed, I could source his counsel on business opportunities and strategic maneuvering, since we were of the same mindset, something that was missing with my partners. I had no idea how vital he would become to my survival.

With half measures the driving fuel behind my intent, the business was being blessed with instant success. I created a flow of business immune to the cyclical nature of buying habits, as well as sourcing key projects in Northern Mexico with the assistance of my family from across the Rio Grande.

All of my good fortune was gladly being recognized as originating from my higher power. My ego was in check and the money started to flow. The energy of the business spawned to the other companies my partners were involved with, and all were realizing the tides to profitability.

It was looking as if my decision a year earlier to pursue integrity over the health of my soul was turning out fruitful, even though the foundation was terminal. I started to drink heavily again to subdue the pain I was feeling inside.

The circus had been reshuffled over the years, but the facts were I was not being genuine with myself, but only a fragment of a shadow of what lay within. I was manipulating myself. The pain and loneliness deepened. I leaned in and waited for some relief. I isolated in darkness while surrounded by the light.

The spiritual war raging within had me straddling the fence of the light and dark in my life. I enjoyed the finer things in life and going to nice places. I loved my church and friends, both old and new. I found new, sophisticated people to drink expensive wine with. I tuned up my golf game with a country club membership, where I could drink and no one cared how much. I would entertain women from all walks of life: attorney, custom homebuilder, pharmaceutical executive, pilot, strippers, entrepreneurs, college students, models, divorced, single with and without children, and married. Hoping with desperation something would change. I tried about everything. I wanted to be normal, not knowing what that entailed. I wanted a family.

I essentially outed myself in my hometown with a new twist in my circus centered on my spiritual walk and a business model designed by faith. The walls of my duality were closing in on me, and I would have to isolate even more not to be found out as a hypocrite. I needed another city to freely exercise my whole being, and a jewel not more than seventy miles north would be an ideal playground for me to sneak away for a night to exercise what I tried so valiantly to snuff from my life.

The seat of government, with a deep history, world-renowned art scene, elegant dining, eclectic characters, bohemian cowboy culture, and an underworld of drugs and alcohol waiting for my insatiable appetite: Santa Fe. I had friends in Santa Fe—well, they were David's friends who became my friends as well: Dennis, Brian, Yurum, Henri, Carl, Dale, Bo, and Rich. But it was the friendship with Jeff that would evolve into a union based on humor, music, honesty, and the outer edges of life lasting a lifetime.

I was returning to the old formula of spinning plates, but this time, it wasn't multiple businesses; rather, it was the spinning of my soul. Even though there were hundreds of experiences representing the tortured nature of my soul and the extreme measures of my current act, one particular sordid attempt to help another framed it all. The intent was forthright and the execution precise, with my reason directing my current act, relying on the old pattern of getting what I wanted and keeping what I had, the heart of my matter. The inability to reconcile the light and dark in my life was beaming brightly when I set out to help another.

The air in my sails, with my spiritual walk leading the way, were taut and full, as was the desire to tap the hidden treasures awaiting myself and those who surrounded my weekly no-holds-barred wrestling match with Hyde. Boolettuce would have been proud. I was fit and experienced at navigating two cities. It was extreme measures with the minimum effort.

The success of the business could not be denied, due to its spiritual foundation, holding steadfast to its tenants and watching it grow one month to the next. The business supported the radio ministry at Calvary with radio spots, not boasting my own lot, but rather communicating to the listeners to support my brother's other business of which I had no interest. Other charities, local food banks, and shelters were also beneficiaries of our good fortune. But in my eyes, it wasn't enough, since I had to help another with my own hands.

A family friend who attended Calvary encouraged me to get involved with a local outreach to the children's detention center. It was where non-adult males were sent to serve out their sentences before turning eighteen to be released back into the community. They were hardened criminals at the tender ages of fourteen, fifteen, and sixteen.

The ministry was simple: lead a Bible study on Friday night every week. I was assigned a pod and provided a table in the middle of the room, and whoever wanted to attend would come out of their cell and sit down. I opened with prayer, read scripture, and talked about how it applied to our life. It was easy to connect with these kids, as I too was a child, not knowing at the time my stunted emotional condition.

It was a match made in heaven. My experiences honed me for this environment, using a seasoned intellect with pragmatism, allowing me to adjust on the fly when communicating to my captive audience. I enjoyed the challenge of young minds involved in their own wrestling match, and my experience, though different, touched them in a way no other could. I not only understood their battle, but was currently dealing with my own while sitting in the pod, testifying to my own changes in life, when in fact, my battle was not reconciled, but disguised in a hypocritical mask. I consciously knew this when walking through the metal detectors every Friday night and, unfortunately for me, able to walk out of the facility several hours later. They were locked in a physical sense, but my self-incarceration was shredding my soul. Who was the prisoner, I kept asking myself. The reflection didn't last long. Ego massaged, box checked, now what about me?

My journey was sapping the vim and vigor for life out of me with the inability to rest comfortably in my own actions and inactions. No one knew what was going on inside the confines of the big tent, me included. And even though I masterminded this charade, the grip on my life and the outcomes were slowly becoming beyond my control.

It was Friday night and my life consisted of Bible study and dinner alone, with no possibility of getting closer to the family of my own that surely would be the answer to all my internal strife. If I had a family, it couldn't be all about me anymore. Right?

The draw to me was insatiable without the distraction of a significant other, I kept reminding myself. If I could only unravel all this self-induced turmoil, my outcome might be different, and the jail cell I'd just exited reminded me of this fact. Drastic measures were needed. The walls that I had erected for safety crept in. I made a decision. Relieving the pressure was crucial for survival. No longer would I retreat home to wallow in loneliness to squander well-intended fun. Relief was only seventy miles north.

As the metal on metal clanging of the prison cell doors echoed in my mind every Friday night to remind me of my tortured soul, I quickly shuttered those feelings of family and being alone with a quick drive up to Santa Fe to lubricate my rusting best friend, Hyde. Fueled by high-grade Peruvian flake, I would catch up with friends in the basement of Evangelo's, shooting pool to see what delights would come my way. Dallas socialites, L.A. hipsters, jet setters, and trust fund babies from the East coast and Europe fit nicely within the capabilities of my circus. I blended in and stood out at the same time because I had no other choice.

A dizzying dance from one establishment to another was my death march, making sure no stone would be left unturned. El Farol, El Nido, Coyote Cantina, The Bell Tower at La Fonda, Hotel Saint Francis Bar, Tommy's, and the Double A. I had only a brief window of opportunity before I returned back to the mask that beamed light, so much needed to be accomplished to satisfy Hyde before he retreated to the basement to wait patiently until Friday night returned. It was an unspoken agreement satisfying the duo of us for the moment.

Saturday morning would come quickly, opening up other possibilities to stretch the circus tent and its performers. The famed Santa Fe Opera, art gallery openings, wine and food festivals, and the ever-present urban spices fueled the engine until I returned home for Bible study on Sunday night. I wanted to stop what was happening to me. I never really tried. Impossible!

The nature of my friendship with Jeff was the rock I held onto when navigating by the coordinates solely guided by Hyde while in Santa Fe. Even though we imbibed in the environment together, it was the honesty we were able to share with one another about the portions of our life we felt uncomfortable sharing with anyone else. I would openly share the duality of my life, and Jeff listened without judgment. We would learn how to scuba dive, venturing to San Pedro, Belize, for my thirtieth birthday celebration. Music would bind us.

The list of vital friends was growing: Kevin, Gregg, Spike, David, Miguel, Tim, and now Jeff. I had more than my fair share. Their value was monumental to my growing isolation in the circus of me, but the energy expelled to connect with anyone beyond this group was deemed non-essential. A tragedy in its reasoning. A furthering of my inability to have intimate relations with other human beings would be the destination I was headed for. I would develop these relationships and drift away when life's tides moved another or me in the opposite direction. I was itching for more again, unsure what that was.

The effort it took to sneak away to Santa Fe every weekend to gorge my appetite was tearing me apart physically, emotionally, and spiritually. And even though the desire to fuel Hyde with amazing people, places, and things would never wane, the toll of this chosen lifestyle since the age of eight was wearing me down. I was exhausted. I was bored with the unordinary!

I couldn't do it with repetition like I used to. It was a young man's game, and I needed to reverse course and drink like a gentleman. I turned thirty-six.

I loved entertaining clients on a weekly basis, where I could showcase my new passion for the expensive grape. I would stumble upon a tiny French Bistro in Albuquerque in a strip mall—Le Café Miche—with eight tables and a small bar, where I would eat and drink wonderful wine alone. It was a safe haven for me, where I could enjoy my love affair with great food served up by this Viking named Klaus, while his wonderful wife Linda tended to the guests. He introduced me to the world of fine wine, and I was hooked in more than one way. I became an oenophile. The hard booze and the recreational drug use were over for the most part, and I was relieved.

One client in particular I would entertain — he had the same proclivity for the culinary arts and wine — would develop into a wonderful friendship. The esteemed senior senator, highly talented architect, tomahawk chop golf swinging, amazing depth of mind and spirit, lover of the song and prose Sir Richard. It became less about business and more about enjoying each other's company on a weekly basis. He stretched my mind as we bantered from one topic to the next, whether it was philosophy, social movement, spiritual enlightenment, history, art, music, and most importantly, the caverns of our own humanity. I loved our friendship, and he came to know the depth of my struggles as I became aware of his own.

We were sharing on a level I had developed with so few, and I acknowledged its scarcity and sacredness, but this didn't stop us from leaning on each other to imbibe in the liquid spirit. Our friendship would be the bridge I needed to freely open up the well of my discontent with my whole life. He knew my biological family, he knew my business partners, and he knew or was introduced to my date du jours. Above all, it was safe to discuss with him with high intellect my troubled nature. He challenged my reasoning with a gentle hand, sharing the depths of his own troubles as his experiences tore him to pieces as well. It wasn't all doom and gloom, as a trust of our secrets shared with each other allowed us to be steadfast for continuing life in the physical sense we both found troubling to keep afloat.

The desire to be alone had deepened, as had the desire to be flailing at all hours of the night, entertaining the next warm body. I was good at it. I was better than good. The capture of my prey was sometimes slow and methodical, and sometimes I struck with a wanting that had my own head spinning. I wasn't interested in a relationship anymore, and the marriage delusion was shifted to another decade, but that was the trivial.

The heart of the matter was the inability to connect with the opposite sex in an intimate fashion outside of sex. I would expel the necessary energy to slither my way into the sheets, and while taking my clothes off, I emotionally and physically detached before I even had the opportunity to experience the only part I knew how to engage in as far as intimacy was concerned. I was crushed by my own selfishness, and I wanted to be alone. I couldn't deceive another. I couldn't deceive myself. But we do! The show must go on.

My friendship with Richard deepened as our solitude grew in the pain of our inability to connect in a meaningful way with the opposite sex. A weekly cache of great wine, great food, silly banter, topped off with a nightcap of whisky and strippers was as far as we could go. It was enough if we held on to each other, a precarious position for either of us when counting on another person to keep the dark from taking complete control. We could never rely on each other completely. Strangely, it was safe. It was all we could engage in at the moment, and then cupid stroked our hearts almost simultaneously.

In my nightly shenanigans, I met Audrey at one of my watering holes and was completely smitten by her sheer beauty. I was uncertain of her heritage, but was sure she was a mix of Asian and Caucasian, with the most stunning hazel, almond-shaped eyes I had ever seen. I was happily surprised by her witty humor and zest for life. I couldn't put my finger on it, but she was unlike anyone I had met. I asked her for her number and she said no! I was a little taken aback, but I liked her spunk. Not getting what I wanted didn't happen very often, and if it did, I wasn't really interested anyway. But this was different, since I was interested and now frozen in disbelief. I didn't necessarily like working for the affection of the opposite sex. I want what I want when I want it. I had only one option: give her my number and see what happened next. I didn't like not having control.

Several weeks lapsed, and in all honesty, I had forgotten about Audrey, when my phone rang with a number I was not familiar with. That was another peculiar trait of mine. I never gave my phone number out unless it was for business, and if so, I would know who was calling me since I had their number first. Control. At least, I thought I was, but in all reality I was out of control. Delusional. Her voice was sweet and soft, with an edge. I quickly invited her to dinner, and she shared with me that she doesn't date much and would consider my invitation. I couldn't figure this girl out. She was beautiful, smart, and witty, and I was convinced there must be a long line of suitors knocking on her door. I was persuasive, and she relented to a Saturday night date.

I was intrigued and, for the first time in a long time, excited about going on a date. I was a little nervous when approaching her house in the university part of town.

Personally, with the windfall from selling my shares at Contract Associates three years earlier, I had purchased a home in the planned community of High Desert at the base of the Sandia Mountains. It was a desperate move when trying to convince Leigh Ann of my desire to have a family, a sad attempt to piece together a family because I thought having a home was one of the building blocks. A large home with three bedrooms, a master suite upstairs, completely empty except for the twin bed, dresser, and a ten-inch television set stuffed in a downstairs bedroom as the only remnant of my delusional thinking. An empty heart preceded an empty home.

As I approached her front door, it was open, with the screen the only barrier to her abode. I knocked, knowing it was futile with the humming of the blow dryer in the distance doing a dance with her silky brunette hair. She was not Asian; she was a mix of Swedish and Spanish. I stood there for a few minutes, just listening, listening for quiet, and when it approached, I leaned in, pressing my lips to the screen door to announce my arrival.

She bellowed back, "Come in. I'm almost ready."

I opened the screen door, shuffling to the center of the small living room, finding myself unsettled and slightly nervous.

"I'm trying to find a pair of shoes to wear. Come back here and talk to me while I figure it out."

Not lacking confidence, I walked to the back of her house and stood in the middle of her bedroom, engaged enough with her banter to respond to any question that might come my way while scanning the room to find out a little more about this person whom I found extremely smart, attractive, and funny. It all seemed normal until I looked beyond her bedroom and saw what I thought was a door to the exterior, only to realize it was a small room with furniture filling its capacity. Pushed to the left rear of the room was a wooden crib. She was a momma! My heart sank and rose at the exact same moment. I took a shallow gasp of air, hoping to hear her next word. My life quickly flashed before my eyes. I've had this experience before, but the roles were reversed. I took a deep breath and continued our conversation. I needed a drink. Drinks!

I whisked us both off to dinner at one of my spots where the waiter knew my preferences, and the wine flowed beautifully to ease our first date uneasiness. We were both a little nervous, and through the course of our dinner, she revealed her situation. She was single mom, recently broken up from the father of her child and ready to move forward with life. She was extremely mature for twenty-three, with thirteen years separating our belly button birthdays.

I thought to myself, I might have more life experiences, but she was definitely more mature than I. She was full of energy and the enormity of life was her stepping stool, and I couldn't keep my eyes off her unique presence. But something else stirred my drink this evening. Could it possibly be the life-long desire to have a family of my own? Was it within my grasp? I wasn't even looking for it. Was she the one?

It had happened in my own life, where a man not of my biology became my friend. I could be her son's friend, and maybe, just maybe if this all worked out, a family of my own was within reach. It was too early to have these thoughts, but I would be lying if I told you otherwise. What I had all but given up on was sitting across the table from me, making me laugh. Her desire was to have a family of her own, unlike the family she grew up with. We were connected in many ways beyond the physical attraction, engaging my interest because in the past, my attention would soon wane when my intellect was not challenged. She challenged me on many levels. Was this an impossible match? I would pursue with respect and purity of intent. New tracks.

The evening wound down and I walked her to her doorstep and hugged her goodbye. She was a young woman, a mother of a son. The me, more and now always present to soothe my ego had been frozen in its well-worn tracks by honoring this human being, wanting to treat her as such by the experience I'd experienced as a child. No kiss, no attempt to sully the moment. This was real life. Was this a possible mirror to my own experience when growing up, and could I do it differently if given the chance? I needed a chance. Desperately.

We would spend a little bit of time together every day for the first few months, except for the days when she would have her son under her care. She was protecting her most sacred jewel, and I concurred. She had no idea about my experience as a child when a man entered my life not of my own biology up until her emotions of our growing connection collided with the fracturing of her recent, although tenuous, family unit. I felt her moving away from our connection, and I had to reach her with my feelings of which I had never sourced before when keeping what I had or getting what I wanted. I was feeling so alive! So scared! I reached out with words not from my mouth, but in the written form and truly opened up to another human being for the first time in my life, sharing with her a piece of me that had been buried forever. I honored her as a mother, as a person revealing my true intent.

It was a fraction of what I was capable of, and the experience was amazing. I didn't have to manipulate or control another human being to fill my needs, and it was a breakthrough I had been longing for my entire life. The electricity between us was contagious, and lo and behold, she had a girlfriend whom we introduced to Richard, and they became one as well.

My heart was healing and the ability to navigate without the circus was in my thoughts. I would no longer chain Hyde in the basement, as he was free to surface when the fun was in play, and when the responsibility of being in a relationship with a mother of a beautiful child was at hand, he gladly stepped aside.

I was at peace except for when I descended from the base of the mountains down to the valley every morning to go to work. Nothing had changed.

With fortunes multiplying and the till filling up, my decision-making paradigm had not changed, but my intent was now in question. I was leaning into the mindset of my partners, feeling like I had to protect my share of the wealth flowing that all along was being provided from above. I'd never cared about money, but now I seemed to care as much as they seemed to care.

My heart sunk with pain as my thoughts moved me closer to positioning myself in their vein of money first and integrity a distant second. I knew what was going on, and it had nothing to do with whom they were but how I was feeling. How I was acting and not acting. Despising this turn in my character, I knew it would be a matter of time before one small disagreement would tear our edifice down.

Ironic in that Juno convinced me to consider the opportunity and a disagreement between the two of us convinced me my stay had been too long. I wanted out and they were glad to have all the spoils for their own. I suggested they give me an offer to buy me out and they did. It was a paltry offer no one in their right mind would accept, and if the shoe was on the other foot, none of my partners could ever accept. But with my recent Dingo Bar lesson learned and my disdain for how the draw to the dollar made me feel, I accepted. It was their terms and their deal. It meant a lot more to them than it ever had to me, and I knew that the first minute I agreed to shutter my dreams in Africa. The heart of what mattered was my dream of helping those that could not help themselves. Unfulfilled.

I was ready to resume what I had chosen not to pursue several years earlier, when my ability to let happen next was sabotaged by inability to let happen, happen next. My next thought was that in a few short months, I would get my settlement and I would be able to manufacture my next experience, providing the delusion I could move back in time and undo what I had done. A tragic mistake under any circumstance, for the simple fact that today is today and it will never be that time again.

At the moment, things seemed simple. I was drinking like a gentleman for the most part. I had a wonderful relationship that had its challenges, but overall it was a blessing, and I was opening up the possibility of tapping the source inside me wanting—or should I say needing—to help another who could not help themselves. Knowing mystically if I didn't unlock this desire welling in my being before my first breath, it would be the death of me.

I had a plan...another tragic mistake!

16

NO MORE MASKS

It is much easier to start something,
Than it is to end something...Jimmy.

loved having a plan and executing it to precision. Risk taking was my passion. My old friend the vascular surgeon was dusting off his rubber gloves hoping to get some face time while executing my new plan of survival.

In all essence, I was only surviving the past thirty-seven years since my magic cure, hoping for so many things but unable to find peace along the way. The ebb and flow of the extremes of my life had stunted my ability to be honest with myself for so long I had trouble deciphering what was real and what was fantasy. I was tired of my circus life, so I did the only thing I knew how to do and kicked forward, since deliberate death by my own hand was out of the question. I was a coward.

My spiritual awakening was intact, although structured on reason and getting what I wanted — a sure sign of an unsustainable relationship with a power greater than I. In all reality I was no longer the same person who was lifted along the way by a cadre of human beings, grateful for their presence and unconditional love. I wanted to share my feelings with them of how they changed my life forever, but I was slowly retreating back to my old tracks of relying on myself and no one else. It didn't have to be this way. They would help if they knew of my desperation. I was a master of disguise. I made every single choice. We all do.

Luckily Hyde was close by with a sole purpose of keeping me from feeling alone, but with a new relationship and a child to think about, I didn't need him as much as before. I wanted more. Everyone around me deserved more.

My relationship with Hyde always weighed heavy on my soul with the inability to reconcile his role in my life once and for all; recognizing my futile attempts in the past by simply chaining him in the basement was a sure recipe for disaster. He was a trusted friend and in most cases my only friend when it really mattered. Our bond was unbreakable.

This would not be the time to sever our relationship. I would need him in these turbulent times—this I was sure of. Life is turbulent. He was a lifesaver.

The tides had changed for the better when a plan of reconstituting my aborted Africa trip several years ago became the perceived saving grace to mend my tattered soul. I was on shaky ground, spiritually, and unfortunately my plan hinged on one vital element—money.

It was a tragic paradox of the grandest proportion, positioning itself directly in front of my serenity while at my weakest moment. Not unlike the unparalleled ideals of love and hate, spiritual matters and money were workable within my wheelhouse of extremes. A circus of many abilities and performers comprised in one breathing body could pull this off. I only needed the dead presidents to sustain the behemoth of a house I purchased, thinking it would bring a family and to support my own ministry while serving those so far away. Naïve.

What I despised and feared the most, relying on another, had me in troubled waters. I was relying on my partners, my family, my brothers, and my father to do the right thing and pay me what they agreed to pay me by their own deal. What I never thought would happen, happened, and I guess I didn't know my customer like I should have. Their safety and comfort, their survival, was solely centered on one and only one element: material wealth. It was the elixir driving them to any means.

The disappointment was not a surprise altogether, as I had watched and participated in the manipulation of another to get what one wants and to keep what one has. The trust for another was at an all-time low, as I waited patiently for the next month to appear, hoping integrity would rule the day and they would do what they had devised and agreed upon.

The desire to connect with my father had faded long ago. The desire to connect with my brother Juno was damaged but reparable. My only hope was the connection with my brother Ralph-David, whom I had spent my whole life with except for a few years here and there. He was the closest idea of family I had going for me. He was my only hope. But a sinister web was being woven, and I was oblivious, as my father's role grew when disagreements occur between siblings. He was working the room, and this case it was his sons against each other, skillfully weaving a web to ensure an imbalance between us all while making sure his own till would be intact and possibly enhanced. He would never be poor, and personal relations or even his own spawn would be fair game to that end.

I was retreating by the hour, by the minute, by each breath to the only thing that ever worked in my life when all else seemed to fail. My self-will. My current relationship would never understand what was going on, and the real tragedy is it might have been possible if I knew how to communicate the emptiness I was feeling inside. Hell, I couldn't understand what was going on at the time. I was embarrassed to acknowledge, even to myself, what was going on, let alone attempt to explain it to another human being.

Dilemma. Reach out or reach in? I was going to fight this obstacle alone like everything else in my life and I was going to do it with integrity and honesty, a sure remnant of my recent spiritual training. I was grateful for my experience at The Dingo Bar, having made the right decision when I found myself in a dispute.

The only person capable of carrying me through this mess was myself, propelling me to communicate and reach out to Ralph-David. I tried. Kept trying. He would go weeks without returning my phone calls. He made me feel like he was doing me a favor by asking for what they had agreed to. What I earned. Heartbroken. Emotionally I crawled into the fetal position. I felt like a child.

Finally a return call and it was not about what we had agreed upon but rather to inform me Juno left the business as well. I guess Juno couldn't take it anymore and his own survival was in the crosshairs when his partnership with those he was most like crumbled. What he was promised was retracted because the deal didn't seem fair anymore now with the fortunes in the black. Ralph-David requested some time to get everything settled. I was compassionate and agreed to a monthly stipend to be subtracted from what they owed me when the waters calmed.

The payment was never on time, and I found myself chasing Ralph-David for weeks as he dodged my phone calls or simply ignored them. I couldn't pay my bills, and this included my mortgage. I was begging.

He was stoic and without compassion. It was about the deal and about winning. The strategy was to wear me down, and if they could pay me less than they agreed to, why not. What I found out later is they purchased another business with the windfall from my endeavors and maybe had nothing at the moment to take care of what they owed me regardless of the amount. Who cares what the reasoning was. It was about integrity. It was absent. Me, more, and now.

The patterns were tired, the tracks were worn, and the method of agreeing to something and changing one's mind for the simple reason it wasn't to their liking anymore was a tune played-out. The payments ceased without a word, and I had no other choice but to pursue legal proceedings, as reason and begging fell on deaf ears. It was out of my hands now, and I had to get back to work to keep my rudderless ship afloat.

My dream was gone. I was shattered and no one knew it. The show must go on!

I had lost all faith in faith by this time. The only thing I trusted to keep me above water was the Hyde, who saved my hide so many times before. I was icy. I was without feelings. I was going to a place even I was unfamiliar with to find comfort. I was surrounded by many who could help, or at least provide comfort, but I was making a choice to rely on what seemed natural, what seemed normal, to be alone even though I was surrounded by the human element the whole time. To be alone when surrounded by people who love you and whom you love is the darkest of moments. Pitch Blackness.

It was no one's fault or actions driving me to where I was now, as my choices had all along been my own and this was another manifestation of acting on the first thought that came to mind. I was back where I started and I felt so dead inside. I had never grown emotionally. I wanted to live. I had a reason—Audrey and her son. I had no business being in a relationship. I wanted to care for them and I did as best I could, but it would never be enough or, at the very least, what they deserved. I was unable to keep my promises.

The only improvements in my life were my golf game and alcohol intake. I whittled down my handicap to single digits and my bar tab up to high triple digits per month. I polished off my résumé and was contacted by a headhunter from the great peach state of Georgia. In a matter of a week I had offers from all over the country. Relief was in sight.

With a short-term loan from Paul, I was able to make it to the New Year and then quickly cashed in my retirement account, paying him back and patching up my sinking ship. It was tenuous at best. The nest egg I was building for the future was gone. I needed to reestablish financial security. I needed to save my house from being taken back by the bank. I needed to survive. I settled on an opportunity in Austin, Texas.

Within a week the offer was accepted and I packed my car, leaving Audrey and her son behind in the house I created for a family. Aborted dream. My relationship was in turmoil. I was afraid to hold on; I was afraid to let go. I was frozen in indecision. I had no choice but to go. I needed to breathe. I inhaled without a plan. Painful.

Austin, Texas. The Third Coast. Keep it Weird. The Longhorns. Texas hippies. Live music capital of the world. Austin City Limits. A blue city in a red state. An amazing and diverse food scene. Farm to table. Food trucks. Lake Austin. Barbecue. The Mean Eyed Cat. Southern hospitality. High-tech. The seat of state government. Guero's. The Greenbelt. Curra's Grill. Zilker Park. Deep Eddy. Barton Springs. Hamilton Pool. Clarksville. 78704. Vintage clothing. Bookstores. Amy's. Whole Foods. Tacodeli. The Yellow Rose. Expose. Cowboy boots. Tattoo parlors. Hip hop, country, folk, rock-n-roll, blues, jazz, Tejano, singer songwriter, acoustic, electric, and everything in between. I had landed on one giant bed of feathered pillows.

After a ten-hour drive I pulled up to the Extended Stay America on 6th and Guadalupe, later to be affectionately known as the uncomfortable inn. I unloaded myself and my luggage to see if I could do business with my new city. I knew not a soul—no connections and no friends from my sordid past other than a few musicians that had roamed The Dingo stage, so long ago. I was alone and was in heaven.

The duality of me was abandoned. I didn't need it anymore. No one knew me, so why all the wasted energy? I was going to let the light and the dark roam freely in my new city and see what happened next. I had to execute professionally, and now with no reason to cut myself into two pieces, I was ready to make this a go.

On my first night I ventured out of my living quarters and stood on the sidewalk facing the famed 6th Street with its nightlife scene on full display. I was looking to fill my belly, not my unquenchable thirst, at least not yet. In the distance I noticed a sign flashing: *Hoffbrau Steaks*. Why not, I loved the meat.

I nestled in at a two-person table at the back of this one room venue, hoping to wrestle with some good vittles. My stewardess shuffled over, gladly regurgitating the menu in about ten seconds. My ear was not yet accustomed to the southern accent, where words blend into one another, so I only caught a glimpse of her prose. I ordered the eighteen-ounce T-bone, medium rare, with the fried wedged potatoes. Now these were not your run of the mill steaks—these were flat iron grilled steaks smothered in a tsunami of butter and lemon. I needed a little green and asked for a salad with blue cheese.

Not a chance. "We have a wet salad smothered in our own garlic dressing, take it or leave it." I took it.

My sky waitress had been working at this venue for twenty-eight years and correctly labeled me a greenhorn to the great state of Texas. I was a resident all of two hours, finding myself knee deep in some home cooking with a heaping scoop of genuine southern hospitality. In an instant I consciously changed the channel from my recent past to this exact moment. I needed it. It provided a sense of grounding. I was seasoned at shifting my feelings so I wouldn't feel what I was feeling. I prayed over my wet salad.

While raising my head to reach for the pepper, I noticed a commotion at the front door when two people walked in and sat next to my table. The couple placed their order while I was sinking my teeth into the most amazing steak I've ever experienced. It felt so good in my mouth. While trying to chew my oversized bite, apparently my military school training was all of naught, when my waitress did the neighborly thing and introduced me to the couple that just sat down for supper. The Governor of Texas, Rick Perry, and his wife, Anita, gave me a warm welcome and insisted on paying for my dinner. I stood up shook both their hands and sat down to finish my vittles.

First night in Texas and I broke bread with the governor and his wife, well sort of. Maybe this was a good move? Or maybe I was extremely lucky? Who cares? I exhaled.

The extraordinary experiences were commonplace in my life, leaving me unfazed by my first night in the Lone Star State. But something deeper was percolating, something on the surface resembling pure luck was not luck at all, but rather a foretelling of what had been missing in my life all along. I had no idea.

I was numb from my experiences over the past thirty-seven years with no ability or desire to slow down to find out what was really going on inside of me. I was doing well, I kept reminding myself. I needed to trudge forward. I needed to dig myself out of another hole. I was great at recovery, just didn't realize at the time how much I needed to recover. Wow!

Regardless of the numerous missteps, aborted opportunities, and calculated deceit—both internal and external—I found myself in a great city with a mystical foundation, stirring an untapped portion of me from my very first experience. I couldn't put my finger on why this place was different. It was floating in the air wherever I went, grasping and tugging at what lay dormant inside of me for my entire breathing life. I knew something was going on, but with a damaged spiritual condition and no faith in the human element whatsoever, I was frozen by my own will. I needed to thaw out. I needed to trust at least one human being. I needed a new friend. I needed hope. I set my sights low and that was about to change.

I was truly scared for the second time in my life. It had been thirty long exhausting years since the magic elixir trickling past my lips vanquished the weight of my sordid childhood dream life. I was due another miracle.

My intent was simple. Work extremely hard, stay connected to Audrey and her son with daily calls and monthly visits, and finally release the whole of me into my new environment to see if I was palatable to a city insisting on keeping it weird. Little did I know my whole experience in Austin would be molded by a sign on a back of a building one short block from the uncomfortable inn.

"Cold Beer, Fried Pies, Frog Legs, Cocktails, Texas Beef, and Air Conditioning."

It was a connection to every part of my life in one short marketing blurb, but something more than the food and the drink were calling me.

Over the next week I curiously passed this building, Ranch 616, everyday as I navigated around my new environment, noticing a new piece to this mystical place viewed only from its exterior. I was drawn by the fifty-foot green rattlesnake lit up in neon on the front of the building with a darting red tongue and the small cactus garden lining the walkway up to the main entrance. If you looked closely, symbols and caricatures were cut into the cacti, revealing a new dimension to an unordinary stand of exotic species.

Overall I was being conservative in my new environment, and Ranch 616 seemed to be a place of safety and comfort on the outside, so why not venture inside to see what made this place call to a space deep within my being? It was only a feeling. I needed what it was offering beyond the food and the drink. But feelings couldn't be trusted. Feelings made me feel unbalanced. I didn't like being vulnerable. It interfered with the circus.

As I approached the front door, I noticed two sea turtle shells illuminated by a single light on the wall, shedding a glowing amber color, furthering its mystical powers. The light was the same exact color I experienced before my first drink at the age of eight and it generated the same feeling. It gave me comfort. I opened the front door and was greeted by an old soda pop machine where you slid back the top to pull out your beverage of choice.

But instead of Coke or Fresca, tiny bottles of Corona were freshly iced to wet your whistle while you waited for your table or an open seat at the concrete half-moon shaped bar. To the immediate right of the front door hung some art and a stunning picture of a beautiful woman.

Mounted deer, boar, a large red fish, and a rattlesnake skin adorned the walls. Dangling from the ceiling to illuminate the patrons at the bar hung pin lights, and attached to each wire were Puta dolls from Mexico, exhilarating the imagination. No more than seventy-five people filled the space to capacity, so the seating was intimate—electrifying the patrons, or should I say patients, of this establishment. Its ambiance made you salivate. The room was filled with beautiful people, chatting, laughing, touching each other. The senses were tantalized. I was envious, as I wanted to be one of them. I knew how to do this. It had been years since my forays in Santa Fe. My circus was on call.

Hanging on the west wall was a twenty-five-foot wide by eight-foot high re-colored photo of a marching band from the twenties by famed Texas artist Bob "Daddy-O" Wade. But it was the spiritual shrine created by Kevin, co-owner, and tended to by Ricky, the waiter-assistant and overall shaman of the space. A Guadalupe statue shrouded with iconic rosary beads and dried flowers and lighted by the glowing flicker of a dozen or so prayer candles was the centerpiece.

This space was more than a high-end watering hole serving South Texas ranch fare with a flare; it was a place for spiritual grounding. A refuge from all that occurred outside its doors was the real sustenance being served—a spiritual/mystical meal and I was famished. I was lured by the dark images on the outside to find a spiritual/mystical home on the inside. It was quite ironic. It represented the completeness of me in every way.

Tracy, Don, Greg, Casey, Miguel, and co-owner Antonio were the caretakers of this gastronomical church, and my life changed when I settled in at the last chair at the bar closest to the kitchen. I was beaten. I was battered. I had lost all connection with humanity and with myself, including the God I had invested so much time getting to know over the last ten years or so. The relationships I encountered were real; the changes in my character were real, but I was dead inside, trying to make it to the next breath. I was hanging on with all my might. No one would know. I couldn't let myself know. I was in grave danger.

I ordered Ranch Water, a tasty beverage of tequila in a tall glass with ice and a Topo Chico mineral water on the side, garnished with lemon and lime. I felt safe for the first time in a very long time, and not an iota of the agave liquid had trickled past my parched lips yet.

In a matter of hours, I had developed an intimate rapport with these strangers and they liked me. It never took long for me to weave my way into a situation, but this was different. It felt good to be free from all the masks and mirrors I had willfully created to survive. The circus was not necessary, I concluded. I was relieved. The whole group took me in like a stray dog and nourished me back physically, emotionally, and spiritually, not knowing I was ready to break at any moment. No walls erected for protection, just me.

I was introduced to all who entered the shrine and in a matter of months knew more about Austin and the intimacy of its real character than most who had lived here their entire lives. I had left the only place I called home, even though it never felt that way, and now I felt like I was home for the very first time in my life. It would have been nice to never look back and I wished it was that simple, but life is a complicated journey and my path more than most. At least it felt that way. We all feel that way.

You see, the only beating part of my broken heart was ten hours away by car in the house I bought so long ago to fill with a family of my own. What my heart so desperately needed and wanted my entire life, I had abandoned for self-survival, and now faced with its reality I could not accept its finality.

What I never experienced when growing up, what I craved, having no idea how to accomplish it—a family to call my own—was so close and yet so far distanced by my inability to provide full measure, which Audrey and her son deserved. I was too selfish to open the door completely to something other than myself. This reality literally ripped me back into two pieces once again. But this time it wasn't the light and the dark jockeying for position—it was love. What I longed for the most.

The bottom line was reality always left a bad taste in my mouth and the only elixir able to cleanse my palate was the drink. It worked every single time in the past, except this time. It was misleading. Hoodwinked. Betrayal. The drink would never be strong enough to mend this unquenchable wound. I escaped the potential of love in my life for so long, the reality of my duality; the desire to be connected to another in a meaningful way or the uncomfortable comfort of being alone could no longer be ignored. I didn't have the words or strength to do the right thing and let them go. I was extremely selfish and willing to do anything for the idea of love and family. Well almost anything.

"Love is not an inner feeling, but an act of the will.
Love can only be known by the action it produces."
–Dietrich Bonhoffer.

I was unwilling to do all the actions necessary to really love another, starting with loving myself. In some ways I didn't know how to love in the way Dietrich Bonhoffer describes above, a sure remnant of not reconciling the completeness of who I really was inside. I didn't want to uncover all of my experiences. I didn't want to change a thing, but at the same time I wanted what I never had. It had to be easy since everything else in life had come easy. I was petrified. The pain was sustainable with my best friend so near. He allowed me to trudge forward. I couldn't let go of my dream.

Audrey and I were both desperately hanging onto the ideal of love and the desire to have a family of at least three, and with a few abandoned attempts to be a family unit in our rearview mirror, we packed up the house in New Mexico and they joined me in Austin.

It was a risky decision for Audrey, as she knew about my struggles, although was oblivious to the depths of the other war rumbling for so long and so deep within my being. How could she have known? I never gave her the chance. If you don't share everything you're feeling, how will someone know? Impossible.

In the human condition we tend to hold onto that vital pea of information perceived as our saving grace, with the illusion it will provide protection and self-preservation, but the holding back only distances us from the truth and any chance of having true communion with another human being. Trust and rapport are not independent. Without one the other is not possible.

The purity of honesty in its unadulterated form can be extremely tough to tap and potentially painful when shared in love with another. What is impossible when not practicing the purity of honesty is internal peace. I wanted to share but did not know how to rip open my chest and reveal the completeness of me. I was emotionally muted.

Unfortunately, I couldn't go to the place where pure honesty resides within me, let alone with Audrey, a sure sign of our relationship's imminent demise. But the heart is an amazing organ, thinking it can overcome any obstacle when faced with the fact it might lose a connection with another. In the human condition, a common trait is to ignore the red flags briskly waving in our immediate vicinity, as we sidestep the raging bull like the matador does in the bull ring, putting our head down to push forward while ignoring the pure truth of the matter. The desire to pursue and capture the heart of another cannot be ignored. Love will blind perfect vision every single time. Love without the purity of honesty is half measures. Selfish.

We played family, and for the most part I kept my drinking in check. But it was gaining speed and surely was ready to take control when all fell apart. I loved taking her son to school every morning and picking him up after school. I loved being his best friend, since he already had a great father. We had some really good times, but Audrey never felt safe and I was the culprit. It takes two to engage, and my half-measures only intensified her pulling back from the hot flame that was sure to burn when fantasy and reality finally collided. Audrey was looking for a way out, and I knew it. How could I blame her? She trusted the heart of her matter.

I was unprepared for the inevitable. The death of the last piece of my beating heart consumed me as our union drifted away. I was alone again, but this time it was different. I was raw, the pain much deeper. The attempt to save love and our family lasted all of six months, and with a few weeks' notice of her impending departure, I collapsed back into me, more and now.

By this time my work efforts over the last year and a half had started to bear fruit. It would be only a matter of time until the deep financial hole created by my last business venture with my family would be filled in.

The legal maneuvering was underway, and the lack of integrity of what really went on during my stay and after my departure was directed by my father to further his and Ralph-David's lot. I never said a word. I never moved away from integrity to get my way or to tilt the scale of justice, family, and public sentiment in my favor. I was fighting two battles at the moment, and the one over integrity would play second fiddle to the one being played out in a two-story home on Sanderling Trail. The battle of the heart trumps any hand.

Three days before Audrey was to depart for good with help from her family, I packed a bag and checked into a motel in the south end of Austin. I knew if I stayed close out of desperation and extreme selfishness, I would ask her to stay, knowing if I did she would stick it out. She was strong-willed, loyal, and believed in the sanctity of commitment like no other. She would love me without condition, and sometimes that is not enough, especially when the receiver of that love is unable to love himself. I was unable.

The toll on the heart is heavy. We all have to make decisions in life, and when it comes to the matters of the heart, those decisions can be very, very tricky. But heartbreaking decisions are critical if the intent is to move toward the possibility of a free and happy heart. No other way is possible, even though our mind and others try to convince us otherwise, but no one can tell you what you feel inside. No one. Heart versus head.

In all reality I could not watch Audrey or her son walk out of my life physically and emotionally, even though my actions over the past year and a half dictated its path. I would pass by our house over the next three days, with tears flowing down my face, to see her car in the driveway; I was hoping for a miracle, but it never came.

It was the first time in my life that I put away my selfishness for a brief moment and let her leave without trying to convince her to stay. I finally did the right thing for someone I loved so deeply, unable to show her how much. Maybe I just did show her?

Her son was gone! Audrey was gone! My hope for family was gone!

Number six! It didn't take long for the compassion in Hyde to come forth to quell the deep raw pain I was experiencing. He was only doing his job, and I was grateful. I found myself in another two-story house, sparsely furnished, but this time with the memory of what I had lost. A quick trip for another bottle of something to rid those feelings from my consciousness and a fender-bender in a parking lot with the wife of the head basketball coach at the University of Texas was all it took to shackle up Hyde and my weakened vessel for the evening. This time we spent the night in jail together. I didn't like lying next to Hyde. I only needed him when he served me, and something needed to change.

I knew where to go, and I found the *Bridge to Shore* meeting on the campus of Riverbend Church. The same church Tim attended as a child when living in Austin. The puzzle to my life was starting to come together, and I needed some more help. I turned to Theri, and she resourced a friend who could help. The links to recovery were deep, with the task at hand equally grand.

I had no time to waste, desperate to change my physical state, so I made an appointment and visited Melanie, hoping to find out what damage had been done over the last thirty-one years of drinking. We talked family, medical history, my current health concerns, and we talked as best I could about what lay beneath all these years of character-building necessary for survival evolving into this circus act my life had become. I was actively pulling the skin and the flesh away from my breastplate, sharing openly with Melanie in a way I had not experienced with another human being. She knew about the drinking and the meetings I was attending, and she knew about the turmoil of my recent relationship and the legal quagmire with my family. But I was still holding onto the pea. The purity of honesty was beyond my reach.

My health improved and luckily there was no apparent long-term damage on my internal organs due to my drinking binges. Emotionally I was feeling some relief. Spiritually I was a mess. Melanie suggested I pursue some acupuncture for my alcohol cravings, allergies, and my inability to sleep more than a handful of hours a week.

I was my own practitioner when it really came down to it, as my cravings were being met by designating one night a week for light drinking. A secret I kept from those who were extending a healing hand. I ventured back to Ranch 616 and to a new fixture on my soul-healing den of food and libations, Uchi. A newly opened sushi restaurant on the south side of Austin with a talented staff headed up by a new friend Tyson. I would drink Brunello with Tyson as he created my dinner from his mind while being expertly tended to by Naomi. A paradox in her own right with beautiful red hair, creamy white skin, and blue eyes and fluent in Japanese. I was smitten. I would find a new family in this gastro delight that by now was getting national recognition for the quality and creativity of its fare.

I had a formula. I had a plan. Meetings a few times a week, bi-monthly sessions with Melanie, and the Friday night release with old and new friends. I was feeling and looking better for sure. But the spiritual element in me needed to be nurtured in a different way than I had experienced over the last ten years. I couldn't go back to what didn't work before. The idea of trying to do the same thing better would surely only reveal short-term improvement and what I was looking for was a sustainable spiritual condition bereft of my reason. I knew I needed to separate the two, as they had been at war my entire life. A truce of sorts was desired.

I finally took up the suggestion of acupuncture, and what appeared as an ancient practice to address my symptoms of addiction and sleep disorder would turn out to be the link to a spiritual healing I could have never imagined. But it wasn't the ancient practice healing my complex spiritual condition, although it was helpful, it was the practitioner of this healing art touching me, extracting from me with her needles and heart what had never been mined before. She allowed and encouraged me to go deeper, to get rawer, and to lean into my unspoken secrets and vulnerabilities. It would be the first time in my life where I could feel the energy of another human being passing through my flesh.

Kimberly would be the spiritual vehicle I had missed since my time with Bob Jefferson. She was from of all places, Silver City, New Mexico. And even though our spiritual traditions were different, we communicated above and beyond the confines of those limitations, allowing for an intimate spiritual discourse not spoken by words but by the energy she was moving in me by encouraging me to seek self-discovery.

I was learning to trust another, and I trusted Kimberley implicitly. It was safe to be in her healing presence. I was able to saw through my breastplate to reveal the completeness of me to a certain extent, although still holding onto the pea, which was keeping me from a peaceful heart.

By this time I had moved back downtown from the family rich community of Westlake to the hustle and bustle of city living. I would find a one bedroom flat in the most luxurious residential high-rise in downtown Austin. The Nakona.

The move was calculated, as I needed to be rid of the desire to have family. I promised myself I would have no relationship with another woman with the idea of family ever again, as long as Hyde was playing an active role in my life. My intent was to never hurt someone again like I hurt Audrey and her son. In my mind, being alone was safe for others, not necessarily for me, and I was cool with that. A risk I needed to take.

The Nakona was filled with academics, entrepreneurs, foreign well-to-doers, the head football and baseball coaches at the University of Texas, Dan Rather, and my next-door neighbor the former Governor of Texas, Ann Richards. Ann and I would meet at the trash chute and while I was separating her recyclables and trash she would tell me stories about her present state of mind. She hated the holidays but she loved people. We would become friends and little did I know but we had another friend in common, well more her friend than mine: my sponsor's grand sponsor, Bill W.

I was surrounded by all who could help. *Bridge to Shore*, Melanie and Kimberley, Ranch 616, and Uchi comprised my new sense of family. A new set of friends at Shoal Creek Saloon: Jeff, Mike, Roy, Tom, Ethan, Billy, Bacon, Renaldo, and the Texas Chili Parlor with Willy, Zach, Kevin, James, Roland, and Zube. The gathering was unique and the healing was possible, but my will was still strong and my way even stronger. Unfortunately, when linked with my inability to be honest and the desire to give half measure to anything, it would eventually quash what was organically evolving. I was kicking backward.

The meetings faded, material fortunes increased, and my new family in Austin continued to grow, as I pleaded guilty to number six. In eighteen months all the consequences would be worked through, looking forward to the end of my drinking career. I was turning forty soon and it was time to move on in life, I kept reminding myself. That day would come and go and without gut-wrenching honesty; change is impossible. I needed and wanted to hoard the pea. It was my faith. I was my faith. I was doomed and I knew it.

You know what you should do.

You know what you want to do.

You know what you're going to do...Eddy.

The inability to crack that last rib to fully spread open my chest and be emotionally naked with my new family and home was so close, and yet the reality of it happening was light years away. I knew what I needed to do. I just didn't want to do it. The idea of what I had become seemed so much more lively than who I was inside all along. I wanted to have intimate relations with other human beings, and I was trying my best, but my best was clearly not nearly enough.

Overall it was an unbalanced balancing act being performed perfectly. I was happy enough; having everything I needed in life with the financial security to do whatever I wanted. No attachments and no real responsibilities. I was resilient and had the ability to recover. I had the experience of starting from a negative position and pulling all the right strings to make me whole again.

But it was a façade. A façade I was willing to stomach for the rest of my life while standing alone wearing the top hat of my circus. The inability to have peace in my life was a forgone conclusion.

The ecstasy of Austin was starting to fade. I needed some type of change. I needed another miracle—at least that's how I was feeling. Deep down I knew I needed to entertain drastic measures. I guess I was fighting for life, rather than the idea of death, that I had become so comfortable with.

The drinking was no longer one night a week but the whole weekend. I had friends and I had a place I loved calling home, but deep down I was still battling the constant thoughts of my life's desire to be free from the battle between my reason and my spiritual condition. Who would be king? The war had been costly with so many innocent victims along the way, not to mention those who had been complicit. I was exhausted. The rabbit's foot was beating.

What could I do to mix up my stagnant life? Unsettled. Anxious. I wasn't looking for excitement anymore, I was looking for the Holy Grail I had been longing for since exiting my mother's womb. Peace!

If I could be challenged again professionally, I would be fine, I reasoned, and out of nowhere an opportunity arose that lifted my spirits commensurate with my insatiable ego. It had to be a challenge. It had to be a huge risk. It had to have high opportunity of failure. It had to be all about me. Nothing had really changed. I was still making the same decisions, only this time they were shrouded in a multitude of experiences and knowledge, which I ignored. I had everything going for me to make a better decision. I was unable to truly reach out for help when I needed it the most. My ego was inflexible.

I wasn't looking to move away from Austin, but an opportunity to move to the Golden State seemed providential, since I was linking up the coincidences to make it as such. My pastor at Calvary Chapel Albuquerque had moved to Southern California and would only be only one hour away for Sunday services. I was desperate to connect spiritually.

The opportunity to navigate back to a place in life I experienced before provided comfort. Spiritually that is. I had been here before and I knew the end result. It was a safe plan. I had the blinders on and I wanted what I wanted. Nothing was going to get in my way. I was willing to leave the only place I called home, the only place I felt safe, the only place where I was begrudgingly working toward the completeness of me. I was surrounded with love and needed to escape. Crazy!

The circus was out of control and the will to keep it going was soaking up all my available energy. Life *had* to be more precious than I had squeezed out of it so far. Death always seemed like a happier place than this life stuff I struggled with each labored breath, and with no real relief in sight I took the plunge and agreed to take a position in San Diego with the firm where Harold worked. I would be reconnecting with an old friend. A trusted friend.

A new challenge of not knowing a soul with the comfort that this time I would leave the drinking behind for good and dive head first into to my spiritual practice. I trusted this path in the past, but this time I was hoping for a different result. I was on shaky ground, again. My faith was deal based again.

I was safe at the Nakona, but it was too close to the nightlife I loved so much, unknowingly allowing me to not connect with another in an intimate fashion. I knew I had to mix it up this time, choosing to find a place without those amenities so near. I searched for a month and with the clock ticking closer to my departure date to San Diego I stumbled upon a cottage in Windansea hoping to find home. A sign was being nailed to the white picket fence. For rent!

La Jolla, California, and La Joya, New Mexico…The Jewel. Regardless of this spelling nuance, my weary vessel landed and settled in for the ride of my life. I turned forty-one.

On my first weekend in my new home it snowed. A strange sign. I was excited about my new adventure until the reality of my decision hit me when the moving truck arrived with the furniture I had dragged from Texas. It was the same furniture I purchased years earlier in New Mexico, hoping a new home and some knick-knacks would lure a family. I was a dreamer and a fool. The reflection was killing me.

The impact of willfully leaving home and my organic family behind for nothing more than a feeling of boredom and an opportunity to feed my enormous ego weighed heavy. As the blood was being pushed through my weakened heart to feed my extremities, I recognized the significance of this decision, feeling the draining of the last possibility of hope in my being with each beat of my broken spirit. Nothing had changed. I was still a scared little kid running from one home to the next, afraid of the possibility it might not be there when I get back. I had no choice but to create the illusion of a higher calling to the Golden State to deceive myself, providing the safety and comfort I desperately needed. I proudly wore the top hat and manipulated the show to keep what I had and get what I wanted.

This feeling of loss overwhelmed my flesh, sapping the will to carry through on my promise to leave the drinking behind and change my life forever. I was debilitated beyond the bone crushing pain I felt when Audrey and her son departed, because this time it was I who gave up on the only thing that ever meant anything to me. The desire to have a family and home was all I ever wanted. I had it unconventionally in Austin, but it was real and now three states away. I didn't think it was possible to feel this alone, but I was wrong. How far could I go? Was it possible I could get so low, so lonely it would be impossible to recover? Remember, I had a plan.

I would drive every Sunday morning seventy-miles to see Skip teach. It wasn't the same as before and how could it be? It was a different time, and change had occurred in me as it does to all of us when we move from one breath to the next. But I was committed to the plan, and it would be doable if I just hung on long enough to get back into the rooms.

My plan crumbled in front of me when Skip announced his decision to go back to New Mexico and the pulpit at Calvary. Expectation. Manipulated providence. I never went to church again. Hyde gladly slid his well-worn footprints into the only pulpit I was assured would never leave me. I needed him more now than ever. He was my only family member left.

My survival instincts took center stage, commanding execution to turn fantasy into reality and make my move to La Jolla a business success, since all else at the moment was utter chaos. I had to reposition my competition and it would be a huge gamble, as I had nothing else to do. I was seasoned at making something out of nothing. Turning fantasy and delusion into reality was my forte. It would be just a matter of time before the hard work would be represented in the sales I was accustomed to and I was steadfast to that end. The work drove me. My ego drove me. It was my only reprieve and all I had left. I was holding on.

Ironically, it was the same yoke my father had been tethered to his whole life, except for the fact I was not my father and my choices in the past had clearly separated me from that reality. But I was in the same boat at the moment and my heart sunk deep into despair, as my will to have sustainable change in my life disappeared with each thunderous thump of the rabbit foot to my soul.

The weekends would be unbearable, especially the early mornings. I successfully patched together my sleepless nights by drinking until I passed out. But my reality was, I still was waking up early and now I needed to kill the pain upon awakening. It was a first. I reached for a new low.

I found my church, not but a short mile from my cottage, with its first service for the lost, lonely, and thirsty starting at six a.m. *London's West End*. I clearly remember my first cocktail served up bright and early by Mac, as it was only the two of us in this odd shaped house of worship. He would mumble to me several weekends later when it would be the two us sitting in an empty bar at opening time that I was too young to be drinking this early. I laughed and he smiled, knowing he knew something about this drinking stuff and where I might be headed.

Mac was an icon and the inspiration for the rag tag bunch of characters making up the *Pump House Gang* chronicled in literary stardom decades before. He would share his childhood memories of creating havoc in La Jolla like driving a flaming car over Torrey Pines cliff to Black's Beach some four hundred feet below, narrowly diving from the vehicle before it careened over the lip. He would a recruit a team of like-minded drinkers to demolish houses for free that were in the way of the new Interstate 5 highway carving its way down the coast. It was an opportunity to have fun and destroy stuff while getting drunk. He was my friend.

But it was the story of a childhood memory that welled tears in his big blue eyes as he took you back in time to share the fright of a young boy when war was in its early stages. He remembered running with his mother for shelter when the Japanese fighter pilots were strafing his home with bullets on that infamous day on December seventh, 1942. This early childhood experience would be with him for the rest of his life, as he too would be collared with the heavy yoke of the rabbit's foot. He would give me a nickname. *Twelve*. I gladly accepted.

Mac soon passed away and it felt like the last piece of hope keeping me from drowning in my own will was being cut. He was the only form other than Hyde that resembled family in my eyes. He was honest with me, knowing his own fate was already sealed. I had a chance in his eyes. I wished I could see through his lens. The purity of his honesty that early morning stayed present with me regardless of how much of the spirit I poured through my frame. I didn't want to shake his words from my spirit. I wanted to live but I also wanted to have peace through death. My own paradox of life haunted me.

I would return to *London's West End* after his passing for one last time. I settled in for a round or two or how many it took to feel numb before heading home. I was uncomfortable, so I struck up a conversation with this cat named Dave and the banter was pleasant and lighthearted. I had a good feeling about this encounter until a young lady approached and wanted to know our profession. I quickly shut down her boring questioning with a non-answer and Dave did as well. She was intoxicated and insistent and after a while our bartender swooshed her away so we could continue our conversation.

Dave was a former Navy Seal and the personal chef to my favorite professional golfer. What I didn't know at the time and would find out soon enough he was one of Eddy's best friends. The friend who would inform the police of where Eddy was holed up that eventually led to his arrest and the long road to his recovery.

For me, the end was near but not the one I wished for, but rather the one intended since my first breath.

Paul arrived in the spring of 2007 to commence his weekly pilgrimage down to Windansea for rest and laughter, as he too was fighting a disease not of his choosing. I loved him being so close and at the same time he elicited the uncomfortable feeling welling in the gutter of my frame of how isolated I had become over the last year. His presence was evocative of all I had wasted, all I took for granted, all I had willfully aborted time after time. I had all the opportunities to have a circus of many but chose otherwise.

The inability to intimately connect with another human being was my demise. It was the heart of my matter. I relied on my will to provide what nothing else could provide. I tried other means with mixed results tragically unwilling to push away from my way, detouring what was intended for me all along. He was here to heal and I was being healed by his presence, but I would not let him know my desperation. Trust was a four-letter word.

The desire and gift of having intimate relations with other human beings was the hot flame I could never embrace. I was afraid to lose something

I thought I never had. Our time together was special and he had no idea how perilous my state would be. I didn't need Hyde when he was around, but what I was unable to control was the extent of my sumptuous swilling after he departed back to New Mexico.

I had lost the will to live, and I knew it. The end was near, and I could not wait to move past all this pain and wastefulness. But hope was lurking around the corner. It would turn out to be my last gasp.

As my desperation grew, news from Nebraska sent me into a tailspin. My connection with Kevin that had its genesis on the rooftop of a four story flat in London some twenty-three years ago was about to be severed, at least in my eyes that is. He called to let me know he was getting married to a wonderful girl from Ireland.

Over the years we would visit each other and the years in between not seeing each other would vanish. We never missed a beat. He was my best friend. A cohort in a lifestyle of excess without limits linked us. With him on this earth I had one last chance of making it out alive. My reason confirmed this thought as insane. I felt insane. I knew that my thoughts were distorted. It was not enough to stop me from me. I would have no one left who understood my way.

Paul had left, connection to my family in Austin had been distanced by my selfishness and ego, and now Kevin was choosing another lifestyle. I wasn't hoping for anything to intervene. It was the end of August. The drinking was especially heavy, trying to fill a bottomless hole. The magic was gone and in a wink everything changed.

Lisa! An angel crafted through her own life experiences. She was God's special tool for a deeply wounded child. She was uniquely suited for the task at hand. No other would suffice. She was magical, a touch of hope, an unexpected boost of life to a soulless body.

The extravagance of our engagements was secondary, tertiary to what emanated from every pore of her being. I had given up, and she was the spark reigniting the flickering flame of my life. What I found completely unbelievable was her ability to tap the marrow of honesty of her past and as each breath left her body in the present. Her honesty was so raw, yet layered in grace and humility.

She was breaking all the rules in the getting to know you stage of a connection between a man and a woman, when your intent is to paint a picture of your life on the most flattering canvass. It was as if a beam of light radiated from within her and drew me into the safety of her energy.

Her ability to shed the pea and truly have intimacy with another human being was beyond remarkable.

What was missing in me my whole lifetime, she represented in the female form. And I couldn't reach out to connect. I was desperate to find the words to express the truth of my experience; the unedited truth as she opened the door so gracefully with her own sharing. The power of when two people willfully open their hearts and share with one another without ulterior motives can foster an intimacy like no other. A circus of two if you will, growing in life as two individuals with a connection grounding them as one. The connection of unconditional love!

But desperation wasn't enough for me. I was still holding onto the pea. I wanted to release my fears. I was trying the best I could. She was near, but I had some decisions to make.

Things were starting to stir the elixir that always muddled my life. The inability to tap the purity of honesty with myself was in the crosshairs, and even though Lisa was heaven-sent, I knew the battle was all my own. The coincidences were becoming less coincidental as I set a new date of starting to change my ways of how Hyde influenced my life. What was happening was neither my will nor my plan.

Upon my arrival in San Diego back in 2006, my old roommate Spike was living a new life as a father and husband. Our connection had been newly minted, and he took me out to show me around his adopted city. He drove me to North Park, Point Loma, Ocean Beach, Mission Beach, Pacific Beach, and La Jolla, pointing out along the way places to eat, drink, and have fun. But it was a place he recommended in Ocean Beach to get a good haircut that would be a place of mystical refuge for me as I separated from the roots I had planted in Austin. It was an odd melding of my Christian beliefs and of a hairstylist who practiced Astrology.

At my first sitting Nicole bantered me up with great conversation when one is trying to establish a connection with a new customer, and I suppose she felt an opening when she asked me if it would be okay to ask me some personal questions. I was game. Before she knew my vitals for proper sighting, she spoke about my recent separation from a place I called home and the necessity to address the one thing I had always struggled with. She did not know what it was, but if I failed to finally address this thing it might be the stumbling block to my personal growth and the freedom I always desired. I was shaking inside as she reeled in my life and in a short hour had pinpointed my Achilles heel. I would visit her often over the next year, excited to see what she would reveal next. I was still holding onto the pea.

It was September first, 2007, and it would be the day I chose to start my life anew. No more drinking and get some help if my ego would relent. But what I wanted most was to be able to connect with another human being in the way Lisa was exposing her life to me. It seemed so natural and freeing to let it all out and see what happens next. She was without expectation, but what she did expect was to be honest with herself and with others regardless of the situation. The truth can be a very powerful tool to get what you want and keep what you have; in fact, more powerful than the entire performer building and shape-shifting I had mastered over the last forty-two years. Her intent wasn't to use the power of honesty for selfish reasons but rather it was a way for her to love another and herself without condition. She was a healer and a teacher.

It was haircut day with a planned visit to my appearance artist/astrologist for some coiffing and some mystical insight, which I was becoming more comfortable with each encounter. As we dabbled in silly banter, a sullen look overcame her otherwise cherub demeanor, as she was connecting my current alignment with the energy of my being and its present condition. She had no idea I had made a sea change of how I would navigate my life going forward. With a slight hesitation she cautiously explained to me that this would be a very critical month for me going forward in my life. Something was going to happen, altering my course forever—unsure of its effect but regardless it was on its way. A collision was going to occur, she just was not sure how or why it would be colliding, or with what. She knew more than she was sharing, but I felt her energy and I knew what it was. What it had always been.

Another sign? It was more than a sign; she was simply connecting me to what I was feeling deeply within my being, allowing me to trust it. I was on the right path. I was in control. I was still wearing the top hat and grasping tightly to the pea. I had a plan. But Lisa had changed my lens forever. I wanted what she had but the task seemed too epic.

Life is complicated and unsuspecting when you least expect it. A different time, another space and Lisa and I could have had a chance to see where our connection would lead us, but she was honest with her current situation and me. Things were very complicated at the moment and she wished we had met one year from then. But the fact was, we had not and I was feeling extremely vulnerable with the feelings I had willfully sequestered away until I cleaned up my act.

Lisa was a mother. I was very aware of my past and did not want to hurt another again. If I could make these changes for my own well-being then the possibility of a connection down the road with Lisa was plausible. I was deal-making with myself and it was conditional. Old patterns, new tricks. I was lacking in the most vital element when loving another without condition…patience.

The connection with Lisa was drifting away as she had the heart of her matter to tend to and I had mine. The difference was she was pure with me and I was unable to reach purity with her. I was honest to the best of my abilities but it wasn't near enough. Half measures.

The turmoil inside was eating me up, and I had not developed an outlet to deal with the feelings gurgling inside my cauldron of loneliness. I wanted Lisa but could not have her, and in my mind the thought of another way out of my life-long struggle for peace vanished with this reality.

On August twenty-first I returned from San Francisco and commenced with drowning myself. Death was near. I was content.

The steps had proved to be essential, allowing me to look back in life and see my experiences for what they were, not what they could have been. I was grateful for each experience along the way, as each experience led me perfectly to the next experience. I would not have had it any other way. It took a perfect storm to get me to my magic couch and it has taken a perfect storm to raise me from said couch.

Windansea has become my spiritual home, with Austin my home of origin. It took thirty-nine years to find home for the first time, and now five short, life-changing years later I now have two places to call home in the physical sense. But the real home I was always searching for was in the last place I ever expected to find it, the last place we in the human condition in the pressures of modernity ever think of looking. In the space that resides in all of us encumbered with the brokenness of being born in the flesh. It's the space deep in each of us standing closest to something greater than ourselves and for me it would be the God of my own understanding.

The relationship with my God was strained. It was an extremely long and complex courtship, having many ups and many downs. It was filled with me leading most of the time and on those rare occasions when I let the energy provided by my higher power lead, if only for a brief moment, it was brilliant.

I knew not how to trust. I was now learning how to. I was always under the delusion my reason protected me from everything and anything, missing out on the reality I had been under the protection of God the whole time. The expense and loss of precious energy expelled in the process of self-protection altered my own experience, and gratefully I was now naked to my environment, seeking progress not perfection. The brilliant light of life could lead me, which is only possible when continually exposing our vulnerability.

My reason is still an asset but no longer desires to lead this life of mine one moment to the next. The fear of keeping what I have and getting what I want has vanished, as I navigate my life today by letting what is going to happen next, happen ncxt.

The unexpected gift is I now have all this beautiful energy to source to healthy self-care, but the true blessing is with an abundance of excess energy I can now direct it toward those who surround me one breath to the next. The king of all addictions, the addiction to self, had released me. I was no longer shackled to my first thought. The summation of the miles was uncountable. Juno was spot on. I was lucky to uncover who I was all along.

I was now a year and a half into wellness, a term used by my Native American brothers in recovery, and I needed to figure out what to do next. I had no time left to waste. I had so many options, so many choices I never realized I had before, and it would be disheartening to choose options I had already experienced in the past, regardless of their perceived success or failure. I had to change everything in my life, and Eddy's words stayed present with each beat of my heart and with each breath inhaled for life.

What I didn't want to do was to be wasteful of the precious gift of life graciously provided from above. In all reality, what I did to myself over those last three days should have killed me. I was alive for a reason and it was no longer all about me. I had another chance at this life and I wanted to be mindful of my next step.

My wellness was on solid ground, but my direction and the source of this newfound peace in life was tenuous. I had to dig deeper. I had to source those beautiful words by Nina and dig until I hit bottom on this particular decision.

The nuance and power of her share was starting to reveal itself to me as I walked through this thing called life. It wasn't just a tool for reflection, but rather it was a tool for everyday living when we need to get to the heart of the matter. It was a tool for continual growth. I needed gut-wrenching honesty with where I should head next without expectation. It was the exact opposite of how I navigated my life in the past. What was going to happen would happen and it would be beyond my wildest imagination if I let it. It's the toughest ego-draining way to navigate life, but essential when peace is the destination.

What were my options? I always wanted a family. I always wanted to have an intimate relationship with a woman. I could have a wife and family. I always wanted to help those who could not help themselves. I could help those suffering from my disease and it would be helpful. I could pull this off.

I had the experiences and the ability now to have intimacy with another including the God of my own understanding, so it would be perfect. Or would it? I had to sharpen the spade. I had to cut deeply at who I really was, not what gave me comfort. I knew this excavation would be tougher than all that I had recently encountered. It was a new perfect storm, and I was challenging the sanctity of my truth. The sanctity of who I really was.

It so happened to be Good Friday, and I reached out to Deborah for her support and to help me sort through this life-threatening decision. It was life and death all over again. It felt that way, and I needed her energy and celestial guidance. We concluded that the option of creating a family and helping others was honorable, but it was not me. It would be the grandest show the circus of one had ever performed and when I pulled it off, all who surrounded me would be standing and applauding with approval. It would be a fitting end to a life lived so selfishly. It was what I wanted, but not who I was. Not an uncommon station in the human experience.

Simply it was not where I was in life at this moment in time, and I knew it without my reason getting in the way. I had to honor what was calling out to me my entire life, and it was something more than always filling my own till. It seemed honorable to help others, but it would still be all about me and what others would see. Nothing would have changed. Maybe in the future a family could be possible, but what was always roaring inside of me had to come out, and I needed a few more days to reconcile my honesty. I needed help.

I reached out to my friend Naomi in Texas and shared with her my heart and what was going on with me. I was being the most vulnerable I had ever been. I needed her lens on my dilemma.

Her words were sound and clear. "If you really want to help someone, you have to tell the whole truth. It will be the only way another can connect with their personal life experience. Just do it. I believe in you."

Her words were comforting. My finances were a challenge.

I needed to eat and I needed to sustain my daily needs, and with the help of Eddy I was able to secure a job washing awnings and cleaning windows. I would ride my beach cruiser five miles at three o'clock every morning to jump in the back of a van for the long ride up to Orange County to clean gargantuan outdoor malls. It was tedious work, and my ego was being crushed daily—and I needed it.

The thoughts of returning to what gave me comfort and safety in the past would filter through my mind, but I knew this thinking would eventually lead me back to my old tracks. It haunted me. The half measures were fruitful and its draw was euphoric.

I hated washing windows, but I was the first one to pick up the squeegee to face the face of who I had become and more importantly who I really was all along. The constant reflection of my face in the window saddened me and at the same time gave me a glimmer of hope. The squeegee became the magic wand I used to wipe away the thoughts of my old ways of navigating life, while my distorted face reflected in the window sprinkled with drops of water. I needed a new path. I wanted to be honest with myself.

As soon as the magic wand wiped the window clean, my face reappeared without delusion, and when I moved to the next window, my face would be sprinkled with the drops of my dishonesty until I wiped it clean again. My work had just begun.

I was ready to be myself. I was changing how I navigated life, with one breath to the next my meter. My face's reflection in the early morning was the reminder I needed to move one breath at a time, having faith for the very first time in something other than myself. I would never feel alone again in a world riddled with loneliness.

What next?

I always wanted to write, but with fear the determining factor, I took the path of least resistance, which in the long run turned out to be neither easy nor painless and wrought full of internal resistance effortlessly ignored or drowned out. The signs were there all along.

I thought I'd write a book with the intent to help just one person, knowing if I set my sights any loftier I would surely start editing my experience to touch a larger audience. I was beginning to understand who I really was and who I had become. The light and dark comprised all of me. I was reconciled. I had only one stumbling block. Money.

I reached out to Eddy once again, and he had another part-time opportunity. He wasn't sure if it would be the right fit for me, but he knew I was hungry and needed the work. My whole life everything came easy and nothing meant anything, and suddenly everything was a struggle and every breath was precious and meant everything. My Papa was close.

Eddy's friends needed someone they could trust to help them run their business. I could help. Art and Adam were brothers but most importantly they cherished the family ideal buttressed by an ancient culture and spiritual tradition. They were Iraqi Christians. Their faith and ideal of family were ancient. I needed what they experienced daily in life more than the job or money itself. I needed to absorb what was passed on from one generation to the next. To be a part of a family with all of its ups and downs as they opened their arms and brought me in as one of their own. Unconditionally.

Nothing else was in my way. I was ready to start writing while washing windows in the early mornings and working late nights at Dick's Liquor & Wine.

How could I script this path? My old lens would never allow this ending. It was impossible. So much had changed.

I finally relented to what was residing deep within me. That sacred space where words, reason, or life experience cannot reconcile.

I was trusting, what was beyond my own understanding. To touch what I could not see, to feel what I could not describe, to allow the next thing to happen in life.

Everything had changed and nothing had changed.

I was who I was all along, without the circus to lean upon.

The good news is the circus of life never ends. It can nourish us when it becomes our ally not our foe. We must make choices and then let happen, happen. I was relieved to know that every moment and experience led perfectly to the next.

My yoke of gratitude was heavy. So many had been vital to my survival and growth. Nothing was wasted. The threshold of having an intimate relationship with myself, another human being, and God had been crossed.

I was freed from what I created. I was grateful to be alive.

I had finally uncovered my Peace!

The only question now was would I allow what was intended for me all along to reveal itself one breath to the next?

I am holding my breath, hoping not to suffocate on the beauty of this thing we call life, since no one knows what will come next...no one.

Here we go again!

ACKNOWLEDGMENTS

Mother, Bob, Theri, Sparky, Uncle Rudy, Uncle Raymond, Peggy, Tim, Paul, Lyn, Eddy, Maria. My Earthly angels: Kim, Deborah, Angela, LoriPop, Kimberly, Cathleen and Cynthia Marie. My yoga teachers: Colleen, Hannah, Kaitlin, Barbra and Mira. Without your support my dream would not be possible.

ABOUT THE AUTHOR

Adam Francis Raby is a writer, yogi, and public speaker living in La Jolla, California. Although not famous for anything but infamous for his desire to explore all the possibilities afforded in the human experience when tethered to the desires of the self. Adam's life-long battle with the drink afforded him the room to navigate life alone. Up until the point when his most trusted friend quit lubricating his loneliness.

His relentless honesty, unflinching self-scrutiny, odd luck, and writing style makes the personal universal—confirming we are all standing on thin ice. Where nothing is for certain no matter your station in life.

Growing up in New Mexico—hounded by the thoughts of an expected early exit from life birthed by a morbid childhood dream life, left him seeking more of anything—Me, more and now! The battle between the sovereignty of his reason and the sovereignty of his spiritual self would slowly stain his soul. Using his reason to manipulate his way through life was the foundation upon which he built a multitude of life experiences.

Adam Raby is a colorful mix of business owner, entrepreneur, social scientist, political junkie, lover of history, music, culture, current events, a good time, and an insatiable desire to consume the foods of the world.

He stakes no claim on "how to" navigate the complexities of life—strange in a world looking for the path of least resistance. His desire is to explore his own experiences in life and to share them in an open, honest, and respectful way while honoring and learning from the experiences of others. It is a method of growth we can all practice—unconditional love. If that sounds appetizing—"let's dig till we hit bottom"—together!

Adam can be contacted at:

Facebook: www.facebook.com/adamfrancisraby

Website: Adam-Francis-Raby.com